CLASSICAL MYTHOLOGY

ILLUSTRATED EDITION

CLASSICAL
MYTHOLOGY

ILLUSTRATED EDITION

HELEN A. GUERBER

FALL RIVER PRESS

New York

FALL RIVER PRESS

New York

An Imprint of Sterling Publishing Co., Inc.
1166 Avenue of the Americas
New York, NY 10036

ISBN 978-1-4351-6685-1

Distributed in Canada by Sterling Publishing Co., Inc.
^{c}/o Canadian Manda Group, 664 Annette Street
Toronto, Ontario M6S 2C8, Canada
Distributed in the United Kingdom by GMC Distribution Services
Castle Place, 166 High Street, Lewes, East Sussex BN7 1XU, England
Distributed in Australia by NewSouth Books
45 Beach Street, Coogee NSW 2034, Australia

For information about custom editions, special sales, and premium and corporate purchases, please contact Sterling Special Sales at 800-805-5489 or specialsales@sterlingpublishing.com.

Manufactured in China

4 6 8 10 9 7 5

sterlingpublishing.com

Cover design by Elizabeth Mihaltse Lindy
Interior design by Kevin Ullrich
Vase painting/cover: © G. NIMATALLAH/DEA/Getty Images
Decorative borders/cover: courtesy of Wikimedia Foundation/Rawpixel
Endpapers by Dover Publications, Inc.

FRONTISPIECE: HOMER AND HIS GUIDE. William-Adolphe Bouguereau.

CONTENTS

III. Juno

IV. Minerva

V. Apollo

VI. Diana

CONTENTS

X. Vulcan

XI. Neptune

XII. Pluto

XIII. Bacchus

CONTENTS

XVIII. Æolus

XIX. Hercules

XX. Perseus

CONTENTS

XXI. Theseus

XXII. Jason

XXIII. The Calydonian Hunt

XXIV. Œdipus

XXV. Bellerophon

CONTENTS

XXVI. Minor Divinities

Following Pages: OLYMPUS, SEAT OF THE GODS. Giulio Romano.

PREFACE

T The myths of Greece and Rome have inspired so much of the best thought in English literature that a knowledge of them is often essential to the understanding of what we read.

"When Byron calls Rome," says Thomas Bulfinch, "'the Niobe of nations,' or says of Venice, 'She looks a Sea-Cybele fresh from Ocean,' he calls up to the mind of one familiar with our subject illustrations more vivid and striking than the pencil could furnish, but which are lost to the reader ignorant of mythology." Literature abounds in such poetic borrowings from the classics, and it is impossible to enjoy fully the works of some of our best writers if we cannot immediately appreciate their imagery.

Again, expressions such as "the heel of Achilles" are part of the common language, but their meaning is lost upon those to whom the myths from which they are derived are unfamiliar.

But apart from the practical utility of the myths, as necessary to the comprehension of much that we read and hear, they have a great aesthetic value, presenting, as they do, a mine of imaginative material whose richness and beauty cannot fail to appeal even to the colder sensibilities of this more prosaic age. It would be difficult, indeed, to exaggerate the importance of these old-world stories, with their wonderful admixture of pagan faith and riotous imagination, in correcting the tendency to mere utilitarianism in the education of the young, and there is need to lay stress upon this because of the increased attention now being given to science and modern languages at the expense of the classics.

Translations of the exquisite writings of the Greek and Latin poets cannot, of course, convey the same rich impressions. They are, at the best, weak and imperfect vehicles for reproducing the literary and imaginative wealth of a golden age; but they are, nevertheless, capable of imparting something of the atmosphere of the great originals, and, in whatever tongue they may be told, the stories themselves cannot easily be spoilt; they will assuredly appeal to thousands to whom the ancient languages of Greece and Rome are as a sealed book.

The writings of many of the great English classical translators, it may be added, are instinct with the spirit of the ancients. We might fancy that they, too, had caught sight of Proteus rising from the sea, and had heard

Old Triton blow his wreathéd horn.

But properly to understand even these translations we first require a knowledge of mythology which it would take a lifetime to acquire piece by piece from general reading, and the aims, therefore, of this book are: first, to present outlines of the stories in a simple form pleasurable to the reader who has no desire further than to obtain a general knowledge of the myths, or to be entertained; and, second, to furnish a practical guide for the student who wishes to prosecute his mythological studies, and who desires to acquire the means whereby he will be enabled to follow intelligently the allusions to other myths which meet him at every turn, and to know something of the origin and significance of the stories.

The numerous quotations throughout will show the way to the noble pasturage from which these "flowers of Parnassus" have been culled, and they will enable the reader to appreciate the great influence of the myths upon our literature. The large selection of reproductions from famous pictures and statuary, also, will show something of the debt which art, both ancient and modern, owes to the same inspiration.

The myths are told as graphically and accurately as possible, great care being taken, however, to avoid the more repulsive features of heathen mythology; and when two or more versions of the same myth occur, the preference has invariably been given to the most popular, that is to say, to the one which has inspired the greatest works.

Both the Latin and the Greek forms of proper names are given, but the Latin names are usually retained throughout the narrative, because more frequently used in poetry and art.

THE BEGINNING OF ALL THINGS

Mythology is the science which treats of the early traditions, or myths, relating to the religion of the ancients, and includes, besides a full account of the origin of their gods, their theory concerning the beginning of all things.

MYTHS OF CREATION

Among all the nations scattered over the face of the earth, the Hebrews alone were instructed by God, who gave them not only a full account of the creation of the world and of all living creatures, but also a code of laws to regulate their conduct. All the questions they fain would ask were fully answered, and no room remained for conjecture.

It was not so, however, with the other nations. The Greeks and Romans, for instance, lacking the definite knowledge which we obtain from the Scriptures, and still anxious to know everything, were forced to construct, in part, their own theory. As they looked about them for some clue to serve as guide, they could not help but observe and admire the wonders of nature. The succession of day and night, summer and winter, rain and sunshine; the fact that the tallest trees sprang from tiny seeds, the greatest rivers from diminutive streams, and the most beautiful flowers and delicious fruits from small green buds,—all seemed to tell them of a superior Being, who had fashioned them to serve a definite purpose.

They soon came to the conclusion that a hand mighty enough to call all these wonders into life, could also have created the beautiful Earth whereon they dwelt. These thoughts gave rise to others; suppositions became certainties; and soon the following myth or fable was evolved, to be handed down from generation to generation.

OPPOSITE PAGE: LA NUIT. William-Adolphe Bouguereau.

At first, when all things lay in a great confused mass,—

> Ere earth, and sea, and covering heavens, were known,
> The face of nature, o'er the world, was one;
> And men have call'd it Chaos; formless, rude,
> The mass; dead matter's weight, inert, and crude;
> Where, in mix'd heap of ill-compounded mold,
> The jarring seeds of things confusedly roll'd.
>
> OVID (Elton's tr.)

The Earth did not exist. Land, sea, and air were mixed up together; so that the earth was not solid, the sea was not fluid, nor the air transparent.

> No sun yet beam'd from yon cerulean height;
> No orbing moon repair'd her horns of light;
> No earth, self-poised, on liquid ether hung;
> No sea its world-enclasping waters flung;
> Earth was half air, half sea, an embryo heap;
> Nor earth was fix'd, nor fluid was the deep;
> Dark was the void of air; no form was traced;
> Obstructing atoms struggled through the waste;
> Where cold, and hot, and moist, and dry rebell'd;
> Heavy the light, and hard the soft repell'd.
>
> OVID (Elton's tr.)

CHAOS AND NYX

Over this shapeless mass reigned a careless deity called Chaos, whose personal appearance could not be described, as there was no light by which he could be seen. He shared his throne with his wife, the dark goddess of Night, named Nyx or Nox, whose black robes, and still blacker countenance, did not tend to enliven the surrounding gloom.

EREBUS, ÆTHER, AND HEMERA

These two divinities wearied of their power in the course of time, and called their son Erebus (Darkness) to their assistance. His first act was to dethrone and supplant

Chaos; and then, thinking he would be happier with a helpmeet, he married his own mother, Nyx. Of course, with our present views, this marriage was a heinous sin; but the ancients, who at first had no fixed laws, did not consider this union unsuitable, and recounted how Erebus and Nyx ruled over the chaotic world together, until their two beautiful children, Æther (Light) and Hemera (Day), acting in concert, dethroned them, and seized the supreme power.

CREATION OF GÆA AND URANUS

Space, illumined for the first time by their radiance, revealed itself in all its uncouthness. Æther and Hemera carefully examined the confusion, saw its innumerable possibilities, and decided to evolve from it a "thing of beauty"; but quite conscious of the magnitude of such an undertaking, and feeling that some assistance would be desirable, they summoned Eros (Amor or Love), their own child, to their aid. By their combined efforts, Pontus (the Sea) and Gæa (Ge, Tellus, Terra), as the Earth was first called, were created.

In the beginning the Earth did not present the beautiful appearance that it does now. No trees waved their leafy branches on the hillsides; no flowers bloomed in the valleys; no grass grew on the plains; no birds flew through the air. All was silent, bare, and motionless. Eros, the first to perceive these deficiencies, seized his life-giving arrows and pierced the cold bosom of the Earth. Immediately the brown surface was covered with luxuriant verdure; birds of many colors flitted through the foliage of the new-born forest trees; animals of all kinds gamboled over the grassy plains; and swift-darting fishes swam in the limpid streams. All was now life, joy, and motion.

Gæa, roused from her apathy, admired all that had already been done for her embellishment, and, resolving to crown and complete the work so well begun, created Uranus (Heaven).

> Her first-born Earth produc'd,
> Of like immensity, the starry Heaven:
> That he might sheltering compass her around
> On every side.
>
> HESIOD (Elton's tr.)

THE EGG MYTH

This version of the creation of the world, although but one of the many current with the Greeks and Romans, was the one most generally adopted; but another, also very popular, stated that the first divinities, Erebus and Nyx, produced a gigantic egg, from which Eros, the god of love, emerged to create the Earth.

In the dreary chaotical closet
Of Erebus old, was a privy deposit,
By Night the primæval in secrecy laid;
A Mystical Egg, that in silence and shade
Was brooded and hatched; till time came about:
And Love, the delightful, in glory flew out.

ARISTOPHANES (Frere's tr.)

MOUNT OLYMPUS AND THE RIVER OCEANUS

The Earth thus created was supposed by the ancients to be a disk, instead of a sphere as science has proved. The Greeks fancied that their country occupied a central position, and that Mount Olympus, a very high mountain, the mythological abode of their gods, was placed in the exact center. Their Earth was divided into two equal parts by Pontus (the Sea,—equivalent to our Mediterranean and Black Seas); and all around it flowed the great river Oceanus in a "steady, equable current," undisturbed by storm, from which the Sea and all the rivers were supposed to derive their waters.

THE HYPERBOREANS

The Greeks also imagined that the portion of the Earth directly north of their country was inhabited by a fortunate race of men, the Hyperboreans, who dwelt in continual bliss, and enjoyed a never-ending springtide. Their homes were said to be "inaccessible by land or by sea." They were "exempt from disease, old age, and death," and were so virtuous that the gods frequently visited them, and even condescended to share their feasts and games. A people thus favored could not fail to be happy, and many were the songs in praise of their sunny land.

OPPOSITE PAGE: L'AMOUR MENAÇANT. Carle Van Loo.

I come from a land in the sun-bright deep,
    Where golden gardens grow;
Where the winds of the north, becalm'd in sleep,
    Their conch shells never blow.

So near the track of the stars are we,
    That oft, on night's pale beams,
The distant sounds of their harmony
    Come to our ears, like dreams.

The Moon, too, brings her world so nigh,
    That when the night-seer looks
To that shadowless orb, in a vernal sky,
    He can number its hills and brooks.

To the Sun god all our hearts and lyres
    By day, by night, belong;
And the breath we draw from his living fires
    We give him back in song.

MOORE

THE ETHIOPIANS AND THE ISLES OF THE BLEST

South of Greece, also near the great river Oceanus, dwelt another nation, just as happy and virtuous as the Hyperboreans,—the Ethiopians. They, too, often enjoyed the company of the gods, who shared their innocent pleasures with great delight.

And far away, on the shore of this same marvelous river, according to some mythologists, were the beautiful Isles of the Blest, where mortals who had led virtuous lives, and had thus found favor in the sight of the gods, were transported without tasting of death, and where they enjoyed an eternity of bliss. These islands had sun, moon, and stars of their own, and were never visited by the cold wintry winds that swept down from the north.

The Isles of the Blest, they say,
    The Isles of the Blest,
Are peaceful and happy, by night and by day,
    Far away in the glorious west.

They need not the moon in that land of delight,
    They need not the pale, pale star;
The sun is bright, by day and night,
    Where the souls of the blessed are.

They till not the ground, they plow not the wave,
    They labor not, never! oh, never!
Not a tear do they shed, not a sigh do they heave,
    They are happy, for ever and ever!

Pindar

Uranus and Gæa

Chaos, Erebus, and Nyx were deprived of their power by Æther and Hemera, who did not long enjoy the possession of the scepter; for Uranus and Gæa, more powerful than their progenitors, soon forced them to depart, and began to reign in their stead. They had not dwelt long on the summit of Mount Olympus, before they found themselves the parents of twelve gigantic children, the Titans, whose strength was such that their father, Uranus, greatly feared them. To prevent their ever making use of it against him, he seized them immediately after their birth, hurled them down into a dark abyss called Tartarus, and there chained them fast.

Titans, Cyclopes, and Centimani

This chasm was situated far under the earth; and Uranus knew that his six sons (Oceanus, Cœus, Crius, Hyperion, Iapetus, and Cronus), as well as his six daughters, the Titanides (Ilia, Rhea, Themis, Thetis, Mnemosyne, and Phœbe), could not easily escape from its cavernous depths. The Titans did not long remain sole occupants of Tartarus, for one day the brazen doors were again thrown wide open to admit the Cyclopes,—Brontes (Thunder), Steropes (Lightning), and Arges (Sheet-lightning),—three later-born children of Uranus and Gæa, who helped the Titans to make the darkness hideous with their incessant clamor for freedom. In due time their number was increased by the three terrible Centimani (Hundred-handed), Cottus, Briareus, and Gyes, who were sent thither by Uranus to share their fate.

Greatly dissatisfied with the treatment her children had received at their father's hands, Gæa remonstrated, but all in vain. Uranus would not grant her request to set the giants free, and, whenever their muffled cries reached his ear, he trembled for his own safety. Angry beyond all expression, Gæa swore revenge, and descended into Tartarus, where she urged the Titans to conspire against their father, and attempt to wrest the scepter from his grasp.

The Titans Revolt

All listened attentively to the words of sedition; but none were courageous enough to carry out her plans, except Cronus, the youngest of the Titans, more familiarly known as Saturn or Time, who found confinement and chains peculiarly galling, and who hated his father for his cruelty. Gæa finally induced him to lay violent hands upon his sire, and, after releasing him from his bonds, gave him a scythe, and bade him be of good cheer and return victorious.

Thus armed and admonished, Cronus set forth, came upon his father unawares, defeated him, thanks to his extraordinary weapon, and, after binding him fast, took possession of the vacant throne, intending to rule the universe forever. Enraged at this insult, Uranus cursed his son, and prophesied that a day would come when he, too, would be supplanted by his children, and would suffer just punishment for his rebellion.

Cronus and Rhea

Cronus paid no heed to his father's imprecations, but calmly proceeded to release the Titans, his brothers and sisters, who, in their joy and gratitude to escape the dismal realm of Tartarus, expressed their willingness to be ruled by him. Their satisfaction was complete, however, when he chose his own sister Rhea (Cybele, Ops) for his consort, and assigned to each of the others some portion of the world to govern at will. To Oceanus and Thetis, for example, he gave charge over the ocean and all the rivers upon earth; while to Hyperion and Phœbe he entrusted the direction of the sun and moon, which the ancients supposed were daily driven across the sky in brilliant golden chariots.

Peace and security now reigned on and around Mount Olympus; and Cronus, with great satisfaction, congratulated himself on the result of his enterprise. One fine morning, however, his equanimity was disturbed by the announcement that a son was born to him. The memory of his father's curse then suddenly returned to his mind. Anxious to avert so great a calamity as the loss of his power, he hastened to his wife, determined to devour the child, and thus prevent him from causing further annoyance. Wholly unsuspicious, Rhea heard him inquire for his son. Gladly she placed him in his extended arms; but imagine her surprise and horror when she beheld her husband swallow the babe!

BIRTH OF JUPITER

Time passed, and another child was born, but only to meet with the same cruel fate. One infant after another disappeared down the capacious throat of the voracious Cronus,—a personification of Time, who creates only to destroy. In vain the bereaved mother besought the life of one little one: the selfish, hard-hearted father would not relent. As her prayers seemed unavailing, Rhea finally resolved to obtain by stratagem the boon her husband denied; and as soon as her youngest son, Jupiter (Jove, Zeus), was born, she concealed him.

Cronus, aware of his birth, soon made his appearance, determined to dispose of him in the usual summary manner. For some time Rhea pleaded with him, but at last pretended to yield to his commands. Hastily wrapping a large stone in swaddling clothes, she handed it to Cronus, simulating intense grief. Cronus was evidently not of a very inquiring turn of mind, for he swallowed the whole without investigating the real contents of the shapeless bundle.

FOLLOWING PAGES: FOUNTAIN OF CYBELE.

> To th' imperial son of Heaven,
> Whilom the king of gods, a stone she gave
> Inwrapt in infant swathes; and this with grasp
> Eager he snatch'd, and in his ravening breast
> Convey'd away: unhappy! nor once thought
> That for the stone his child behind remain'd
> Invincible, secure; who soon, with hands
> Of strength o'ercoming him, should cast him forth
> From glory, and himself th' immortals rule.
>
> HESIOD (Elton's tr.)

Ignorant of the deception practiced upon him, Cronus then took leave, and the overjoyed mother clasped her rescued treasure to her breast. It was not sufficient, however, to have saved young Jupiter from imminent death: it was also necessary that his father should remain unconscious of his existence.

JUPITER'S INFANCY

To insure this, Rhea intrusted her babe to the tender care of the Melian nymphs, who bore him off to a cave on Mount Ida. There a goat, Amalthea, was procured to act as nurse, and fulfilled her office so acceptably that she was eventually placed in the heavens as a constellation, a brilliant reward for her kind ministrations. To prevent Jupiter's cries being heard in Olympus, the Curetes (Corybantes), Rhea's priests, uttered piercing screams, clashed their weapons, executed fierce dances, and chanted rude war songs.

The real significance of all this unwonted noise and commotion was not at all understood by Cronus, who, in the intervals of his numerous affairs, congratulated himself upon the cunning he had shown to prevent the accomplishment of his father's curse. But all his anxiety and fears were aroused when he suddenly became aware of the fraud practiced upon him, and of young Jupiter's continued existence. He immediately tried to devise some plan to get rid of him; but, before he could put it into execution, he found himself attacked, and, after a short but terrible encounter, signally defeated.

JUPITER'S SUPREMACY

Jupiter, delighted to have triumphed so quickly, took possession of the supreme power, and aided by Rhea's counsels, and by a nauseous potion prepared by Metis, a daughter of Oceanus, compelled Cronus to produce the unfortunate children he had swallowed; i.e., Neptune, Pluto, Vesta, Ceres, and Juno.

Following the example of his predecessor, Jupiter gave his brothers and sisters a fair share of his new kingdom. The wisest among the Titans—Mnemosyne, Themis, Oceanus, and Hyperion—submitted to the new sovereign without murmur, but the others refused their allegiance; which refusal, of course, occasioned a deadly conflict.

> When gods began with wrath,
> And war rose up between their starry brows,
> Some choosing to cast Cronus from his throne
> That Zeus might king it there, and some in haste
> With opposite oaths that they would have no Zeus
> To rule the gods forever.
>
> E. B. BROWNING

THE GIANTS' WAR

Jupiter, from the top of Mount Olympus, discerned the superior number of his foes, and, quite aware of their might, concluded that reënforcements to his party would not be superfluous. In haste, therefore, he released the Cyclopes from Tartarus, where they had languished so long, stipulating that in exchange for their freedom they should supply him with thunderbolts,—weapons which only they knew how to forge. This new engine caused great terror and dismay in the ranks of the enemy, who, nevertheless, soon rallied, and struggled valiantly to overthrow the usurper and win back the sovereignty of the world.

During ten long years the war raged incessantly, neither party wishing to submit to the dominion of the other, but at the end of that time the rebellious Titans were obliged to yield. Some of them were hurled into Tartarus once more, where they were carefully secured by Neptune, Jupiter's brother, while the young conqueror joyfully proclaimed his victory.

> League all your forces then, ye powers above,
> Join all, and try th' omnipotence of Jove:

Let down our golden everlasting chain,
Whose strong embrace holds heaven and earth and main:
Strive all, of mortal and immortal birth,
To drag, by this, the Thunderer down to earth,
Ye strive in vain! if I but stretch this hand,
I heave the gods, the ocean, and the land;
I fix the chain to great Olympus' height,
And the vast world hangs trembling in my sight!
For such I reign, unbounded and above;
And such are men and gods, compar'd to Jove.

                              HOMER (Pope's tr.)

The scene of this mighty conflict was supposed to have been in Thessaly, where the country bears the imprint of some great natural convulsion; for the ancients imagined that the gods, making the most of their gigantic strength and stature, hurled huge rocks at each other, and piled mountain upon mountain to reach the abode of Jupiter, the Thunderer.

Mountain on mountain, as the Titans erst,
My brethren, scaling the high seat of Jove,
Heaved Pelion upon Ossa's shoulders broad
In vain emprise.

                              LOWELL

Saturn, or Cronus, the leader and instigator of the revolt, weary at last of bloodshed and strife, withdrew to Italy, or Hesperia, where he founded a prosperous kingdom, and reigned in peace for many long years.

THE DEATH OF TYPHŒUS

Jupiter, having disposed of all the Titans, now fancied he would enjoy the power so unlawfully obtained; but Gæa, to punish him for depriving her children of their birthright, created a terrible monster, called Typhœus, or Typhon, which she sent to attack him. This Typhœus was a giant, from whose trunk one hundred dragon heads arose; flames shot from his eyes, nostrils, and mouths; while he incessantly uttered such blood-curdling screams, that the gods, in terror, fled from Mount Olympus and sought refuge in Egypt. In mortal fear lest this terror-inspiring monster would pursue them, the gods there assumed the forms of different animals; and Jupiter became a ram, while Juno, his sister and queen, changed herself into a cow.

The king of the gods, however, soon became ashamed of his cowardly flight, and resolved to return to Mount Olympus to slay Typhœus with his terrible thunder-bolts. A long and fierce struggle ensued, at the end of which, Jupiter, again victorious, viewed his fallen foe with boundless pride; but his triumph was very short-lived.

DEFEAT OF ENCELADUS

Enceladus, another redoubtable giant, also created by Gæa, now appeared to avenge Typhœus. He too was signally defeated, and bound with adamantine chains in a burning cave under Mount Ætna. In early times, before he had become accustomed to his prison, he gave vent to his rage by outcries, imprecations, and groans: sometimes he even breathed forth fire and flames, in hopes of injuring his conqueror. But time, it is said, somewhat cooled his resentment; and now he is content with an occasional change of position, which, owing to his huge size, causes the earth to tremble over a space of many miles, producing what is called an earthquake.

> 'Tis said, that thunder-struck Enceladus,
> Groveling beneath the incumbent mountain's weight,
> Lies stretched supine, eternal prey of flames;
> And, when he heaves against the burning load,
> Reluctant, to invert his broiling limbs,
> A sudden earthquake shoots through all the isle,
> And Ætna thunders dreadful under ground,
> Then pours out smoke in wreathing curls convolved,
> And shades the sun's bright orb, and blots out day.
>
> ADDISON

JUPITER DIVIDES HIS REALM

Jupiter had now conquered all his foes, asserted his right to the throne, and could at last reign over the world undisturbed; but he knew that it would be no small undertaking to rule well heaven, earth, and sea, and resolved to divide the power with his brothers. To avoid quarrels and recriminations, he portioned the world out into lots, allowing each of his brothers the privilege of drawing his own share.

Neptune thus obtained control over the sea and all the rivers, and immediately expressed his resolve to wear a symbolic crown, composed exclusively of marine shells and aquatic plants, and to abide within the bounds of his watery realm.

Pluto, the most taciturn of the brothers, received for his portion the scepter of Tartarus and all the Lower World, where no beam of sunlight was ever allowed to find its way; while Jupiter reserved for himself the general supervision of his brothers' estates, and the direct management of Heaven and Earth.

Peace now reigned throughout all the world. Not a murmur was heard, except from the Titans, who at length, seeing that further opposition would be useless, grew reconciled to their fate.

In the days of their prosperity, the Titans had intermarried. Cronus had taken Rhea "for better or for worse"; and Iapetus had seen, loved, and wedded the fair Clymene, one of the ocean nymphs, or Oceanides, daughters of Oceanus. The latter pair became the proud parents of four gigantic sons,—Atlas, Menetius, Prometheus (Forethought), and Epimetheus (Afterthought),—who were destined to play prominent parts in Grecian mythology.

STORY OF PROMETHEUS

At the time of the creation, after covering the new-born Earth with luxuriant vegetation, and peopling it with living creatures of all kinds, Eros perceived that it would be necessary to endow them with instincts which would enable them to preserve and enjoy the life they had received. He therefore called the youngest two sons of Iapetus to his aid, and bade them make a judicious distribution of gifts to all living creatures, and create and endow a superior being, called Man, to rule over all the others.

Prometheus's and Epimetheus's first care was, very naturally, to provide for the beings already created. These they endowed with such reckless generosity, that all their favors were soon dispensed, and none remained for the endowment of man. Although they had not the remotest idea how to overcome this difficulty, they proceeded to fashion man from clay.

> Prometheus first transmuted
> Atoms culled for human clay.
> HORACE

They first molded an image similar in form to the gods; bade Eros breathe into its nostrils the spirit of life, and Minerva (Pallas) endow it with a soul; whereupon man lived, and moved, and viewed his new domain.

Justly proud of his handiwork, Prometheus observed man, and longed to bestow upon him some great power, unshared by any other creature of mortal birth, which would raise him far above all other living beings, and bring him nearer to the perfection of the immortal gods. Fire alone, in his estimation, could effect this; but fire was the special possession and prerogative of the gods, and Prometheus knew they would never willingly share it with man, and that, should any one obtain it by stealth, they would never forgive the thief. Long he pondered the matter, and finally determined to obtain fire, or die in the attempt.

One dark night, therefore, he set out for Olympus, entered unperceived into the gods' abode, seized a lighted brand, hid it in his bosom, and departed unseen, exulting in the success of his enterprise. Arrived upon earth once more, he consigned the stolen treasure to the care of man, who immediately adapted it to various purposes, and eloquently expressed his gratitude to the benevolent deity who had risked his own life to obtain it for him.

> Of Prometheus, how undaunted
> On Olympus' shining bastions
> His audacious foot he planted,
> Myths are told and songs are chanted,
> Full of promptings and suggestions.
> Beautiful is the tradition
> Of that flight through heavenly portals,
> The old classic superstition
> Of the theft and the transmission
> Of the fire of the Immortals.
> LONGFELLOW

FOLLOWING PAGES: THE FORMATION OF MAN BY PROMETHEUS WITH THE AID OF MINERVA. Louis de Silvestre.

From his lofty throne on the topmost peak of Mount Olympus Jupiter beheld an unusual light down upon earth. Anxious to ascertain its exact nature, he watched it closely, and before long discovered the larceny. His anger then burst forth, terrible to behold; and the gods all quailed when they heard him solemnly vow he would punish the unhappy Prometheus without mercy. To seize the offender in his mighty grasp, bear him off to the Caucasian Mountains, and bind him fast to a great rock, was but a moment's work. There a voracious vulture was summoned to feast upon his liver, the tearing of which from his side by the bird's cruel beak and talons caused the sufferer intense anguish. All day long the vulture gorged himself; but during the cool night, while the bird slept, Prometheus's suffering abated, and the liver grew again, thus prolonging the torture, which bade fair to have no end.

Disheartened by the prospect of long years of unremitting pain, Prometheus at times could not refrain from pitiful complaints; but generation after generation of men lived on earth, and died, blessing him for the gift he had obtained for them at such a terrible cost. After many centuries of woe, Hercules, son of Jupiter and Alcmene, found Prometheus, killed the vulture, broke the adamantine chains, and liberated the long-suffering god.

STORY OF EPIMETHEUS AND PANDORA

The first mortals lived on earth in a state of perfect innocence and bliss. The air was pure and balmy; the sun shone brightly all the year; the earth brought forth delicious fruit in abundance; and beautiful, fragrant flowers bloomed everywhere. Man was content. Extreme cold, hunger, sickness, and death were unknown. Jupiter, who justly ascribed a good part of this beatific condition to the gift conferred by Prometheus, was greatly displeased, and tried to devise some means to punish mankind for the acceptance of the heavenly fire.

With this purpose in view, he assembled the gods on Mount Olympus, where, in solemn council, they decided to create woman; and, as soon as she had been artfully fashioned, each one endowed her with some special charm, to make her more attractive.

> The crippled artist-god,
> Illustrious, molded from the yielding clay
> A bashful virgin's image, as advis'd
> Saturnian Jove.

*   *   *   *   *

> But now when the fair mischief, seeming-good,
> His hand had perfected, he led her forth
> Exulting in her grac'd attire, the gift
> Of Pallas, in the midst of gods and men.
> On men and gods in that same moment seiz'd
> The ravishment of wonder, when they saw
> The deep deceit, th' inextricable snare.
>
> HESIOD (Elton's tr.)

Their united efforts were crowned with the utmost success. Nothing was lacking, except a name for the peerless creature; and the gods, after due consideration, decreed she should be called Pandora. They then bade Mercury take her to Prometheus as a gift from heaven; but he, knowing only too well that nothing good would come to him from the gods, refused to accept her, and cautioned his brother Epimetheus to follow his example. Unfortunately Epimetheus was of a confiding disposition, and when he beheld the maiden he exclaimed, "Surely so beautiful and gentle a being can bring no evil!" and accepted her most joyfully.

The first days of their union were spent in blissful wanderings, hand in and, under the cool forest shade; in weaving garlands of fragrant flowers; and in refreshing themselves with the luscious fruit, which hung so temptingly within reach.

One lovely evening, while dancing on the green, they saw Mercury, Jupiter's messenger, coming towards them. His step was slow and weary, his garments dusty and travel-stained, and he seemed almost to stagger beneath the weight of a huge box which rested upon his shoulders. Pandora immediately ceased dancing, to speculate with feminine curiosity upon the contents of the chest. She nudged Epimetheus, and in a whisper begged him to ask Mercury what brought him thither. Epimetheus complied with her request; but Mercury evaded the question, asked permission to deposit his burden in their dwelling for safekeeping, professing himself too weary to convey it to its destination that day, and promised to call for it shortly. The permission was promptly granted. Mercury, with a sigh of relief, placed the box in one corner, and then departed, refusing all hospitable offers of rest and refreshment.

He had scarcely crossed the threshold, when Pandora expressed a strong desire to have a peep at the contents of the mysterious box; but Epimetheus, surprised and shocked, told her that her curiosity was unseemly, and then, to dispel the frown and pout seen for the first time on the fair face of his beloved, he entreated her to come

out into the fresh air and join in the merry games of their companions. For the first time, also, Pandora refused to comply with his request. Dismayed, and very much discouraged, Epimetheus sauntered out alone, thinking she would soon join him, and perhaps by some caress atone for her present willfulness.

Left alone with the mysterious casket, Pandora became more and more inquisitive. Stealthily she drew near, and examined it with great interest, for it was curiously wrought of dark wood, and surmounted by a delicately carved head, of such fine workmanship that it seemed to smile and encourage her. Around the box a glittering golden cord was wound, and fastened on top in an intricate knot. Pandora, who prided herself specially on her deft fingers, felt sure she could unfasten it, and, reasoning that it would not be indiscreet to untie it if she did not raise the lid, she set to work. Long she strove, but all in vain. Ever and anon the laughing voices of Epimetheus and his companions, playing in the luxuriant shade, were wafted in on the summer breeze. Repeatedly she heard them call, and beseech her to join them; yet she persisted in her attempt. She was just on the point of giving it up in despair, when suddenly the refractory knot yielded to her fumbling fingers, and the cord, unrolling, dropped on the floor.

Pandora had repeatedly fancied that sounds like whispers issued from the box. The noise now seemed to increase, and she breathlessly applied her ear to the lid to ascertain whether it really proceeded from within. Imagine, therefore, her surprise when she distinctly heard these words, uttered in the most pitiful accents: "Pandora, dear Pandora, have pity upon us! Free us from this gloomy prison! Open, open, we beseech you!"

Pandora's heart beat so fast and loud, that it seemed for a moment to drown all other sounds. Should she open the box? Just then a familiar step outside made her start guiltily. Epimetheus was coming, and she knew he would urge her again to come out, and would prevent the gratification of her curiosity. Precipitately, therefore, she raised the lid to have one little peep before he came in.

Now, Jupiter had malignantly crammed into this box all the diseases, sorrows, vices, and crimes that afflict poor humanity; and the box was no sooner opened, than all these ills flew out, in the guise of horrid little brown-winged creatures, closely resembling moths. These little insects fluttered about, alighting, some upon Epimetheus, who had just entered, and some upon Pandora, pricking and stinging them most unmercifully. Then they flew out through the open door and windows, and fastened

OPPOSITE PAGE: PANDORA. John William Waterhouse.

upon the merrymakers without, whose shouts of joy were soon changed into wails of pain and anguish.

Epimetheus and Pandora had never before experienced the faintest sensation of pain or anger; but, as soon as these winged evil spirits had stung them, they began to weep, and, alas! quarreled for the first time in their lives. Epimetheus reproached his wife in bitterest terms for her thoughtless action; but in the very midst of his vituperation he suddenly heard a sweet little voice entreat for freedom. The sound proceeded from the unfortunate box, whose cover Pandora had dropped again, in the first moment of her surprise and pain. "Open, open, and I will heal your wounds! Please let me out!" it pleaded.

The tearful couple viewed each other inquiringly, and listened again. Once more they heard the same pitiful accents; and Epimetheus bade his wife open the box and set the speaker free, adding very amiably, that she had already done so much harm by her ill-fated curiosity, that it would be difficult to add materially to its evil consequences, and that, perchance, the box contained some good spirit, whose ministrations might prove beneficial.

It was well for Pandora that she opened the box a second time, for the gods, with a sudden impulse of compassion, had concealed among the evil spirits one kindly creature, Hope, whose mission was to heal the wounds inflicted by her fellow-prisoners.

> Hope sole remain'd within, nor took her flight,
> Beneath the vessel's verge conceal'd from light.
> HESIOD (Elton's tr.)

Lightly fluttering hither and thither on her snowy pinions, Hope touched the punctured places on Pandora's and Epimetheus's creamy skin, and relieved their suffering, then quickly flew out of the open window, to perform the same gentle office for the other victims, and cheer their downcast spirits.

Thus, according to the ancients, evil entered into the world, bringing untold misery; but Hope followed closely in its footsteps, to aid struggling humanity, and point to a happier future.

> Hope rules a land forever green:
> All powers that serve the bright-eyed Queen
>   Are confident and gay;
> Clouds at her bidding disappear;
> Points she to aught?——the bliss draws near,
>   And Fancy smooths the way.
>
> WORDSWORTH

During many centuries, therefore, Hope continued to be revered, although the other divinities had ceased to be worshiped.

According to another version, Pandora was sent down to man, bearing a vase in which the evil spirits were imprisoned, and on the way, seized by a fit of curiosity, raised the cover, and allowed them all to escape.

THE FOUR AGES

Little by little the world was peopled; and the first years of man's existence upon earth were, as we have seen, years of unalloyed happiness. There was no occasion for labor, for the earth brought forth spontaneously all that was necessary for man's subsistence. "Innocence, virtue, and truth prevailed; neither were there any laws to restrict men, nor judges to punish." This time of bliss has justly borne the title of Golden Age, and the people in Italy then throve under the wise rule of good old Saturn, or Cronus.

Unfortunately, nothing in this world is lasting; and the Golden Age was ollowed by another, not quite so prosperous, hence called the Silver Age, when the year was first divided into seasons, and men were obliged to toil for their daily bread.

> Succeeding times a silver age behold,
> Excelling brass, but more excell'd by gold.
> Then summer, autumn, winter, did appear,
> And spring was but a season of the year;
> The sun his annual course obliquely made,
> Good days contracted, and enlarg'd the bad.
> The air with sultry heats began to glow,
> The wings of winds were clogg'd with ice and snow;
> And shivering mortals into houses driven,

HOPE IN A PRISON OF DESPAIR.
Evelyn De Morgan.

Sought shelter from the inclemency of heaven.
Those houses, then, were caves or homely sheds,
With twining osiers fenc'd, and moss their beds.
Then plows, for seed, the fruitful furrows broke,
And oxen labor'd first beneath the yoke.

OVID (Dryden's tr.)

Yet, in spite of these few hardships, the people were happy, far happier than their descendants during the Age of Brass, which speedily followed, when strife became customary, and differences were settled by blows.

But by far the worst of all was the Iron Age, when men's passions knew no bounds, and they even dared refuse all homage to the immortal gods. War was waged incessantly; the earth was saturated with blood; the rights of hospitality were openly violated; and murder, rape, and theft were committed on all sides.

THE DELUGE

Jupiter had kept a close watch over men's actions during all these years; and this evil conduct aroused his wrath to such a point, that he vowed he would annihilate the human race. But the modes of destruction were manifold, and, as he could not decide which would eventually prove most efficacious, he summoned the gods to deliberate and aid him by their counsels. The first suggestion offered, was to destroy the world by fire, kindled by Jupiter's much-dreaded thunderbolts; and the king of gods was about to put it into instant execution, when his arm was stayed by the objection that the rising flames might set fire to his own abode, and reduce its magnificence to unsightly ashes. He therefore rejected the plan as impracticable, and bade the gods devise other means of destruction.

After much delay and discussion, the immortals agreed to wash mankind off the face of the earth by a mighty deluge. The winds were instructed to gather together the rain clouds over the earth. Neptune let loose the waves of the sea, bidding them rise, overflow, and deluge the land. No sooner had the gods spoken, than the elements obeyed: the winds blew; the rain fell in torrents; lakes, seas, rivers, and oceans broke their bonds; and terrified mortals, forgetting their petty quarrels in a common impulse to flee from the death which threatened them, climbed the highest mountains, clung to uprooted trees, and even took refuge in the light skiffs they had constructed in happier days. Their efforts were all in vain, however; for the waters rose higher and higher, overtook them one after another in their ineffectual efforts to escape, closed over the homes where they might have been so happy, and drowned their last despairing cries in their seething depths.

> Now hills and vales no more distinction know,
> And level'd nature lies oppress'd below;
> The most of mortals perish in the flood.
>
> OVID (Dryden's tr.)

STORY OF DEUCALION AND PYRRHA

The rain continued to fall, until, after many days, the waves covered all the surface of the earth except the summit of Mount Parnassus, the highest peak in Greece. On this mountain, surrounded by the ever-rising flood, stood the son of Prometheus, Deucalion, with his faithful wife Pyrrha, a daughter of Epimetheus and Pandora. From thence they, the sole survivors, viewed the universal desolation with tear-dimmed eyes.

In spite of the general depravity, the lives of this couple had always been pure and virtuous; and when Jupiter saw them there alone, and remembered their piety, he decided not to include them in the general destruction, but to save their lives. He therefore bade the winds return to their cave, and the rain to cease. Neptune, in accordance with his decree, blew a resounding blast upon his conch shell to recall the wandering waves, which immediately returned within their usual bounds.

> At length the world was all restor'd to view,
> But desolate, and of a sickly hue;
> Nature beheld herself, and stood aghast,
> A dismal desert and a silent waste.
>
> OVID (Dryden's tr.)

Deucalion and Pyrrha followed the receding waves step by step down the steep mountain side, wondering how they should repeople the desolate earth. As they talked, they came to the shrine of Delphi, which alone had been able to resist the force of the waves. There they entered to consult the wishes of the gods. Their surprise and horror were unbounded, however, when a voice exclaimed, "Depart from hence with veiled heads, and cast your mother's bones behind you!" To obey such a command seemed sacrilegious in the extreme; for the dead had always been held

DEUCALION AND PYRRHA. Peter Paul Rubens.

in deep veneration by the Greeks, and the desecration of a grave was considered a heinous crime, and punished accordingly. But, they reasoned, the gods' oracles can seldom be accepted in a literal sense; and Deucalion, after due thought, explained to Pyrrha what he conceived to be the meaning of this mysterious command.

"The Earth," said he, "is the mother of all, and the stones may be considered her bones." Husband and wife speedily decided to act upon this premise, and continued their descent, casting stones behind them. All those thrown by Deucalion were immediately changed into men, while those cast by Pyrrha became women.

Thus the earth was peopled for the second time with a blameless race of men, sent to replace the wicked beings slain by Jupiter. Deucalion and Pyrrha shortly after became the happy parents of a son named Hellen, who gave his name to all the Hellenic or Greek race; while his sons Æolus and Dorus, and grandsons Ion and Achæus, became the ancestors of the Æolian, Dorian, Ionian, and Achaian nations.

Other mythologists, in treating of the deluvian myths, state that Deucalion and Pyrrha took refuge in an ark, which, after sailing about for many days, was stranded on the top of Mount Parnassus. This version was far less popular with the Greeks, although it betrays still more plainly the common source whence all these myths are derived.

> Who does not see in drown Deucalion's name,
> When Earth her men and Sea had lost her shore,
> Old Noah!
>
> FLETCHER

JUPITER

JUPITER'S TITLES

Jupiter, Jove, or Zeus, king of the gods, supreme ruler of the universe, the special deity of mankind, the personification of the sky and of all the phenomena of the air, and the guardian of political order and peace, was the most prominent of all the Olympian divinities: the others were obliged to submit to his will, and trembled at his all-powerful nod.

> He, whose all-conscious eyes the world behold,
> The eternal Thunderer sat, enthroned in gold.
> High heaven the footstool of his feet he makes,
> And wide beneath him all Olympus shakes.
>
> He spoke, and awful bends his sable brows,
> Shakes his ambrosial curls, and gives the nod,
> The stamp of fate and sanction of the god:
> High heaven with trembling the dread signal took,
> And all Olympus to the center shook.
>
> HOMER (Pope's tr.)

The Fates and Destiny alone dared oppose Jupiter's sovereign will, and they continued to issue their irrevocable decrees, even after he supplanted his father and began to rule over all.

In common with all other Greek and Roman divinities, Jupiter, though immortal, was subject to pleasure, pain, grief, and anger, and a prey to all the passions which rule the hearts of men.

It was he who presided at the councils held on the top of "many-peaked Olympus," and summoned the gods whenever he wished to discuss with them any matter of importance, or to indulge in a sumptuous repast, when they ate the celestial ambrosia and quaffed the fragrant nectar.

He is generally represented as a fine majestic figure, with long curling hair and beard, clad in flowing drapery, his redoubtable thunderbolts or scepter in one hand, and a statue of Victory in the other. The world is his footstool; and the eagle, emblem of strength and power, is generally seen close beside him.

JUPITER'S ATTENDANTS

Jupiter had his own special attendants, such as Victoria, or Nice, the goddess of victory, who was ever ready to obey his slightest behest, and it is said her master loved her so dearly, that he generally held an image of her in his hand.

JUPITER GIVING FIRE TO VESUVIUS. Francois Joseph Heim.

The hundred-tongued goddess of fame, Fama, trumpet in hand, proclaimed, at his bidding, anything he wished, never questioning whether it were true or false.

Fame than who never plague that runs
    Its way more swiftly wins:
Her very motion lends her power:
She flies and waxes every hour.
At first she shrinks, and cowers for dread:
    Ere long she soars on high:
Upon the ground she plants her tread,
    Her forehead in the sky.
              VIRGIL (Conington's tr.)

Close by Jupiter's side was sometimes seen Fortuna, goddess of fortune, poised on a constantly revolving wheel, whereon she journeyed throughout the world, scattering with careless hands her numerous gifts, and lavishing with indifference her choicest smiles; while Hebe, or Juventas, the goddess of youth, was ever ready at his wish to pour out the nectar, in which the gods were wont to pledge each other.

> Hebe, honored of them all,
> Ministered nectar, and from cups of gold
> They pledged each other.
>
> HOMER (Bryant's tr.)

But this fair goddess awkwardly tripped and fell on a solemn occasion, and was forced to resign her office. To replace her, the father of the gods was obliged to go in quest of another cup-bearer.

To facilitate his search, he assumed the form of an eagle, and winged his flight over the earth. He had not flown far, before he beheld a youth of marvelous beauty, alone on a neighboring hill. To swoop down, catch him up in his mighty talons, and bear him safely off to Olympus, was but a moment's work; and there the kidnapped youth Ganymede, the son of a king of Troy, was carefully instructed in the duties he was called upon to perform in the future.

> And godlike Ganymede, most beautiful
> Of men; the gods beheld and caught him up
> To heaven, so beautiful was he, to pour
> The wine to Jove, and ever dwell with them.
>
> HOMER (Bryant's tr.)

STORY OF PHILEMON AND BAUCIS

Solicitous for the welfare of mankind, Jupiter often visited the earth, taking great care to assume some disguise which would enable him to ascertain all he wished without any risk of detection. One day he and Mercury, his special messenger and favorite among the gods, took the forms of needy, belated travelers, and entered the lowly hut of a worthy old couple, Philemon and Baucis.

OPPOSITE PAGE: GANYMEDE ABDUCTED BY THE EAGLE.
Antonio da Correggio.

Eager to offer their best to the strangers, these poor people decided to kill their sole remaining goose; but their efforts to secure it were vain, and finally the persecuted fowl took refuge between Jupiter's knees. Touched with their zeal, yet anxious to prevent the death of the confiding goose, Jupiter revealed himself to his faithful worshipers, and in gratitude for their intended sacrifice bade them ask any boon, promising by the great river Styx—the most binding and solemn oath a god could utter—to grant their request.

Contrary to the custom current in similar cases, Philemon and Baucis made a modest and judicious choice, and proffered a timid request that they might serve the gods as long as life and strength endured, and finally die together. This most reasonable wish was immediately granted; and Jupiter, moreover, changed their humble abode into a superb temple, where they could offer daily sacrifices on his altars.

> Their little shed, scarce large enough for two,
> Seems, from the ground increased, in height and bulk to grow.
> A stately temple shoots within the skies,
> The crotches of their cot in columns rise;
> The pavement polish'd marble they behold,
> The gates with sculpture grac'd, the spires and tiles of gold.
>
> OVID (Dryden's tr.)

After many years of faithful service, when age had made them long for death, Philemon and Baucis were transformed into majestic oaks, which stood for many a century in front of the temple, monuments of the love and faith which had bound the pair through life.

Although married to Juno, Jupiter often indulged in love affairs with other goddesses, and even with mortal maidens. The ancients themselves did not practice polygamy, but their gods were supposed to be able to indulge all their passions with impunity. As the personification of the sky, Jupiter, therefore, consorted at times with Juno (the Atmosphere), with Dione (Moisture), with Themis (Justice), etc., without incurring any reproach; for these marriages, in their estimation, were all symbolical.

But Juno being of a jealous disposition, Jupiter was forced to conduct his courtships with great secrecy and circumspection, and therefore generally adopted the precaution of a disguise. To win Europa, the fair daughter of Agenor, for instance, he became a bull.

> The gods themselves,
> Humbling their deities to love, have taken
> The shapes of beasts upon them. Jupiter
> Became a bull, and bellow'd.
>
> SHAKESPEARE

JUPITER KIDNAPS EUROPA

One day Europa was playing in her father's meadows with her three brothers, Cadmus, PhŒnix, and Cilix, when she suddenly saw a white bull coming towards her; not with fiery eyes and lowered horns, but gently, as if to express a mute request to be petted. The maiden, delighted, stroked the beast, and decked him with bright garlands of meadow-blossoms. Then, seeing him kneel, as if to invite her to mount, she lightly sprang upon his broad back, calling to her companions to follow her example; but, before they could do as she wished, the bull had risen to his feet, and galloped off towards the sea with his fair burden on his back.

Instead of turning when he saw the foam-crested waves, he plunged into the midst of them, and in a few minutes disappeared from view, so rapidly did he swim away. To reassure the frightened girl, the bull now spoke in gentle accents, bidding her dismiss all fear, for he was the great Jupiter in disguise.

> Take courage, gentle maid! nor fear the tide:
> I, though near-seen a bull, am heavenly Jove:
> I change my shape at will.
>
> MOSCHUS (Elton's tr.)

Pleased with the novelty of her situation, and flattered by the god's evident admiration, Europa ceased to struggle, wound her arms more closely around the bull's neck to prevent the waves from washing her off her perilous seat, and allowed herself to be carried away.

Jupiter finally deposited his fair burden upon the shores of a new land, to which he gallantly gave her name, Europe. He then resumed his wonted form, explained at length his reasons for so unceremoniously kidnapping her, and finally won her consent to their union. Their three sons were Minos, Rhadamanthus, and Sarpedon. The two former were subsequently appointed judges in the Infernal Regions, while the third found an early but glorious death during the Trojan war.

SEARCH FOR EUROPA

All unconscious of their sister's fate, the young princes had returned in haste to their father's palace to announce her sudden involuntary departure. Agenor, whose favorite she had always been, rent his garments for grief, and bade his sons go forth and seek her, and not to return till they had found her. Accompanied by their mother, Telephassa, they immediately set out on their journey, inquiring of all they met if they had seen their sister. Search and inquiry proved equally fruitless.

At last, weary of this hopeless quest, Phœnix refused his further aid, and allowed his sorrowing relatives to continue without him, remaining in a land which from him was called Phœnicia. Cilix, too, soon followed his example, and settled in a fertile country which they had reached, hence called Cilicia; and finally Telephassa, worn out with grief and fatigue, lay down to die, charging her oldest son to go on alone.

Cadmus wandered on till he came to Delphi, where he consulted the oracle; but, to his great dismay, the only reply he received was, "Follow the cow, and settle where she rests."

In deep perplexity he left the temple, and, from force of habit, journeyed on, patiently questioning all he met. Soon he perceived a cow leisurely walking in front of him, and, mindful of the oracle, he ceased his search and followed her. Urged by curiosity, many adventurers joined him on the way, and, when the cow at last lay down in the land since called Bœotia, they all promised to aid Cadmus, their chosen leader, to found their future capital, which was to be called Thebes.

FOUNDING OF THEBES

Parched with thirst after their long walk, the men then hastened to a neighboring spring, but, to Cadmus's surprise, time passed and still they did not return. Armed with his trusty sword, he finally went down to the spring to discover the cause of their delay, and found that they had all been devoured by a huge dragon, which lived in the hollow. The prince raised his sword to avenge their death, and dealt the dragon such a deadly blow upon the head, that he put an immediate end to its existence.

While Cadmus stood there contemplating his lifeless foe, a voice bade him extract the dragon's teeth, and sow them in the ground already broken for his future

OPPOSITE PAGE: THE RAPE OF EUROPA. Simon Vouet.

city. No human being was within sight: so Cadmus knew the order proceeded from the immortal gods, and immediately prepared to obey it. The dragon's teeth were no sooner planted, than a crop of giants sprang from the soil, full grown, and armed to the teeth. They were about to fall upon Cadmus, when the same voice bade him cast a stone in the midst of their close-drawn phalanx. Cadmus, seeing the giants were almost upon him, and that no time was to be lost, quickly threw a stone. The effect produced was almost instantaneous; for the giants, each fancying it had been thrown by his neighbor, began fighting among themselves. In a few minutes the number of giants was reduced to five, who sheathed their bloodstained weapons, and humbly tendered their services to Cadmus. With their aid, the foundations of the city were laid; but their labor was not very arduous, as the gods caused some of the public buildings to rise up out of the ground, all complete, and ready for use.

To reward Cadmus for his loving and painstaking search for Europa, Jupiter gave him the hand of the fair princess Harmonia, a daughter of Mars and Venus, in marriage. Cadmus, the founder of Thebes, is supposed to have invented the alphabet, and introduced its use into Greece. Although his career was very prosperous at first, he finally incurred the wrath of the gods by forgetting, on a solemn occasion, to offer them a suitable sacrifice; and, in anger at his dereliction, they changed him and Harmonia into huge serpents.

WORSHIP OF JUPITER

Jupiter was, of course, very widely and generally worshiped by the ancients; and his principal temples—the Capitol at Rome, and the shrine of Jupiter Ammon in Libya— have been world-renowned. He also had a noted temple at Dodona, where an oak tree gave forth mysterious prophecies, which were supposed to have been inspired by the king of gods; this long lost shrine has recently been discovered.

> Oh, where, Dodona! is thine aged grove,
> Prophetic fount, and oracle divine?
> What valley echoed the response of Jove?
> What trace remaineth of the Thunderer's shrine?
> All, all forgotten!
>
> BYRON

A magnificent temple at Olympia, on the Peloponnesus, was also dedicated to Jupiter; and here every fifth year the people of Greece were wont to assemble to celebrate games, in honor of Jupiter's great victory over the Titans. These festivals were known as the Olympian Games; and the Greeks generally reckoned time by olympiads, that is to say, by the space of time between the celebrations. Within the temple at Olympia stood a wonderful statue of gold and ivory, the work of Phidias. Its proportions and beauty were such, that it was counted one of the Seven Wonders of the ancient world. It is said, too, that the artist, having completed this masterpiece, longed for some sign of approval from heaven, and fervently prayed for a token that the god accepted his labor. Jupiter, in answer to this prayer, sent a vivid flash of lightning, which played about the colossal image, illuminating it, but leaving it quite unharmed.

The Greeks were indebted to Phidias for many of their most exquisite statues of the gods; but none of the others equaled this figure of Jupiter in size, dignity of attitude, or elaborate finish.

> Wise Phidias, thus his skill to prove,
> Through many a god advanc'd to Jove,
> And taught the polish'd rocks to shine
> With airs and lineaments divine;
> Till Greece, amaz'd, and half afraid,
> Th' assembled deities survey'd.
>
> ADDISON

JUNO

JUNO'S MARRIAGE

Juno (Hera, Here), queen of heaven, and goddess of the atmosphere and of marriage, was the daughter of Cronus and Rhea, and consequently the sister of Jupiter; but, as soon as the latter had dethroned his parents and seized the scepter, he began to look about him for a suitable helpmate. Juno won his affections by her great beauty; and he immediately began his courtship, which he carried on in the guise of a cuckoo, to infuse a little romance into it. He evidently found favor in her sight, and won her consent to share his throne; for shortly afterward their wedding was celebrated with great pomp on Mount Olympus. It was on this solemn occasion that the immortal conclave of the gods declared that Juno should be henceforth honored as goddess of marriage.

> Juno, who presides
> Supreme o'er bridegrooms and o'er brides.
> VIRGIL (Conington's tr.)

But although in the beginning this union seemed very happy, there soon arose subjects for contention; for unfortunately Jupiter was inclined to be faithless, and Juno jealous, and, like the element she personified, exceedingly variable in her moods. On such occasions she gave way to her violent temper, and bitterly reproached her husband, who, impatient of her censure, punished her severely, and, instead of reforming, merely continued his numerous intrigues with renewed zest.

OPPOSITE PAGE: JUPITER AND JUNO ON MOUNT IDA. James Barry.

Story of Callisto and Arcas

On one occasion he fell deeply in love with a maiden named Callisto, gentle, fair, and slender; but, in spite of all the precautions which he took when visiting her, Juno discovered the object of his affections. Night and day she thought and planned, until she devised a species of revenge which seemed adequate. The graceful girl was suddenly bereft of speech, changed into a rough, ungainly bear, and driven out into the solitudes of the great forests, which were from that time forth to be her home. Jupiter vainly sought his missing ladylove, and it was only long afterward that he discovered her and her little bear son Arcas. In pity for all they had suffered, he transferred them both to the sky, where they are still known as the constellations of the Great and Little Bear.

Juno's Attendant

Juno, like her husband, had also her special attendant, Iris (the Rainbow), whom she frequently employed as messenger,—a task which this deity accomplished with as much celerity as Mercury. Her flight through the air was so rapid, that she was seldom seen; and no one would have known she had passed, had it not been for the brilliant trail her many-colored robe left behind her in the sky.

> Like fiery clouds, that flush with ruddy glare,
> Or Iris, gliding through the purple air;
> When loosely girt her dazzling mantle flows,
> And 'gainst the sun in arching colors glows.
>
> Flaccus (Elton's tr.)

Juno is the mother of Mars, Hebe, and Vulcan, and is always described and represented as a beautiful, majestic woman, clad in flowing robes, with a diadem and scepter. The peacock and cuckoo were both sacred to her, and are therefore often seen at her side.

Worship of Juno

Her principal places of worship were at Mycenæ, Sparta, Argos, Rome, and Heræum. She had also numerous other sanctuaries scattered throughout the ancient world,

Opposite Page: AIR. Acislo Antonio Palomino y Velasco.

and was worshiped in the same temples as Jupiter. Many fine statues of this goddess were found in Greece and Italy, some of which are still extant, and serve to show the ancients' exalted conception of the Queen of Heaven.

STORY OF CLEOBIS AND BITON

Juno's festivals, the Matronalia, in Rome, were always celebrated with great pomp. Less important feasts were held in each city where a temple was dedicated to her. On one of these occasions an old priestess was very anxious to go to the temple at Argos, where she had ministered to the goddess for many years, and which she had left only to be married. The way was long and dusty: so the aged woman, who could no longer walk such a distance, bade her sons, Cleobis and Biton, harness her white heifers to her car. The youths hastened to do her bidding; but, although they searched diligently, the heifers could not be found. Rather than disappoint their aged mother, who had set her heart upon attending the services, these kind-hearted sons harnessed themselves to the cart, and drew her through the city to the temple gates, amid the acclamations of all the people, who admired this trait of filial devotion.

The mother was so touched by her sons' affection, that, as she knelt before the altar, she fervently prayed Juno to bestow upon them the greatest boon in her power. At the conclusion of the services the ex-priestess went into the portico, where her sons had thrown themselves to rest after their unwonted exertions; but instead of finding them merely asleep, as she expected, she found them dead. The Queen of Heaven had transported them while asleep to the Elysian Fields, the place of endless bliss, where such as they enjoyed eternal life.

MINERVA

BIRTH OF MINERVA

Although immortal, the gods were not exempt from physical pain. One day Jupiter suffered intensely from a sudden headache, and, in hopes that some mode of alleviation would be devised, he summoned all the gods to Olympus. Their united efforts were vain, however; and even the remedies suggested by Apollo, god of medicine, proved inefficacious. Unwilling, or perchance unable, to endure the racking pain any longer, Jupiter bade one of his sons, Vulcan, cleave his head open with an ax. With cheerful alacrity the dutiful god obeyed; and no sooner was the operation performed, than Minerva (Pallas, Athene) sprang out of her father's head, full-grown, clad in glittering armor, with poised spear, and chanting a triumphant song of victory.

> From his awful head
> Whom Jove brought forth, in warlike armor drest,
> Golden, all radiant.
>
> SHELLEY

The assembled gods recoiled in fear before this unexpected apparition, while at the same time a mighty commotion over land and sea proclaimed the advent of a great divinity.

The goddess, who had thus joined the inhabitants of Olympus, was destined to preside over peace, defensive war, and needlework, to be the incarnation of wisdom, and to put to flight the obscure deity called Dullness, who until then had ruled the world.

FOLLOWING PAGES: THE BIRTH OF MINERVA. René-Antoine Houasse.

Ere Pallas issu'd from the Thund'rer's head,
Dullness o'er all possess'd her ancient right,
Daughter of Chaos and eternal Night.

POPE

Minerva, having forced her unattractive predecessor to beat an ignominious retreat, quickly seized the scepter, and immediately began to rule in her stead.

NAMING OF ATHENS

Not long after her birth, Cecrops, a Phœnician, came to Greece, where he founded a beautiful city in the province since called Attica. All the gods watched his undertaking with great interest; and finally, seeing the town promised to become a thriving place, each wished the privilege of naming it. A general council was held, and after some deliberation most of the gods withdrew their claims. Soon none but Minerva and Neptune were left to contend for the coveted honor.

To settle the quarrel without evincing any partiality, Jupiter announced that the city would be intrusted to the protection of the deity who would create the most useful object for the use of man. Raising his trident, Neptune struck the ground, from which a noble horse sprang forth, amid the exclamations of wonder and admiration of all the spectators. His qualities were duly explained by his proud creator, and all thought it quite impossible for Minerva to surpass him. Loudly they laughed, and scornfully too, when she, in her turn, produced an olive tree; but when she had told them the manifold uses to which wood, fruit, foliage, twigs, etc., could be applied, and explained that the olive was a sign of peace and prosperity, and therefore far more desirable than the horse, the emblem of war and wretchedness, they could but acknowledge her gift the most serviceable, and award her the prize.

To commemorate this victory over her rival, Minerva gave her own name of Athene to the city, whose inhabitants, from that time forth, were taught to honor her as their tutelary goddess.

Ever at Jupiter's side, Minerva often aided him by her wise counsels, and in times of war borrowed his terrible shield, the Ægis, which she flung over her shoulder when she sallied forth to give her support to those whose cause was just.

> Her shoulder bore
> The dreadful Ægis with its shaggy brim
> Bordered with Terror. There was Strife, and there
> Was Fortitude, and there was fierce Pursuit,
> And there the Gorgon's head, a ghastly sight,
> Deformed and dreadful, and a sign of woe.
>
> HOMER (Bryant's tr.)

The din of battle had no terrors for this doughty goddess, and on every occasion she was wont to plunge into the thickest of the fray with the utmost valor.

STORY OF ARACHNE

These virile tastes were, however, fully counterbalanced by some exclusively feminine, for Minerva was as deft with her needle as with her sword. In Greece there lived in those olden times a maiden by the name of Arachne. Pretty, young, and winsome, she would have been loved by all had it not been for her inordinate pride, not in her personal advantages, but in her skill as a needlewoman.

Arachne, in her conceit, fancied that no one could equal the work done by her deft fingers, so she boasted far and wide that she would have no fear to match her skill with Minerva's. She made this remark so loudly and so frequently, that the goddess was finally annoyed, and left her seat in high Olympus to come down upon earth and punish the maiden. In the guise of an old crone, she entered Arachne's house, seated herself, and began a conversation. In a few minutes the maiden had resumed her usual strain, and renewed her rash boast. Minerva gently advised her to be more modest, lest she should incur the wrath of the gods by her presumptuous words; but Arachne was so blinded by her conceit, that she scorned the well-meant warning, saucily tossed her head, and declared she wished the goddess would hear her, and propose a contest, in which she would surely be able to prove the truth of her assertions. This insolent speech so incensed Minerva, that she cast aside her disguise and accepted the challenge.

Both set up their looms, and began to weave exquisite designs in tapestry: Minerva choosing as her subject her contest with Neptune; and Arachne, the kidnapping of

FOLLOWING PAGES: DISPUTE BETWEEN MINERVA AND NEPTUNE OVER THE
NAMING OF THE CITY OF ATHENS.
René-Antoine Houasse.

Europa. In silence the fair weavers worked, and their webs grew apace under their practiced fingers. The assembled gods, the horse, the olive tree, seemed to live and move under Minerva's flashing shuttle.

> Emongst these leaves she made a Butterflie,
> With excellent device and wondrous slight,
> Fluttring among the Olives wantonly,
> That seem'd to live, so like it was in sight:
> The velvet nap which on his wings doth lie,
> The silken downe with which his backe is dight,
> His broad outstretched hornes, his hayrie thies,
> His glorious colours, and his glistering eies.
>
> SPENSER

Arachne, in the mean while, was intent upon her swimming bull, against whose broad breast the waves splashed, and upon a half-laughing, half-frightened girl, who clung to the bull's horns, while the wind played with her flowing tresses and garments.

> Sweet Europa's mantle blew unclasp'd,
> From off her shoulder backward borne:
> From one hand droop'd a crocus: one hand grasp'd
> The mild bull's golden horn.
>
> TENNYSON

The finishing touches all given, each turned to view her rival's work, and at the very first glance Arachne was forced to acknowledge her failure. To be thus out-stripped, after all her proud boasts, was humiliating indeed. Bitterly did Arachne now repent of her folly; and in her despair she bound a rope about her neck, and hung her-self. Minerva saw her discomfited rival was about to escape: so she quickly changed her dangling body into a spider, and condemned her to weave and spin without ceasing,— a warning to all conceited mortals.

WORSHIP OF MINERVA

Minerva, the goddess of wisdom, was widely worshiped. Temples and altars without number were dedicated to her service, the most celebrated of all being the Parthenon at Athens. Naught but the ruins of this mighty pile now exist; but they suffice to testify to the beauty of the edifice, which served, in turn, as temple, church, mosque, and finally as powder magazine.

> Fair Parthenon! yet still must Fancy weep
> For thee, thou work of nobler spirits flown.
> Bright, as of old, the sunbeams o'er thee sleep
> In all their beauty still—and thine is gone!
> Empires have sunk since thou wert first revered,
> And varying rites have sanctified thy shrine.
> The dust is round thee of the race that rear'd
> Thy walls; and thou—their fate must soon be thine!
>
> HEMANS

Statues of Minerva—a beautiful, majestic woman, fully clothed and armed— were very numerous. The most celebrated of all, by the renowned Greek sculptor Phidias, measured full forty feet in height. Festivals were celebrated in honor of Minerva wherever her worship was held,—some, the Greek Panathenæa, for instance, only every four years; others, such as the Minervalia and Quinquatria, every year. At these festivals the Palladium, a statue of the goddess, said to have fallen from heaven, was carried in procession through the city, where the people hailed its appearance with joyful cries and songs of praise.

APOLLO

The most glorious and beautiful among all the gods was Apollo (Phœbus, Sol, Helios, Cynthius, Pytheus), god of the sun, of medicine, music, poetry, and all fine arts.

> Bright-hair'd Apollo!—thou who ever art
> A blessing to the world—whose mighty heart
> Forever pours out love, and light, and life;
> Thou, at whose glance, all things of earth are rife
> With happiness; to whom, in early spring,
> Bright flowers raise up their heads, where'er they cling
> On the steep mountain side, or in the vale
> Are nestled calmly. Thou at whom the pale
> And weary earth looks up, when winter flees,
> With patient gaze: thou for whom wind-stripped trees
> Put on fresh leaves, and drink deep of the light
> That glitters in thine eye: thou in whose bright
> And hottest rays the eagle fills his eye
> With quenchless fire, and far, far up on high
> Screams out his joy to thee, by all the names
> That thou dost bear—whether thy godhead claims
> Phœbus or Sol, or golden-hair'd Apollo,
> Cynthian or Pythian, if thou dost follow
> The fleeing night, oh, hear
> Our hymn to thee, and willingly draw near!
>
> Pike

Opposite Page: APOLLO CROWNED BY VICTORY. Noël Coypel.

Apollo was the son of Jupiter and Latona, or Leto, the goddess of dark nights. Juno's jealousy had been aroused by Jupiter's preference for her rival. To avenge herself, she banished Latona to earth, and declared that if any one, mortal or immortal, showed her any pity or gave her any assistance, he would incur her lasting resentment.

After long, painful wanderings on earth, poor Latona, weary and parched with thirst, drew near a small pool by the wayside to refresh herself; but, urged by Juno, some reapers bade her pass on, and then, seeing she paid no heed to their commands, they sprang into the shallow waters, and stirred up the mud at the bottom until it was quite unpalatable. With tear-dimmed eyes, Latona prayed these cruel men might never leave the spot whereon they now stood; and Jupiter, in answer to her prayer, immediately transformed them into huge green frogs, which creatures have since then showed great preference for muddy pools.

Driven on once more by Juno's unrelenting hatred, Latona finally came to the seashore, where she stretched out imploring hands to Neptune, who sent a dolphin to bear her in safety to the floating island of Delos, raised in her behalf from the depths of the sea. The rocking motion, however, proving disagreeable to the goddess, Neptune chained the island fast in the Ægean Sea; and there in that delightful climate, justly praised by poets, were born to Jupiter and Latona twin children, Apollo and Diana, the divinities of the sun and moon.

Story of Coronis

Apollo, having attained manhood, could not avoid the usual lot of the gods, as well as of mortal men,—the pangs of love. They were first inspired by Coronis, a fair maiden, who kindled within his breast an ardent flame. The sun god wooed the girl warmly and persistently, and at length had the deep satisfaction of seeing his affections returned. His bliss, however, proved but fleeting; for Coronis, reasoning, that, if one lover were so delightful, two would be doubly so, secretly encouraged another suitor.

> Flirted with another lover
> (So at least the story goes)
> And was wont to meet him slyly,
> Underneath the blushing rose.
> SAXE

Although so cleverly managed, these trysts could not escape the bright eyes of Apollo's favorite bird, the snowy raven,—for such was his hue in those early times,—so *he* flew off in haste to his master to report the discovery he had made. Desperate with love and jealousy, Apollo did not hesitate, but, seizing his bow and deadly arrows, shot Coronis through the heart.

The deed was no sooner accomplished, than all his love returned with tenfold power; and, hastening to Coronis's side, he vainly tried all his remedies (he was god of medicine) to recall her to life.

> The god of Physic
> Had no antidote; alack!
> He who took her off so deftly
> Couldn't bring the maiden back!
>
> SAXE

Bending over the lifeless body of his beloved one, he bewailed his fatal haste, and cursed the bird which had brought him the unwelcome tidings of her faithlessness.

> Then he turned upon the Raven,
> "Wanton babbler! see thy fate!
> Messenger of mine no longer,
> Go to Hades with thy prate!
>
> "Weary Pluto with thy tattle!
> Hither, monster, come not back;
> And—to match thy disposition—
> Henceforth be thy plumage black!"
>
> SAXE

ÆSCULAPIUS

The only reminder of this unfortunate episode was a young son of Apollo and Coronis, Æsculapius (Asklepios), who was carefully instructed by Apollo in the healing art. The disciple's talent was so great, that he soon rivaled his master, and even, it is said, recalled the dead to life. Of course, these miracles did not long remain concealed from Jupiter's all-seeing eye; and he, fearing lest the people would forget him and worship their physician, seized one of his thunderbolts, hurled it at the clever youth, and thus brought to an untimely end his brilliant medical career.

> Then Jove, incensed that man should rise
> From darkness to the upper skies,
> The leech that wrought such healing hurled
> With lightning down to Pluto's world.
>
> VIRGIL (Conington's tr.)

Æsculapius's race was not entirely extinct, however, for he left two sons—Machaon and Podalirius, who inherited his medical skill—and a daughter, Hygeia, who watched over the health of man.

ADMETUS AND ALCESTIS

Maddened with grief at the unexpected loss of his son, Apollo would fain have wreaked his vengeance upon the Cyclopes, the authors of the fatal thunderbolt; but ere he could execute his purpose, Jupiter interfered, and, to punish him, banished him to earth, where he entered the service of Admetus, King of Thessaly. One consolation alone now remained to the exiled god,—his music. His dulcet tones soon won the admiration of his companions, and even that of the king, who listened to his songs with pleasure, and to reward him gave him the position of head shepherd.

> Then King Admetus, one who had
>   Pure taste by right divine,
> Decreed his singing not too bad
> To hear between the cups of wine:
>
> And so, well pleased with being soothed
>   Into a sweet half sleep
> Three times his kingly beard he smoothed
> And made him viceroy o'er his sheep.
>
> LOWELL

Time passed. Apollo, touched by his master's kindness, wished to bestow some favor in his turn, and asked the gods to grant Admetus eternal life. His request was complied with, but only on condition, that, when the time came which had previously been appointed for the good king's death, some one should be found willing to die in his stead. This divine decree was reported to Alcestis, Admetus's beautiful young wife, who in a passion of self-sacrifice offered herself as substitute, and cheerfully gave her life for her husband. But immortality was too dearly bought at such a price; and Admetus mourned until Hercules, pitying his grief, descended into Hades, and brought her back from the tomb.

> Did not Hercules by force
> Wrest from the guardian Monster of the tomb
> Alcestis, a reanimated Corse,
> Given back to dwell on earth in vernal bloom?
>
> WORDSWORTH

THE WALLS OF TROY

Apollo, after endowing Admetus with immortality, left his service, and went to assist Neptune, who had also been banished to earth, to build the walls of Troy. Scorning to perform any menial tasks, the God of Music seated himself near by, and played such inspiring tunes that the stones waltzed into place of their own accord.

APOLLO SLAYS PYTHON

Then, his term of exile being ended, he returned to heaven, and there resumed his wonted duties. From his exalted position he often cast loving glances down upon men, whose life he had shared for a short time, whose every privation he had endured; and, in answer to their prayers, he graciously extended his protection over them, and delivered them from misfortunes too numerous to mention. Among other deeds done for men was the slaying of the monster serpent Python, born from the slime and stagnant waters which remained upon the surface of the earth after the Deluge. None had dared approach the monster; but Apollo fearlessly drew near, and slew him with his golden shafts. The victory over the terrible Python won for Apollo the surname of Pytheus (the Slayer), by which appellation he was frequently invoked.

FOLLOWING PAGES: APOLLO AND THE PYTHON. Cornelis de Vos.

This annihilation of Python is, of course, nothing but an allegory, illustrating the sun's power to dry up marshes and stagnant pools, thus preventing the lurking fiend malaria from making further inroads.

Apollo has always been a favorite subject for painters and sculptors. The most beautiful statue of him is the Apollo Belvedere, which represents him at the moment of his conquest of the Python.

APOLLO AND HYACINTHUS

Although successful in war, Apollo was very unfortunate indeed in friendship. One day he came down to earth to enjoy the society of a youth of mortal birth, named Hyacinthus. To pass the time agreeably, the friends began a game of quoits, but had not played long, before Zephyrus, god of the south wind, passing by, saw them thus occupied. Jealous of Apollo, for he too loved Hyacinthus, Zephyrus blew Apollo's quoit aside so violently that it struck his playmate, and felled him to the ground. Vainly Apollo strove to check the stream of blood which flowed from the ghastly wound. Hyacinthus was already beyond aid, and in a few seconds breathed his last in his friend's arms. To keep some reminder of the departed, Apollo changed the fallen blood drops into clusters of flowers, ever since called, from the youth's name, hyacinths; while Zephyrus, perceiving too late the fatal effect of his jealousy, hovered inconsolable over the sad spot, and tenderly caressed the dainty flowers which had sprung from his friend's lifeblood.

> Zephyr penitent,
> Who now, ere Phœbus mounts the firmament,
> Fondles the flower.
>
> KEATS

APOLLO AND CYPARISSUS

To divert his mind from the mournful fate of Hyacinthus, Apollo sought the company of Cyparissus, a clever young hunter; but this friendship was also doomed to a sad end, for Cyparissus, having accidentally killed Apollo's pet stag, grieved so sorely over this mischance, that he pined away, and finally died. Apollo then changed his lifeless clay into a cypress tree, which he declared should henceforth be used to shade the graves of those who had been greatly beloved through life.

Above: THE DEATH OF HYACYNTHUS. Giovanni Battista Tiepolo.

Apollo and Daphne

Some time after this episode, Apollo encountered in the forest a beautiful nymph by the name of Daphne, the daughter of the river god Peneus. Love at first sight was the immediate consequence on Apollo's part, and he longed to speak to the maid and win her affections. He first tried to approach her gently, so as not to frighten her; but, before he could reach her side, she fled, and he, forgetful of all else, pursued her flying footsteps. As he ran, he called aloud to Daphne, entreating her to pause were it only for a moment, and promising to do her no harm.

> Abate, fair fugitive, abate thy speed,
> Dismiss thy fears, and turn thy beauteous head;
> With kind regard a panting lover view;
> Less swiftly fly, less swiftly I'll pursue:
> Pathless, alas! and rugged is the ground,
> Some stone may hurt thee, or some thorn may wound.
>
> You fly, alas! not knowing whom you fly;
> No ill-bred swain, nor rustic clown, am I.
>
> PRIOR

The terrified girl paid no heed to promises or entreaties, but sped on until her strength began to fail, and she perceived, that, notwithstanding her utmost efforts, her pursuer was gaining upon her. Panting and trembling, she swerved aside, and rushed down to the edge of her father's stream, calling out loudly for his protection. No sooner had she reached the water's edge, than her feet seemed rooted to the ground. A rough bark rapidly inclosed her quivering limbs, while her trembling hands were filled with leaves. Her father had granted her prayer by changing her into a laurel tree.

Apollo, coming up just then with outstretched arms, clasped nothing but a rugged tree trunk. At first he could not realize that the fair maiden had vanished from his sight forever; but, when the truth dawned upon him, he declared that from henceforth the laurel would be considered his favorite tree, and that prizes awarded to poets, musicians, etc., should consist of a wreath of its glossy foliage.

Opposite Page: APOLLO AND DAPHNE. Giovanni Battista Tiepolo.

I espouse thee for my tree:
Be thou the prize of honor and renown;
The deathless poet, and the poem, crown;
Thou shalt the Roman festivals adorn,
And, after poets, be by victors worn.

OVID (Dryden's tr.)

This story of Apollo and Daphne was an illustration of the effect produced by the sun (Apollo) upon the dew (Daphne). The sun is captivated by its beauty, and longs to view it more closely; the dew, afraid of its ardent lover, flies, and, when its fiery breath touches it, vanishes, leaving nothing but verdure in the selfsame spot where but a moment before it sparkled in all its purity.

CEPHALUS AND PROCRIS

The ancients had many analogous stories, allegories of the sun and dew, amongst others the oft-quoted tale of Cephalus and Procris. Cephalus was a hunter, who fell in love with and married one of Diana's nymphs, Procris. She brought him as dowry a hunting dog, Lelaps, and a javelin warranted never to miss its mark. The newly married pair were perfectly happy; but their content was viewed with great displeasure by Eos (Aurora), goddess of dawn, who had previously tried, but without success, to win Cephalus's affections, and who now resolved to put an end to the bliss she envied.

All day long Cephalus hunted in the forest, and, when the evening shadows began to fall, joined his loving wife in their cozy dwelling. Her marriage gifts proved invaluable, as Lelaps was swift of foot, and tireless in the chase. One day, to test his powers, the gods from Olympus watched him course a fox, a special creation of theirs; and so well were both animals matched in speed and endurance, that the chase bade fair to end only with the death of one or both of the participants. The gods, in their admiration for the fine run, declared the animals deserved to be remembered forever, and changed them into statues, which retained all the spirited action of the living creatures.

In the warm season, when the sun became oppressive, Cephalus was wont to rest during the noon hour in some shady spot, and as he flung himself down upon the short grass he often called for a breeze, bidding it cool his heated brow.

A hunter once in that grove reclin'd,
To shun the noon's bright eye,

And oft he woo'd the wandering wind,
    To cool his brow with its sigh.
While mute lay ev'n the wild bee's hum,
    Nor breath could stir the aspen's hair,
His song was still, "Sweet air, oh come!"
    While Echo answer'd, "Come, sweet air!"

MOORE

Eos heard of this habit, and was fully aware that he merely addressed the passing wind; nevertheless she sought Procris, and informed her that her husband was faithless, and paid court to a fair maid, who daily met him at noonday in the forest solitudes. Procris, blinded by sudden jealousy, gave credit to the false story, and immediately resolved to follow her husband.

The morning had well-nigh passed, and the sun was darting its perpendicular rays upon the earth, when Cephalus came to his usual resort, near which Procris was concealed.

"Sweet air, oh come!" the hunter cried; and Procris, cut to the heart by what she considered an infallible proof of his infidelity, sank fainting to the ground. The rustle caused by her swoon attracted Cephalus's attention. Under the mistaken impression that some wild beast was lurking there, ready to pounce upon him, he cast his unerring javelin into the very midst of the thicket, and pierced the faithful bosom of his wife. Her dying moan brought him with one bound to her side; ere she breathed her last, an explanation was given and received; and Procris died with the blissful conviction that her husband had not deserved her unjust suspicions, and that his heart was all her own.

There are, of course, many other versions of these selfsame myths; but one and all are intended to illustrate the same natural phenomena, and are subject to the same interpretation.

Apollo's principal duty was to drive the sun chariot. Day after day he rode across the azure sky, nor paused on his way till he reached the golden boat awaiting him at the end of his long day's journey, to bear him in safety back to his eastern palace.

Helios all day long his allotted labor pursues;
    No rest to his passionate heart and his panting horses given,
From the moment when roseate-fingered Eos kindles the dews
    And spurns the salt sea-floors, ascending silvery the heaven,

Until from the hand of Eos Hesperos, trembling, receives
His fragrant lamp, and faint in the twilight hangs it up.

OWEN MEREDITH

CLYTIE

A fair young maiden, named Clytie, watched Apollo's daily journey with strange per-
sistency; and from the moment when he left his palace in the morning until he came to
the far western sea in the evening, she followed his course with loving eyes, thought
of the golden-haired god, and longed for his love. But, in spite of all this fervor, she
never won favor in Apollo's eyes, and languished until the gods, in pity, changed her
into a sunflower.

Even in this altered guise, Clytie could not forget the object of her love; and now,
a fit emblem of constancy, she still follows with upturned face the glowing orb in its
daily journey across the sky.

No, the heart that has truly lov'd never forgets,
But as truly loves on to the close;
As the sunflower turns on her god when he sets
The same look which she turn'd when he rose.

MOORE

APOLLO AND MARSYAS

A young shepherd, lying in the cool grass one summer afternoon, became
aware of a distant sound of music, so sweet, so thrilling, that he fairly held his breath
to listen. These weird, delightful tones were produced by Minerva, who, seated by
the banks of a small stream, was trying her skill on the flute. As she bent over the
limpid waters, she suddenly beheld her puffed cheeks and distorted features, and
impetuously threw the instrument into the water, vowing never to touch it again.

Hence, ye banes of beauty, hence!
What? shall I my charms disgrace
By making such an odious face?

MELANIPPIDES

The sudden break in the entrancing music caused the youth, Marsyas, to start from his abstraction and look about him. He then perceived the rejected flute sailing gently down the stream past his feet. To seize the instrument and convey it to his lips was the work of an instant; and no sooner had he breathed into it, than the magic strain was renewed. No recollection of his pastoral duties could avail to tear Marsyas away from his new-found treasure; and so rapidly did his skill increase, that he became insufferably conceited, and boasted he could rival Apollo, whom he actually challenged to a musical contest.

Intending to punish him for his presumption, Apollo accepted the challenge, and selected the nine Muses—patronesses of poetry and music—as umpires. Marsyas was first called upon to exhibit his proficiency, and charmed all by his melodious strains.

> So sweet that alone the south wind knew,
> By summer hid in green reeds' jointed cells
> To wait imprisoned for the south wind's spells,
> From out his reedy flute the player drew,
> And as the music clearer, louder grew,
> Wild creatures from their winter nooks and dells,
> Sweet furry things with eyes like starry wells,
> Crept wanderingly out; they thought the south wind blew.
> With instant joyous trust, they flocked around
> His feet who such a sudden summer made,
> His eyes, more kind than men's, enthralled and bound
> Them there.
>
> H. H.

The Muses bestowed much deserved praise, and then bade Apollo surpass his rival if he could. No second command was necessary. The god seized his golden lyre, and poured forth impassioned strains. Before pronouncing their decision, the Muses resolved to give both musicians a second hearing, and again both strove; but on this occasion Apollo joined the harmonious accents of his godlike voice to the tones of his instrument, causing all present, and the very Muses too, to hail him as conqueror.

> And, when now the westering sun
> Touch'd the hills, the strife was done,
> And the attentive Muses said:

"Marsyas, thou art vanquished!"
MATTHEW ARNOLD

According to a previous arrangement,—that the victor should have the privilege of flaying his opponent alive,—Apollo bound Marsyas to a tree, and slew him cruelly. As soon as the mountain nymphs heard of their favorite's sad death, they began to weep, and shed such torrents of tears, that they formed a new river, called Marsyas, in memory of the sweet musician.

APOLLO AND PAN

The mournful termination of this affair should have served as a warning to all rash mortals. Such was not the case, however; and shortly after, Apollo found himself engaged in another musical contest with Pan, King Midas's favorite flute player. Upon this occasion Midas himself retained the privilege of awarding the prize, and, blinded by partiality, gave it to Pan, in spite of the marked inferiority of his playing. Apollo was so incensed by this injustice, that he determined to show his opinion of the dishonest judge by causing generous-sized ass's ears to grow on either side of his head.

> The god of wit, to show his grudge,
> Clapt asses' ears upon the judge;
> A goodly pair, erect and wide,
> Which he could neither gild nor hide.
>
> SWIFT

Greatly dismayed by these new ornaments, Midas retreated into the privacy of his own apartment, and sent in hot haste for a barber, who, after having been sworn to secrecy, was admitted, and bidden to fashion a huge wig, which would hide the deformity from the eyes of the king's subjects. The barber acquitted himself deftly, and, before he was allowed to leave the palace, was again charged not to reveal the secret, under penalty of immediate death.

But a secret is difficult to keep; and this one, of the king's long ears, preyed upon the poor barber's spirits, so that, incapable of enduring silence longer, he sallied out into a field, dug a deep hole, and shouted down into the bosom of the earth—

> "King Midas wears
> (These eyes beheld them, these) such ass's ears!"
>
> HORACE

Unspeakably relieved by this performance, the barber returned home. Time passed. Reeds grew over the hole, and, as they bent before the wind which rustled through their leaves, they were heard to murmur, "Midas, King Midas, has ass's ears!" and all who passed by caught the whisper, and noised it abroad, so that the secret became the general topic of all conversations.

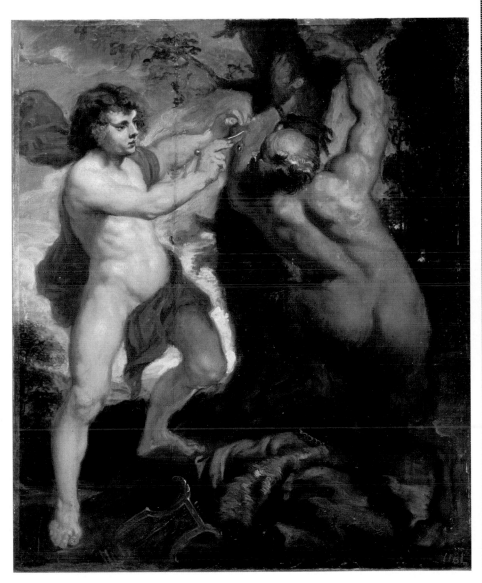

ABOVE: APOLLO AND MARSYAS. Peter Paul Rubens.

ORPHEUS AND EURYDICE

As Apollo had frequent opportunities of meeting the Muses, it is not to be wondered at that he fell a victim to the charms of the fair Calliope, who, in her turn, loved him passionately, and even wrote verses in his honor. This being the state of her feelings, she readily consented to their union, and became the proud mother of Orpheus, who inherited his parents' musical and poetical gifts.

> Orpheus with his lute made trees,
> And the mountain-tops, that freeze,
>   Bow themselves when he did sing:
> To his music plants and flowers
> Ever sprung; as sun and showers
>   There had made a lasting spring.
>
> Everything that heard him play,
> Even the billows of the sea,
>   Hung their heads, and then lay by.
>
> SHAKESPEARE

This talent waxed greater as the years passed by, and became so remarkable, that the youth's fame was very widespread; and when he fell in love with Eurydice, he brought all his skill into play to serenade her, and wooed her with voice and glance and with tender, passionate music. Eurydice was touched by his courtship, and ere long requited the love lavished upon her by conferring her hand upon Orpheus.

Shortly after their union, while walking alone in the fields, the bride encountered a youth named Aristæus, whose bold admiration proved so distasteful, that she fled from him as quickly as possible. In her haste she accidentally trod upon a venomous serpent lurking in the long grass, which immediately turned upon her, and bit her heel. A short period of agonized suffering ensued; then Eurydice died, and her spirit was conducted down into the gloomy realms of Pluto, leaving Orpheus broken-hearted.

Plaintive, heartrending laments now replaced the joyous wedding strains; but even the charms of music failed to make life endurable, and Orpheus wandered off to Olympus, where he so piteously implored Jupiter to restore his wife to his longing arms, that the great god's heart was moved to compassion. He gave him permission, therefore, to go down into the Infernal Regions to seek his wife, but warned him at the same time that the undertaking was perilous in the extreme.

Nothing daunted, Orpheus hastened to the entrance of Hades, and there saw the fierce three-headed dog, named Cerberus, who guarded the gate, and would allow no living being to enter, nor any spirit to pass out of Hades. As soon as this monster saw Orpheus, he began to growl and bark savagely, to frighten him away; but Orpheus merely paused, and began to play such melting chords, that Cerberus's rage was appeased, and he finally allowed him to pass into Pluto's dark kingdom.

The magic sounds penetrated even into the remote depths of Tartarus, where the condemned suspended their toil for a moment, and hushed their sighs and groans to listen.

> E'en Tantalus ceased from trying to sip
> The cup that flies from his arid lip;
> Ixion, too, the magic could feel,
> And, for a moment, blocked his wheel;
> Poor Sisyphus, doomed to tumble and toss
> The notable stone that gathers no moss,
> Let go his burden, and turned to hear
> The charming sounds that ravished his ear.
>
> SAXE

No living being had ever before penetrated thus into the Infernal Regions, and Orpheus wandered on until he came to the throne of Pluto, king of these realms, whereon the stern ruler sat in silence, his wife Proserpina beside him, and the relentless Fates at his feet.

Orpheus made known his errand in operatic guise, and succeeded in moving the royal pair to tears, whereupon they graciously consented to restore Eurydice to life and to her fond husband's care.

> Hell consented
> To hear the Poet's prayer:
> Stern Proserpine relented,
> And gave him back the fair.
> Thus song could prevail
> O'er death, and o'er hell,

ORPHEUS AND EURYDICE. Jean Raoux.

A conquest how hard and how glorious!
　　Tho' fate had fast bound her
　　With Styx nine times round her,
Yet music and love were victorious.

POPE

But one condition was imposed before he was allowed to depart; i.e., that he should leave the Infernal Regions without turning once to look into his beloved wife's face.

Orpheus accepted the condition joyfully, and wended his way out of Hades, looking neither to the right nor to the left, but straight before him; and as he walked he wondered whether Eurydice were changed by her sojourn in these rayless depths. His longing to feast his eyes once more upon her loved features made him forget the condition imposed by Pluto, and turn just before he reached the earth; but he only beheld the vanishing form of the wife he had so nearly snatched from the grave.

All was now over. He had tried and failed. No hope remained. In despair, the lonely musician retreated to the forest solitudes, and there played his mournful laments,—

Such strains as would have won the ear
Of Pluto, to have quite set free
His half-regained Eurydice.

MILTON

But there were none to hear except the trees, winds, and wild beasts in the forest, who strove in their dumb way to comfort him as he moved restlessly about, seeking a solace for his bursting heart. At times it seemed to his half-delirious fancy that he could discern Eurydice wandering about in the dim distance, with the selfsame mournful expression of which he had caught a mere glimpse as she drifted reluctantly back into the dark shadows of Hades.

At that elm-vista's end I trace
Dimly thy sad leave-taking face,
Eurydice! Eurydice!
The tremulous leaves repeat to me
Eurydice! Eurydice!

LOWELL

At last there dawned a day when some Bacchantes overtook him in the forest, and bade him play some gay music, so they might indulge in a dance. But poor Orpheus, dazed with grief, could not comply with their demands; and the sad notes which alone he now could draw from his instrument so enraged the merrymakers, that they tore him limb from limb, and cast his mangled remains into the Hebrus River.

As the poet-musician's head floated down the stream, the pallid lips still murmured, "Eurydice!" for even in death he could not forget his wife; and, as his spirit drifted on to join her, he incessantly called upon her name, until the brooks, trees, and fountains he had loved so well caught up the longing cry, and repeated it again and again.

Nothing was now left to remind mortals of the sweet singer who had thus perished, except his lute, which the gods placed in the heavens as a bright constellation, Lyra, also called by Orpheus's name.

Another musician celebrated in mythological annals is Amphion, whose skill was reported to be but little inferior to Orpheus's.

> 'Tis said he had a tuneful tongue,
>   Such happy intonation,
> Wherever he sat down and sung
>   He left a small plantation;
> Wherever in a lonely grove
>   He set up his forlorn pipes,
> The gouty oak began to move,
>   And flounder into hornpipes.
>
> TENNYSON

STORY OF AMPHION

This musician, a son of Jupiter and Antiope, had a twin brother Zethus, who, however, shared none of his artistic tastes. Hearing that their mother Antiope had been repudiated by her second husband, Lycus, so that he might marry another wife by the name of Dirce, these youths hastened off to Thebes, where they found the state of affairs even worse than represented; for poor Antiope was now imprisoned, and subject to her rival's daily cruel treatment.

Zethus and Amphion, after besieging and taking the city, put Lycus to death, and, binding Dirce to the tail of a wild bull, let him loose to drag her over briers and stones until she perished. This punishment inflicted upon Dirce is the subject of the famous group once belonging to the Farnese family, and now called by their name.

Amphion's musical talent was of great use to him when he subsequently became King of Thebes, and wished to fortify his capital by building a huge rampart all around it; for the stones moved in rhythmic time, and, of their own volition, marched into their places.

ARION

Second to him only, in musical fame, was Arion, the musician who won untold wealth by his talent. On one occasion, having gone to Sicily to take part in a musical contest which had attracted thither the most famous musicians from all points of the compass, he resolved to return home by sea.

Unfortunately for him, the vessel upon which he had embarked was manned by an avaricious, piratical crew, who, having heard of his treasures, resolved to murder him to obtain possession of them. He was allowed but scant time to prepare for death; but, just as they were about to toss him overboard, he craved permission to play for the last time. The pirates consented. His clear notes floated over the sea, and allured a school of dolphins, which came and played about the ship. The pirates, terrified by the power of his music, and in dread lest their hearts should be moved, quickly laid hands upon him, and hurled him into the water, where he fell upon the broad back of a dolphin, who bore him in safety to the nearest shore.

> Then was there heard a most celestiall sound
> Of dainty musicke, which did next ensew
> Before the spouse: that was Arion crownd;
> Who, playing on his harpe, unto him drew
> The eares and hearts of all that goodly crew,
> That even yet the Dolphin, which him bore
> Through the Agean seas from Pirates vew,
> Stood still by him astonisht at his lore,
> And all the raging seas for joy forgot to rore.
>
> SPENSER

To commemorate this miracle, the gods placed Arion's harp, together with the dolphin, in the heavens, where they form a constellation.

In the sunny plains of Greece there once dwelt Clymene, a fair nymph. She was not alone, however, for her golden-haired little son Phaeton was there to gladden her heart with all his childish graces.

STORY OF PHAETON

Early in the morning, when the sun's bright orb first appeared above the horizon, Clymene would point it out to her boy, and tell him that his father, Apollo, was setting out for his daily drive. Clymene so often entertained her child with stories of his father's beauty and power, that at last Phaeton became conceited, and acquired a habit of boasting rather loudly of his divine parentage. His playmates, after a time, wearied of his arrogance, and, to avoid the constant repetition of his vain speeches, bade him show some proof of his divine origin, or keep his peace.

Stung to the quick by some insolent taunts which they added, Phaeton hastened to his mother, and begged her to direct him to his father, that he might obtain the desired proof. Clymene immediately gave him all necessary information, and bade him make haste if he would reach his father's palace in the far east before the sun chariot passed out of its portals to accomplish its daily round. Directly eastward Phaeton journeyed, nor paused to rest until he came in view of the golden and jeweled pinnacles and turrets of his father's abode.

> The sun's bright palace, on high columns rais'd
> With burnish'd gold and flaming jewels blaz'd,
> The folding gates diffus'd a silver light,
> And with a milder gleam refresh'd the sight.
>
> ADDISON

Quite undazzled by this splendor, the youth still pressed on, straining his eyes to catch the first glimpse of the godly father, whose stately bearing and radiant air his mother had so enthusiastically described.

Apollo, from his golden throne, had watched the boy's approach, and, as he drew nearer, recognized him as his own offspring. Timidly now Phaeton advanced to the steps of his father's throne, and humbly waited for permission to make his errand known. Apollo addressed him graciously, called him his son, and bade him speak with-

OPPOSITE PAGE: FARNESE BULL.

out fear. In a few minutes the youth impetuously poured out the whole story, and watched with pleasure the frown which gathered on Apollo's brow when he repeated his companions' taunts. As soon as he had finished his tale, Apollo exclaimed that he would grant him any proof he wished, and confirmed these words by a solemn oath.

> "By the terrible Styx" said the angry sire,
>   While his eyes flashed volumes of fury and fire,
> "To prove your reviler an infamous liar,
>   I swear I will grant you whate'er you desire!"
>
> SAXE

This oath was the most solemn any god could utter, and in case of perjury he was obliged to drink the waters of this river, which would lull him into senseless stupidity for one whole year. During nine years following he was deprived of his office, banished from Olympus, and not allowed to taste of the life-giving nectar and ambrosia.

With a flash of triumph in his dark eyes, Phaeton, hearing this oath, begged permission to drive the sun chariot that very day, stating that all the world would be sure to notice his exalted position, and that none would ever dare doubt his veracity after such a signal mark of Apollo's favor.

When the god heard this presumptuous request, he started back in dismay, for he alone could control the four fiery steeds which drew the golden-wheeled sun car. Patiently he then explained to Phaeton the great danger of such an undertaking, earnestly begging him to select some other, less fatal boon.

> Choose out a gift from seas, or earth, or skies,
> For open to your wish all nature lies;
> Only decline this one unequal task,
> For 'tis a mischief, not a gift, you ask.
>
> ADDISON

But Phaeton, who, like many another conceited youth, fancied he knew better than his sire, would not give heed to the kindly warning, and persisted in his request, until Apollo, who had sworn the irrevocable oath, was obliged to fulfill his promise.

The hour had already come when the Sun usually began his daily journey. The pawing, champing steeds were ready; rosy-fingered Aurora only awaited her master's signal to fling wide the gates of morn; and the Hours were ready to escort him as usual.

Apollo, yielding to pressure, quickly anointed his son with a cooling essence to preserve him from the burning sunbeams, gave him the necessary directions for his journey, and repeatedly and anxiously cautioned him to watch his steeds with the utmost care, and to use the whip but sparingly, as they were inclined to be very restive.

The youth, who had listened impatiently to cautions and directions, then sprang into the seat, gathered up the reins, signaled to Aurora to fling the gates wide, and dashed out of the eastern palace with a flourish.

For an hour or two Phaeton bore in mind his father's principal injunctions, and all went well; but later, elated by his exalted position, he became very reckless, drove faster and faster, and soon lost his way. In finding it again he drove so close to the earth, that all the plants shriveled up, the fountains and rivers were dried in their mossy beds, the smoke began to rise from the parched and blackened earth, and even the people of the land over which he was passing were burned black,— a hue retained by their descendants to this day.

Terrified at what he had done, Phaeton whipped up his steeds, and drove so far away, that all the vegetation which had survived the intense heat came to an untimely end on account of the sudden cold.

The cries of mortals rose in chorus, and their clamors became so loud and importunate, that they roused Jupiter from a profound sleep, and caused him to look around to discover their origin. One glance of his all-seeing eye sufficed to reveal the damaged earth and the youthful charioteer. How had a beardless youth dared to mount the sun chariot? Jupiter could scarcely credit what he saw. In his anger he vowed he would make the rash mortal expiate his presumption by immediate death. He therefore selected the deadliest thunderbolt in his arsenal, aimed it with special care, and hurled it at Phaeton, whose burned and blackened corpse fell from his lofty seat down into the limpid waves of the Eridanus River.

> And Phaethon, caught in mid career,
> And hurled from the Sun to utter sunlessness,
> Like a flame-bearded comet, with ghastliest hiss,
> Fell headlong in the amazed Eridanus,
> Monarch of streams, who on the Italian fields
> Let loose, and far beyond his flowery lips
> Foam-white, ran ruinous to the Adrian deep.
>
> WORSLEY

THE HELIADES

The tidings of his death soon reached poor Clymene, who mourned her only son, and refused to be comforted; while the Heliades, Phaeton's sisters, three in number,—Phaetusa, Lampetia, and Ægle,—spent their days by the riverside, shedding tears, wringing their white hands, and bewailing their loss, until the gods, in pity, transformed them into poplar trees, and their tears into amber, which substance was supposed by the ancients to flow from the poplar trees like teardrops. Phaeton's intimate friend, Cycnus, piously collected his charred remains, and gave them an honorable burial. In his grief he continually haunted the scene of his friend's death, and repeatedly plunged into the river, in the hope of finding some more scattered fragments, until the gods changed him into a swan; which bird is ever sailing mournfully about, and frequently plunging his head into the water to continue his sad search.

Apollo, as the dearly loved leader of the nine Muses,—daughters of Jupiter and Mnemosyne, goddess of memory,—was surnamed Musagetes.

AURORA. Guido Reni.

Whom all the Muses loved, not one alone;—
Into his hands they put the lyre of gold,
    And, crowned with sacred laurel at their fount,
    Placed him as Musagetes on their throne.

LONGFELLOW

Although the Muses united at times in one grand song, they had each separate duties assigned them.

The Nine Muses

Clio, the Muse of history, recorded all great deeds and heroic actions, with the names of their authors, and was therefore generally represented with a laurel wreath and a book and stylus, to indicate her readiness to note all that happened to mortal men or immortal gods.

Euterpe, the graceful "Mistress of Song," was represented with a flute, and garlands of fragrant flowers.

Thalia, Muse of pastoral poetry, held a shepherd's crook and mask, and wore a crown of wild flowers.

> Mild pastoral Muse!
> That, to the sparkling crown Urania wears,
> And to her sister Clio's laurel wreath,
> Preferr'st a garland culled from purple heath!
>
> Wordsworth

Her graver sister, Melpomene, who presided over tragedy, wore a crown of gold, and wielded a dagger and a scepter; while Terpsichore, the light-footed Muse of dancing, was represented treading an airy measure.

Erato, who preferred lyric poetry to all other styles of composition, was pictured with a lyre; and Polyhymnia, Muse of rhetoric, held a scepter to show that eloquence rules with resistless sway.

Calliope, Muse of heroic poetry, also wore a laurel crown; and Urania, Muse of astronomy, held mathematical instruments, indicative of her love of the exact sciences.

This glorious sisterhood was wont to assemble on Mount Parnassus or on Mount Helicon, to hold their learned debates on poetry, science, and music.

Apollo's favorite attendant was Eos (Aurora), the fair goddess of dawn, whose rose-tipped fingers opened wide the eastern gates of pearl, and who then flashed across the sky to announce her master's coming.

Opposite Page: APOLLO AND TWO MUSES.
Pompeo Batoni.

Hail, gentle Dawn! mild blushing goddess, hail!
Rejoiced I see thy purple mantle spread
O'er half the skies; gems pave thy radiant way,
And orient pearls from every shrub depend.

SOMERVILLE

STORY OF AURORA AND TITHONUS

This dainty goddess loved and married Tithonus, Prince of Troy, and won from the
gods the boon of everlasting life to confer upon him. Alas! however, she forgot to
ask at the same time for continued youth; and her husband grew older and older, and
finally became so decrepit, that he was a burden to her. Knowing he would never die,
and wishing to rid herself of his burdensome presence, she changed him into a grass-
hopper.

At this time the goddess fell in love with Cephalus, the young hunter, and
frequently visited him on Mount Hymettus.

"Come," Phœbus cries, "Aurora, come—too late
Thou linger'st slumbering with thy wither'd mate!
Leave him, and to Hymettus' top repair!
Thy darling Cephalus expects thee there!"
The goddess, with a blush, her love betrays,
But mounts, and, driving rapidly, obeys.

KEATS

WORSHIP OF APOLLO

The principal temples dedicated to the worship of Apollo were at Delos, his birthplace, and at Delphi, where a priestess called Pythia gave out mysterious oracles
purporting to have come from the god. The ancients everywhere could not fail to
recognize the sun's kindly influence and beneficent power, and were therefore ever
ready to worship Apollo.

I marvel not, O sun! that unto thee
In adoration man should bow the knee,
   And pour his prayers of mingled awe and love;
For like a God thou art, and on thy way
Of glory sheddest with benignant ray,
   Beauty, and life, and joyance from above.

SOUTHEY

The most renowned among the numerous festivals held in honor of Apollo were, without exception, the Pythian Games, celebrated at Delphi every three years.

A manly, beardless youth of great beauty, Apollo is generally crowned with laurels, and bears either a bow or a lyre.

Lord of the unerring bow,
The God of life, and poesy, and light—
The Sun in human limbs array'd, and brow
All radiant from his triumph in the fight;
The shaft hath just been shot—the arrow bright
With an immortal's vengeance; in his eye
And nostril beautiful disdain, and might
And majesty, flash their full lightnings by,
Developing in that one glance the Deity.

BYRON

One of the Seven Wonders of the ancient world, the famous Colossus of Rhodes, was a statue of Apollo, his head encircled with a halo of bright sunbeams, and his legs spread wide apart to allow vessels, with all their sails spread, to pass in and out of the harbor, whose entrance he guarded for many a year.

DIANA

D iana (Cynthia, Phœbe, Selene, Artemis), the fair twin sister of Apollo, was not only goddess of the moon, but also of the chase.

> "Goddess serene, transcending every star!
> Queen of the sky, whose beams are seen afar!
> By night heaven owns thy sway, by day the grove,
> When, as chaste Dian, here thou deign'st to rove."
>
> BYRON

In works of art this goddess is generally represented as a beautiful maiden, clad in a short hunting dress, armed with a bow, a quiver full of arrows at her side, and a crescent on her well-poised head.

Proud of her two children, Apollo and Diana, Latona boasted far and wide that such as hers had never been, for they excelled all others in beauty, intelligence, and power.

STORY OF NIOBE

The daughter of Tantalus, Niobe, heard this boast, and laughed in scorn; for she was the mother of fourteen children,—seven manly sons and seven beautiful daughters. In her pride she called aloud to Latona, and taunted her because her offspring numbered but two.

OPPOSITE PAGE: DIANA AND ENDYMION. Giovani Pistor the Younger.

Shortly after, Niobe even went so far as to forbid her people to worship Apollo and Diana, and gave orders that all the statues representing them in her kingdom should be torn down from their pedestals, and destroyed. Enraged at this insult, Latona called her children to her side, and bade them go forth and slay all her luckless rival's offspring.

Provided with well-stocked quivers, the twins set out to do her bidding; and Apollo, meeting the seven lads out hunting, cut their existence short with his unfailing arrows.

> Phœbus slew the sons
> With arrows from his silver bow, incensed
> At Niobe.
>
> HOMER (Bryant's tr.)

With all proverbial speed the tidings reached Niobe, whose heart failed when she heard that her seven sons, her pride and delight, had fallen under Apollo's shafts, and that they now lay cold and stiff in the forest, where they had eagerly hastened a few hours before, to follow the deer to its cover.

As she mourned their untimely death, she thought her cup of sorrow was full; but long ere her first passion of grief was over, Diana began to slay her daughters.

> But what is this? What means this oozing flood?
> Her daughters, too, are weltering in their blood:
> One clasps her mother's knees, one clings around
> Her neck, and one lies prostrate on the ground;
> One seeks her breast; one eyes the coming woe
> And shudders; one in terror crouches low.
>
> MELEAGER

In vain the poor girls sought to escape the flying arrows. In vain Niobe sought to protect them, and called upon all the gods of Olympus. Her daughters fell one by one, never to rise again. The last clung convulsively to her mother's breast; but, even in that fond mother's passionate embrace, death found and claimed her. Then the gods, touched by the sight of woe so intense, changed Niobe into stone, just as she stood, with upturned face, streaming eyes, and quivering lips.

This statue was placed on Mount Sipylus, close to a stream of running water; and it was said that tears continually flowed down the marble cheeks, for, though changed, Niobe still felt, and wept for her great loss.

This story is an allegory, in which Niobe, the mother, represents winter, hard, cold, and proud; until Apollo's deadly arrows, the sunbeams, slay her children, the winter months. Her tears are emblems of the natural thaw which comes in spring, when winter's pride has melted.

DIANA'S AVOCATIONS

As soon as the young Goddess of the Moon had been introduced in Olympus, all the gods expressed a wish to marry her; but she refused to listen to their entreaties, begged her father's permission to remain single all her life, and pleaded her cause so ably, that Jupiter was forced to grant her request.

Every evening, as soon as the Sun had finished his course, Diana mounted her moon car, and drove her milk-white steeds across the heavens, watched over and loved by the countless stars, which shone their brightest to cheer her on her way; and as she drove she often bent down to view the sleeping earth, so shadowy and dreamlike, and to breathe the intoxicating perfume of the distant flowers. It always seemed to her then as if Nature, so beautiful during the day, borrowed additional charms from the witching hours of the night.

> 'Twas now the time when Phœbus yields to night,
> And rising Cynthia sheds her silver light,
> Wide o'er the world in solemn pomp she drew
> Her airy chariot hung with pearly dew.

STORY OF ENDYMION

One evening, as she was driving noiselessly along, she suddenly checked her steeds; for there on the hillside she saw a handsome young shepherd, fast asleep, his upturned face illumined by the moon's soft light. Diana wonderingly gazed upon his beauty, and before long felt her heart beat with more than admiration. Gliding gently from her chariot, she floated to his side, bent slowly, and dropped an airy kiss upon his slightly parted lips.

The youth Endymion, only partially awakened by this demonstration, half raised his fringed lids, and for a moment his sleep-dimmed eyes rested wonderingly upon the

FOLLOWING PAGES: CHILDREN OF NIOBE. Jacques-Louis David.

beautiful vision. That one glance, although it drove Diana away in great haste, kindled in his heart an inextinguishable passion. He rose with a start, and rubbed his sleepy eyes; but when he saw the moon, which he fancied close beside him, sailing away across the deep-blue sky, he felt sure the whole occurrence had been but a dream, but so sweet a dream that he cast himself down upon the sward, hoping to woo it to visit him once more.

It did not come again that night, however; but the next night, as he lay on the self-same spot, it recurred in all its sweetness; and night after night it was repeated when the pale moonbeams fell athwart his sleeping face.

> Then, as the full orb poised upon the peak,
> There came a lovely vision of a maid,
> Who seemed to step as from a golden car
> Out of the low-hung moon.
>
> LEWIS MORRIS

Diana, fully as enamored as he, could not bear to pass him by without a caress, and invariably left her car for a moment, as it touched the mountain peak, to run to him and snatch a hasty kiss.

> Chaste Artemis, who guides the lunar car,
> The pale nocturnal vigils ever keeping,
> Sped through the silent space from star to star,
> And, blushing, stooped to kiss Endymion sleeping.
>
> BOYESEN

But, even when asleep, Endymion watched for her coming, and enjoyed the bliss of her presence; yet a spell seemed to prevent his giving any sign of consciousness.

Time passed thus. Diana, who could not bear to think of the youth's beauty being marred by want, toil, and exposure, finally caused an eternal sleep to fall upon him, and bore him off to Mount Latmus, where she concealed him in a cave held sacred to her, and never profaned by human gaze. There each night the goddess paused to gaze enraptured upon his beloved countenance, and to press a soft kiss upon his unconscious lips. Such is the tale of Diana and her lowly sweetheart, which has inspired poets of all ages.

Queen of the wide air; thou most lovely queen
Of all the brightness that mine eyes have seen!
As thou exceedest all things in thy shrine,
So every tale, does this sweet tale of thine.

KEATS

STORY OF ORION

Endymion was not, however, the only mortal loved by Diana, for mythologists report that her affections were also bestowed upon a young hunter by the name of Orion. All day long this youth scoured the forest, his faithful dog Sirius at his heels.

One day, in the dense shade of the forest, he met a group of Diana's nymphs, the seven Pleiades, daughters of Atlas. These fair maidens needed but to be seen to be passionately loved, and Orion's heart burned as he sought to approach them; but they were very coy, and, as he drew near and addressed them, turned and fled.

Afraid lest he should never see them again were he now to lose sight of them, he pursued them hotly; but the nymphs sped on, until, their strength failing, they called upon their patroness's aid. Their prayer was no sooner heard than answered, and Orion, panting and weary, came up just in time to see seven snow-white pigeons wing their way up into the azure sky.

There a second transformation overtook the Pleiades, who were changed into a constellation, composed of seven bright stars, and there they shone undimmed for ages; but when Troy fell into the enemy's hands, all grew pale with grief, and one, more timid and impressionable than the rest, withdrew from sight to hide her anguish from the curious eyes of men.

And is there glory from the heavens departed?—
O void unmark'd!—thy sisters of the sky
Still hold their place on high,
Though from its rank thine orb so long hath started
Thou, that no more art seen of mortal eye!

HEMANS

Orion, like a fickle youth, was soon consoled for their disappearance and loved Merope, daughter of Œnopion, King of Chios, who consented to their union on condition that his future son-in-law should win his bride by some heroic deed. Now, as

Orion was anything but a patient man, the delay was very unwelcome indeed, and he made up his mind to abduct his bride instead of marrying her openly; but the plan was frustrated by Œnopion's watchfulness, and Orion was punished by the loss not only of his bride, but also of shis eyesight.

Blind, helpless, and alone, he now wandered from place to place, hoping to find some one capable of restoring his sight. At last he reached the Cyclopes's cave, and one of them took pity on him, and led him to the Sun, from whose radiance he borrowed a store of light,—

> When, blinded by Œnopion,
> He sought the blacksmith at his forge,
> And, climbing up the mountain gorge,
> Fixed his blank eyes upon the sun.
>
> LONGFELLOW

Happy once more, he resumed his favorite sport, and hunted from morn till eve. Diana met him in the forest, and, sharing his tastes, soon learned to love him; but this affection was viewed with great displeasure by Apollo, from whose piercing glance nothing that occurred by day could be hidden, and he resolved to put an end to his sister's infatuation. He therefore summoned her to his side. To divert her suspicions, he began to talk of archery, and, under the pretext of testing her skill as a markswoman, bade her shoot at a dark speck rising and falling far out at sea.

Diana seized her bow, feathered her arrow, and sent it with such force and accurate aim, that she touched the point, and saw it vanish beneath the waves, little suspecting that the dark head of Orion, who was refreshing himself by a sea bath, was given her as a target. When she discovered her error, she mourned his loss with many tears, vowed never to forget him, and placed him and his faithful dog Sirius as constellations in the sky.

STORY OF ACTÆON

When Diana had finished her nightly journey in her moon car, she seized her bow and arrows, and, attended by her nymphs, was wont to sally forth to hunt the wild beasts in the forest.

One summer afternoon, after an unusually long and exciting pursuit, Diana and her followers came to one of the still mountain pools where they had often resorted to

enjoy a plunge. The cool waters rippled so invitingly, that the goddess and her attendants hastened to divest themselves of their short hunting garments, and lave their
heated limbs.

But unfortunately the goddess and her attendant nymphs had not been the only
ones out hunting that day. Actæon, the huntsman, had risen at dawn to stalk the deer;
and now, weary and parched with thirst, he too sought the well-known mountain spring,

> Deep in the cool recesses of the wood,
> Where the cold crystal of a mossy pool
> Rose to the flowery marge, and gave again
> The soft green lawn where ofttimes, overspent,
> I lay upon the grass and eager bathed
> My limbs in the clear lymph.
>
> LEWIS MORRIS

As he drew near the accustomed spot, Actæon fancied he heard bursts of silvery
laughter: so he crept on very cautiously, and soon, gently parting the thick branches of
the underbrush, beheld the sporting group.

At the selfsame moment Diana turned to ascertain the cause of the rustle which
had caught her practiced ear, and met the admiring gaze of the astonished young
hunter. Speechless with indignation that a mortal had beheld her thus, she caught some
water in her hollow palm, flung it in his face, and bade him go and declare, if he could,
that he had seen Diana disrobed.

The glittering drops had no sooner touched the young man's face, than he turned
to obey her command, and found himself transformed into a stag, with slender, sin-
ewy limbs, furry skin, and wide-branching antlers. Nothing remained of his former self
except the woeful consciousness of his transformation; and as he stood there, motionless and dismayed, the distant baying of his hounds coming to join him fell upon his ear.

An electric thrill of fear shot through every vein, as, mindful of his new form, he
bounded away through the forest. Alas! too late; for the pack had caught one glimpse
of his sleek sides, and were after him in full cry.

In vain poor Actæon strained every muscle. His limbs refused their support, and,
as he sank exhausted to the ground, the hounds sprang at his quivering throat.

Nearer they came and nearer, baying loud,
With bloodshot eyes and red jaws dripping foam;
And when I strove to check their savagery,
Speaking with words, no voice articulate came,
Only a dumb, low bleat. Then all the throng
Leapt swift on me, and tore me as I lay!

LEWIS MORRIS

Diana was widely worshiped, and temples without number were dedicated to her service; among others, the world-renowned sanctuary of Ephesus. The ancients also celebrated many festivals in honor of this fair goddess of the moon, who was ever ready to extend her protection over all deserving mortals.

VENUS

VENUS'S BIRTH

Venus (Dione, Aphrodite, Cytherea), the goddess of beauty, love, laughter, and marriage, is said by some mythologists to be the daughter of Jupiter and Dione, goddess of moisture: others report that she sprang from the foam of the sea.

> Look, look, why shine
> Those floating bubbles with such light divine?
> They break, and from their mist a lily form
> Rises from out the wave, in beauty warm.
> The wave is by the blue-veined feet scarce press'd,
> Her silky ringlets float about her breast,
> Veiling its fairy loveliness; while her eye
> Is soft and deep as the blue heaven is high.
> The Beautiful is born; and sea and earth
> May well revere the hour of that mysterious birth.
>
> SHELLEY

The ocean nymphs were the first to discover her, cradled on a great blue wave; and they carried her down into their coral caves, where they tenderly nursed her, and taught her with the utmost care. Then, her education being completed, the sea nymphs judged it time to introduce her to the other gods, and, with that purpose in view, carried her up to the surface of the sea—where Tritons, Oceanides, and Nereides all crowded around her, loudly expressing their ardent admiration—and offered her pearls and choice bits of coral from the deep, as a tribute to her charms.

FOLLOWING PAGES: THE BIRTH OF VENUS. Sandro Botticelli.

Then they pillowed her softly on a great wave, and intrusted her to the care of Zephyrus, the soft south wind, who blew a gentle breath, and wafted her to the Island of Cyprus.

The four beautiful Horæ (the Seasons), daughters of Jupiter and Themis, goddess of justice, stood there on the shore to welcome her.

> An ethereal band
> Are visible above: the Seasons four,—
> Green-kirtled Spring, flush Summer, golden store
> In Autumn's sickle, Winter frosty hoar.
>
> KEATS

And they were not alone to watch for her coming, for the three Charites (Graces, or Gratiæ) were also present.

> "These three on men all gracious gifts bestow,
> Which decke the body or adorne the mynde,
> To make them lovely or well-favoured show;
> As comely carriage, entertainement kynde,
> Sweete semblaunt, friendly offices that bynde,
> And all the complements of curtesie:
> They teach us how to each degree and kynde
> We should our selves demeane, to low, to hie,
> To friends, to foes; which skill men call Civility."
>
> SPENSER

Daughters of Jupiter and Eurynome, these maidens, who bore the respective names of Aglaia, Euphrosyne, and Thalia, longed to show their love for their new mistress. When the wave upon which she reclined came nearer still, the "rosy-bosomed Hours, fair Venus's train," appeared. The wind finally brought the fair goddess in safety to the shore; and, as soon as her foot touched the white sand, all bent in homage to her surpassing beauty, and reverentially watched her dry her hair.

> Idalian Aphrodite beautiful,
> Fresh as the foam, new-bathed in Paphian wells,
> With rosy slender fingers backward drew

From her warm brows and bosom her deep hair
Ambrosial, golden round her lucid throat
And shoulder: from the violets her light foot
Shone rosy-white, and o'er her rounded form
Between the shadows of the vine bunches
Floated the glowing sunlights, as she moved.

TENNYSON

This hasty and somewhat primitive toilet completed, Venus and her followers set out for Mount Olympus, and on their way thither were joined by Himerus, god of the desire of love; Pothos, god of the amities of love; Suadela, god of the soft speech of love; and Hymen, god of marriage.

VENUS AND VULCAN

A throne had been prepared for the expected goddess, and, when she suddenly appeared to take possession of it, the assembled gods could not restrain a rapturous murmur of admiration. Her beauty took them by storm, and her grace won their hearts; but, although they one and all expressed a desire to marry her, Venus scornfully rejected their proposals. Even the king of gods was slighted, and, to punish her for her pride, he decreed she should marry Vulcan, god of the forge, the most ill-favored of all the heavenly council.

This compulsory union was anything but a happy one; for Venus never showed any affection for her deformed consort, and, instead of being a faithful wife, soon deserted him, and openly declared she would please herself.

STORY OF ALECTRYON

Her first fancy was for Mars, the handsome god of war, who was not slow in reciprocating the fair goddess's affections, and many and sweet were the secret interviews they enjoyed. Yet, fearful lest some of the gods passing by should discover them together, Mars always placed his attendant Alectryon on guard, bidding him give due warning

FOLLOWING PAGES: PRIMAVERA. Sandro Botticelli.

SLEEPING CUPID. Francesco Albani.

of any one's approach, and especially to call him before the sun rose, as the lovers were particularly anxious that Apollo should not witness their parting caresses.

All prospered according to their desires, until one night the unfortunate Alectryon fell asleep; and so profound were his slumbers, that he did not even stir when Aurora flung open the gates of the east, and Apollo flashed forth to receive the melodious greetings of the feathered denizens of the forest.

The sun god drove rapidly on, glancing right and left, and taking note of all he saw. Nothing escaped his bright and piercing eye, as it flashed its beams hither and thither, and he was soon aware of the sleeping watchman and of the guilty lovers. As fast as his fleet-footed steeds could carry him, Apollo hastened to Vulcan, to whom he vividly described the sight which had greeted his eyes.

The irate husband lost no time, but, seizing a net of linked steel, went in search of his runaway wife. Stealthily he approached the lovers' bower, and deftly flung the net over both sleepers, who were caught in its fine meshes, and could not escape; and there he kept them imprisoned, in spite of their entreaties, until all the gods had seen their humiliating plight, and turned them into ridicule. But when he at last set them free, Mars darted away, vowing vengeance upon the negligent sentinel, who was still blissfully sleeping. Pouncing upon him, Mars awakened him roughly, administered a sharp reproof, changed him into a cock, banished him into the barnyard, and condemned him to give daily warning of the sun's approach.

> And, from out a neighboring farmyard,
> Loud the cock Alectryon crowed.
>   LONGFELLOW

VENUS'S CHILDREN

Several beautiful children were born to Mars and Venus. Hermione, or Harmonia, their daughter, married Cadmus, King of Thebes; and Cupid (Cupido, Eros, Amor), their little son, was appointed god of love. Although nursed with tender solicitude, this second-born child did not grow as other children do, but remained a small, rosy, chubby child, with gauzy wings and roguish, dimpled face. Alarmed for his health, Venus consulted Themis, who oracularly replied, "Love cannot grow without Passion."

In vain the goddess strove to catch the concealed meaning of this answer. It was only revealed to her when Anteros, god of passion, was born. When with his brother, Cupid grew and flourished, until he became a handsome, slender youth; but when separated from him, he invariably resumed his childish form and mischievous habits.

VENUS AND ADONIS

Venus, however, did not lavish all her love upon Mars, for she is said to have felt a tender passion for a young man named Adonis, a bold young hunter, whose rash pursuit of dangerous game caused Venus many anxious alarms. In vain she besought him to forego the pleasures of the chase and remain with her. He laughingly escaped, and continued to join the other hunters in his favorite sport. But, alas! one day, after an exciting pursuit, he boldly attacked a wild boar, which, goaded to madness, turned upon him, buried his strong tusk in the youth's unprotected side, and trampled him to death.

The white tusk of a boar has transpierced his white thigh.

*   *   *   *   *

The youth lieth dead while his dogs howl around,
And the nymphs weep aloud from the mists of the hill.

BION (Mrs. Browning's tr.)

Venus ran straight to the scene of his tragic death, rushing through underbrush and briers, tearing her delicate skin, and her blood tingeing all the white roses along her way to a faint pink. When she arrived, she found her beloved Adonis cold in death, and her passionate caresses met with no response. Then she burst into such a passion of tears, that the wood and water nymphs, the gods, men, and all nature in fact, joined with her to mourn the beloved youth.

Her loss the Loves deplore:
Woe, Venus, woe! Adonis is no more.

BION (Elton's tr.)

Very reluctantly Mercury at last appeared to lead the soul of the departed down into the Infernal Regions, where it was welcomed by Proserpina, queen of the realm, and led to the place where pure and virtuous mortals enjoyed an eternity of bliss. Venus, still inconsolable, shed countless tears, which, as they dropped upon the ground, were changed to anemones, while the red drops which had fallen from Adonis's side were transformed into red roses.

As many drops as from Adonis bled,
So many tears the sorrowing Venus shed:
For every drop on earth a flower there grows:
Anemones for tears; for blood the rose.

BION (Elton's tr.)

As time did not soften Venus's grief, but, on the contrary, made it more and more unendurable, she went to Olympus, where she fell at Jupiter's feet, imploring him to release Adonis from death's embrace, or allow her to share his lot in Hades.

To allow Beauty to desert the earth was not possible, nor could he resist her pleading: so he finally decreed that Adonis should be restored to her longing arms. But Pluto, whose subject he had now become, refused to yield up Adonis; and after much dispute a compromise was agreed upon, by virtue of which Adonis was allowed to spend one half of the year on earth, providing he spent the remaining six months in the Elysian Fields.

In early spring, therefore, Adonis left the Lower World, and came with bounding tread to join his beloved. On his path the flowers bloomed and the birds sang, to show their joy at his coming. An emblem of vegetation, which rises from the ground in early spring to deck the earth with beautiful foliage and flowers, and cause the birds to sing for gladness, Adonis reluctantly returned to Hades, when Winter, the cruel boar, slew him again with his white tusk, and made nature again droop, and mourn his departure.

> But even in death, so strong is Love,
> I could not wholly die; and year by year,
> When the bright springtime comes, and the earth lives,
> Love opens these dread gates, and calls me forth
> Across the gulf.
>
> LEWIS MORRIS

VENUS AND ANCHISES

The Goddess of Beauty also loved Anchises, Prince of Troy, but, ashamed of lavishing favors upon a mere mortal, extorted from him a promise that he would never reveal their secret marriage. Unfortunately, however, Anchises was of a boastful disposition, and ere long yielded to temptation and revealed the secret, incurring her wrath to such an extent, that some mythologists accuse her of borrowing one of Jupiter's thunderbolts and slaying him. Others, however, report that Anchises lived to a ripe old age, and escaped from burning Troy on his son Æneas's back. Venus's love was, however, all transferred to her son Æneas, whom she signally protected throughout his checkered career.

STORY OF HERO AND LEANDER

Venus's most ardent admirers and faithful worshipers were the young people, for she delighted in their youthful sentiments, and was ever ready to lend a helping hand to all true lovers when apparently insurmountable obstacles appeared on their path.

This was the case with a lovely maiden by the name of Hero, who was dedicated by her parents to Venus's service, and, as soon as old enough, spent all her time in the temple, ministering to the goddess, or in a lonely tower by the sea, where she dwelt alone with her aged nurse.

> Honey-sweet Hero, of a princely race,
> Was priestess to Queen Venus in that place;
> And at her father's tower, by the sea set—
> Herself a Queen of Love, though maiden yet—
> Dwelt.
>
> EDWIN ARNOLD

The maiden's beauty increased with her years, until the fame of her loveliness spread throughout her native city Sestus, and even passed over the Hellespont and reached Abydus, where Leander, the bravest and handsomest youth of the town, was fired with a desire to view the charming young priestess.

Just at that time a solemn festival in honor of Venus was to be celebrated at Sestus, to which all the youths and maidens were cordially invited. Under pretext of paying homage to the goddess, Leander entered her temple, and saw the young priestess, whose charms far surpassed all descriptions.

Venus, as has already been stated, was always deeply interested in young lovers; and when she saw these two, so well matched in beauty and grace, she bade Cupid pierce them with his love darts, which behest the mischief-loving god immediately obeyed.

> God Eros, setting notch to string,
> Wounded two bosoms with one shaft-shooting,
> A maiden's and a youth's—Leander he,
> And lovely Hero, Sestos' sweetest, she;
> She of her town, and he of his, the boast;
> A noble pair!
>
> EDWIN ARNOLD

An undying passion was thus simultaneously kindled in both young hearts; and, thanks to Venus's assistance, Leander managed to exchange a few words with Hero, declared his love, implored her to view his suit kindly, and, above all, to grant him a private interview, or he would surely die.

The maiden listened to his pleading with mingled joy and terror, for she knew her parents would never consent to their union. Then, afraid lest some one should notice that she was talking to a stranger, she bade him depart; but he refused to go until he had learned where she lived, and proposed to swim across the Hellespont when the shades of night had fallen, and none could see his goal, and pay her a visit in her lonely tower.

"Sweet! for thy love," he cried, "the sea I'd cleave,
Though foam were fire, and waves with flame did heave,
I fear not billows if they bear to thee;
Nor tremble at the hissing of the sea!
And I will come—oh! let me come—each night,
Swimming the swift flood to my dear delight:
For white Abydos, where I live, doth front
Thy city here, across our Hellespont."

EDWIN ARNOLD

At last his prayers overcame the maiden's scruples, and she arranged to receive him in her sea-girt tower, promising at a given hour to light a torch and hold it aloft to guide him safely across the sea. Then only he departed.

Night came on; darkness stole over the earth; and Leander impatiently paced the sandy shore, and watched for the promised signal, which no sooner appeared, than he exultantly plunged into the dark waves, and parted them with lusty strokes, as he hastened across the deep to join his beloved. At times the huge billows towered above his head; but when he had escaped their threatening depths, and rose up on their foamy crests, he could catch a glimpse of the torch burning brightly, and pictured to himself the shy, sweet blushes which would dye Hero's cheek as he clasped her to his passionate heart.

Leander had no fear—he cleft the wave—
What is the peril fond hearts will not brave!

LANDON

Venus, from the top of "many-peaked Olympus," smilingly viewed the success of her scheme, and nerved Leander's arm to cleave the rapid current. At last he reached the tower steps, and was lovingly greeted by Hero, whose heart had throbbed with anxiety at the thought of the perils her lover was braving for the sake of seeing her once more.

It was only when the dawn began to whiten the east, that the lovers finished their interview and parted, he to return to Abydus, and she to prepare for the daily duties which would soon claim her attention. But separation by day was all these fond lovers could endure, and night after night, as soon as the first stars appeared, Hero lighted her torch, and Leander hastened to her, to linger by her side till dawn.

Thus pass'd the summer shadows in delight:
Leander came as surely as the night,
And when the morning woke upon the sea,
It saw him not, for back at home was he.

HUNT

No one suspected their meetings; and all went well until the first fierce storms of winter swept down over the Hellespont. Hero, in the gray dawn of a winter's morning, besought her lover not to leave her to battle against the waves, which beat so violently against the stone tower; but he gently laughed at her fears, and departed, promising to return at night as usual.

The storm, which had raged so fiercely already in the early morning, increased in violence as the day wore on, until the waves were lashed into foam, while the wind howled more and more ominously as the darkness came on again; but none of these signs could deter Leander from visiting Hero.

HERO AND LEANDER. Domenico Fetti.

> There came one night, the wildest of the year,
> When the wind smote like edge of hissing spear,
> And the pale breakers thundered on the beach.
>
> EDWIN ARNOLD

All day long Hero had hoped that her lover would renounce his nightly journey; but still, when evening came, she lighted her torch to serve as beacon, should he risk all to keep his word. The wind blew so fiercely, that the torch wavered and flickered, and nearly went out, although Hero protected its feeble flame by standing over it with outstretched robes.

At sight of the wonted signal, Leander, who had already once been beaten back by the waves, made a second attempt to cross the strait, calling upon the gods to lend him their aid. But this time his prayers were unheard, drowned in the fury of the storm; yet he struggled on a while longer, with Hero's name on his lips.

At last, exhausted and ready to sink, he lifted his eyes once more to view the cheering light. It was gone, extinguished by a passing gust of wind. Like a stone Leander sank, once, twice, thrice, and the billows closed forever over his head.

Hero in the mean while had relighted her torch, and, quite unconscious of the tragedy which had taken place, stood on the tower, straining her eyes to pierce the darkness. All night long she waited and watched for the lover who did not come; and, when the first sunbeams shone over the tossing sea, she cast an anxious glance over the waters to Abydus. No one was in sight as far as she could see. She was about to descend to pursue her daily tasks, when, glancing at the foot of the tower, she saw her lover's corpse heaving up and down on the waves.

> As shaken on his restless pillow,
> His head heaves with the heaving billow;
> That hand, whose motion is not life,
> Yet feebly seems to menace strife,
> Flung by the tossing tide on high,
>   Then level'd with the wave.
>
> BYRON

Hero's heart broke at this sad sight, and she longed to die, too, that she might not be parted from Leander. To hasten their meeting, she threw herself into the sea, and perished in the waves, close by his side. Thus lived and died the faithful lovers, whose attachment has passed into a proverb.

Byron, the celebrated English bard, attempted Leander's feat of swimming across the Hellespont, and, on his return from that dangerous venture, wrote the following lines, which are so familiar to all English-speaking people:—

> The winds are high on Helle's wave,
>   As on that night of stormy water
> When Love, who sent, forgot to save
> The young, the beautiful, the brave,
>   The lonely hope of Sestos' daughter.
> Oh! when alone along the sky
> Her turret torch was blazing high,

Though rising gale, and breaking foam,
And shrieking sea-birds warn'd him home;
And clouds aloft and tides below,
With signs and sounds, forbade to go,
He could not see, he would not hear,
Or sound or sign foreboding fear;
His eye but saw that light of love,
The only star it hail'd above;
His ear but rang with Hero's song,
"Ye waves, divide not lovers long!"
That tale is old, but love anew
May nerve young hearts to prove as true.

PYRAMUS AND THISBE

An equally loving and unfortunate pair were Pyramus and Thisbe. Although no waves divided them, and they had the good fortune to occupy adjoining houses in Babylon, their parents having quarreled, they were forbidden to see or speak to each other. This decree wrung their tender hearts; and their continuous sighs finally touched Venus, who prepared to give them her aid. Thanks to this goddess's kind offices, a crack was discovered in the party wall, through which the lovers could peep at each other, converse, and even, it is said, exchange a kiss or two.

Sundry stolen interviews through this crack made them long for uninterrupted and unrestrained meetings: so they made an appointment to meet on a certain day and hour, under a white mulberry tree, just without the city gates.

Thisbe, anxious to see her lover, was the first to reach the trysting place, and, as she slowly paced back and forth to while away the time of waiting, she wondered what had happened to delay Pyramus. Her meditation was suddenly broken by a rustling sound in some neighboring bushes; and, thinking Pyramus was concealed there, she was about to call to him that he was discovered, when, instead of her lover, she saw a lion emerge from the thicket and come towards her, slowly lashing his sides with his tail, and licking his bloody jaws. With one terrified shriek the girl ran away, dropping her veil, which the lion caught in his bloody mouth and tore to shreds, before beating a retreat into the forest.

Shortly after, Pyramus came rushing up, out of breath, and full of loving excuses for Thisbe, who was not there, however, to receive them. Wondering at her absence,

Pyramus looked around, and after a short investigation discerned the lion's footprints and the mangled veil. These signs sufficed to convince him that Thisbe had perished, and in a fit of despair he drew his dagger from its sheath and thrust it into his heart.

A few minutes later, Thisbe cautiously drew near, peering anxiously about to discover whether the lion were still lurking near. Her first glance showed her Pyramus stretched dead beneath the mulberry tree, with her bloody veil pressed convulsively to his lips. With a cry of terror she flew to his side, and tried to revive him; but, when assured that all her efforts were in vain, she drew the dagger from his breast, and, plunging it into her own bosom, fell beside him quite lifeless.

> In her bosom plunged the sword,
> All warm and reeking from its slaughtered lord.
>
> OVID (Eusden's tr.)

Since that ominous day the fruit of the mulberry tree, which had been white, assumed a blood-like hue, dyed by the blood which flowed from the death wounds of Pyramus and Thisbe.

ECHO AND NARCISSUS

The lovely and talkative nymph Echo lived free from care and whole of heart until she met Narcissus, hunting in the forest. This frivolous young lady no sooner beheld the youth, than she fell deeply in love with him, and was proportionately grieved when she saw that he did not return her affections.

All her blandishments were unavailing, and, in her despair at his hard-heartedness, she implored Venus to punish him by making him suffer the pangs of unrequited love; then, melancholy and longing to die, she wandered off into the mountains, far from the haunts of her former companions, and there, brooding continually over her sorrow, pined away until there remained naught of her but her melodious voice.

The gods, displeased at her lack of proper pride, condemned her to haunt rocks and solitary places, and, as a warning to other impulsive maidens, to repeat the last sounds which fell upon her ear.

But her voice is still living immortal,—
    The same you have frequently heard
In your rambles in valleys and forests,
    Repeating your ultimate word.

SAXE

Venus alone had not forgotten poor Echo's last passionate prayer, and was biding her time to punish the disdainful Narcissus. One day, after a prolonged chase, he hurried to a lonely pool to slake his thirst.

In some delicious ramble, he had found
A little space, with boughs all woven round;
And in the midst of all, a clearer pool
Than e'er reflected in its pleasant cool
The blue sky here, and there, serenely peeping
Through tendril wreaths fantastically creeping.

KEATS

Quickly he knelt upon the grass, and bent over the pellucid waters to take a draught; but he suddenly paused, surprised. Down near the pebbly bottom he saw a face so passing fair, that he immediately lost his heart, for he thought it belonged to some water nymph gazing up at him through the transparent flood.

With sudden passion he caught at the beautiful apparition; but, the moment his arms touched the water, the nymph vanished. Astonished and dismayed, he slowly withdrew to a short distance, and breathlessly awaited the nymph's return.

The agitated waters soon resumed their mirror-like smoothness; and Narcissus, approaching noiselessly on tiptoe, and cautiously peeping into the pool, became aware first of curly, tumbled locks, and then of a pair of beautiful, watchful, anxious eyes. Evidently the nymph had just concluded to emerge from her hiding place to reconnoiter.

More prudent this time, the youth gradually bent further over the pool; and, reassured by his kindly glances, the nymph's whole head appeared. In gentle tones the youth now addressed her; and her ruby lips parted and moved as if she were answering, though not a sound came to his ear. In his excitement he began to gesticulate, whereupon two snowy arms repeated his every gesture; but when, encouraged by her loving glances and actions, he tried once more to clasp her in his arms, she vanished as rapidly as the first time.

Time and again the same pantomime was enacted, and time and again the nymph eluded his touch; but the enamored youth could not tear himself away from the spot haunted by this sweet image, whose sensitive face reflected his every emotion, and who grew as pale and wan as he,—evidently, like him, a victim to love and despair.

Even the shades of night could not drive Narcissus away from his post, and, when the pale moonbeams illumined his retreat, he bent over the pool to ascertain whether she too were anxious and sleepless, and saw her gazing longingly up at him.

There Narcissus lingered day and night, without eating or drinking, until he died, little suspecting that the fancied nymph was but his own image reflected in the clear waters. Echo was avenged; but the gods of Olympus gazed compassionately down upon the beautiful corpse, and changed it into a flower bearing the youth's name, which has ever since flourished beside quiet pools, wherein its pale image is clearly reflected.

> A lonely flower he spied,
> A meek and forlorn flower, with naught of pride,
> Drooping its beauty o'er the watery clearness,
> To woo its own sad image into nearness:
> Deaf to light Zephyrus it would not move;
> But still would seem to droop, to pine, to love.
>
> KEATS

PYGMALION AND GALATEA

Pygmalion, King of Cyprus, was a very celebrated sculptor. All his leisure moments were spent in the faithful portrayal of the gods and goddesses. One day his practiced hand fashioned an image of Galatea. It was so beautiful that even before it was entirely finished its author loved it. When completed, Pygmalion admired it still more, deemed it too beautiful to remain inanimate, and besought Venus to give it life, stating that he wished a wife just like it.

As Pygmalion had always been an obdurate bachelor, and had frequently declared he would never marry, Venus was delighted to see him at last a victim of the tender passion, and resolved to grant his request. Pygmalion clasped the exquisite image to his breast to infuse some of his own warmth into the icy bosom, and pressed kiss after kiss upon the chiseled lips, until at last they grew soft and warm at his touch, and a faint color flushed the pale cheeks, as a breath dilated her lungs, and sent her blood coursing along her veins—

> As once with prayers in passion flowing,
> Pygmalion embraced the stone,
> Till, from the frozen marble glowing,
> The light of feeling o'er him shone.
>
> SCHILLER

Pygmalion's delight at seeing his fair image a living and breathing maiden was unbounded, and after a short but passionate wooing the object of his affections became his happy wife.

CUPID AND PSYCHE

In those same remote ages of "sweet mythology" there lived a king whose three daughters were world-renowned on account of their matchless beauty. Psyche, the youngest of the sisters, was so lovely, that her father's subjects declared her worthy to be called the Goddess of Beauty, and offered to pay homage to her instead of to Venus. Offended by this proposal, which Psyche had good sense enough to refuse, Venus resolved to demonstrate forcibly to that benighted race that the maiden was mortal. She therefore bade her son Cupid slay her.

Armed with his bow and arrows, and provided with a deadly poison, Cupid set out to do her bidding, and at nightfall reached the palace, crept noiselessly past the sleeping guards, along the deserted halls, and came to Psyche's apartment, into which he glided unseen. Stealthily he approached the couch upon which the fair maiden was sleeping, and bent over her to administer the poisoned dose.

A moonbeam falling athwart her face revealed her unequaled loveliness, and made Cupid start back in surprise; but, as he did so, one of his own love arrows came into contact with his rosy flesh, and inflicted a wound, from which he was to suffer for many a weary day.

All unconscious of the gravity of his hurt, he hung enraptured over the sleeping maiden, and let her fair image sink into his heart; then, noiselessly as he had entered, he stole out again, vowing he would never harm such innocence and beauty.

Morning dawned. Venus, who had expected to see the sun illumine her rival's corpse, saw her sporting as usual in the palace gardens, and bitterly realized that her first plan had completely failed. She therefore began to devise various torments of a petty kind, and persecuted the poor girl so remorselessly, that she fled from home with the firm intention of putting an end to the life she could no longer enjoy in peace.

To achieve this purpose, Psyche painfully toiled up a rugged mountain, and, creeping to the very edge of a great precipice, cast herself down, expecting to be dashed to pieces on the jagged rocks below; but Cupid, who had indignantly though helplessly seen all his mother's persecutions, had followed Psyche unseen, and, when he perceived her intention to commit suicide, he called to Zephyrus (the South Wind), and entreated him to catch the maiden in his strong yet gentle arms, and bear her off to a distant isle.

Consequently, instead of a swift, sharp fall and painful death, Psyche felt herself gently wafted over hill and dale, across sparkling waters; and, long before she wearied of this new mode of travel, she was gently laid on a flowery bank, in the midst of an exquisite garden.

Bewildered, she slowly rose to her feet, rubbed her pretty eyes to make sure she was not dreaming, and wonderingly strolled about the beautiful grounds. Ere long she came to an enchanted palace, whose portals opened wide to receive her, while gentle voices bade her enter, and invisible hands drew her over the threshold and waited upon her.

When night came, and darkness again covered the earth, Cupid appeared in search of his beloved Psyche. In the perfumed dusk he confessed his love, and tenderly begged for some return.

Now, although the fading light would not permit her to discern the form or features of her unknown lover, Psyche listened to his soft tones with unconcealed plea-sure, and soon consented to their union. Cupid then entreated her to make no attempt to discover his name, or to catch a glimpse of his face, warning her that if she did so he would be forced to leave her, never to return.

> "Dear, I am with thee only while I keep
>   My visage hidden; and if thou once shouldst see
>   My face, I must forsake thee: the high gods
>   Link Love with Faith, and he withdraws himself
>   From the full gaze of Knowledge."
>
> LEWIS MORRIS

Psyche solemnly promised to respect her mysterious lover's wishes, and gave her-self up entirely to the enjoyment of his company. All night long they talked; and when the first faint streak of light appeared above the horizon, Cupid bade Psyche farewell, promising to return with the welcome shades of night. All day long Psyche thought of him, longed for him, and, as soon as the sun had set, sped to the bower where the birds were sleepily trilling forth their evening song, and breathlessly waited until he came to join her.

> Now on broad pinions from the realms above
> Descending Cupid seeks the Cyprian grove;
> To his wide arms enamor'd Psyche springs,
> And clasps her lover with aurelian wings.
> A purple sash across His shoulder bends,
> And fringed with gold the quiver'd shafts suspends.
>
> DARWIN

Although the hours of day seemed interminable, spent as they were in complete solitude, Psyche found the hours of night all too short in the sweet society of Love. Her every wish was gratified almost as soon as expressed; and at last, encouraged by her lover's evident anxiety to please her, she gave utterance to her longing to see and converse with her sisters once more. The ardent lover could not refuse to grant this request, yet Psyche noticed that his consent seemed somewhat hesitating and reluctant.

The next morning, while enjoying a solitary stroll, Psyche suddenly encountered her two sisters. After rapturous embraces and an incoherent volley of questions and answers, they settled down to enjoy a long talk. Psyche related her desperate attempt at suicide, her miraculous preservation from certain death, her aërial journey, her entrance into the enchanted palace, her love for her mysterious nightly visitor— all, in short, that had happened since she had left her father's home.

Now, the elder sisters had always been jealous of Psyche's superior beauty; and when they saw her luxurious surroundings, and heard her raptures about her lover, they were envious, and resolved to mar the happiness which they could not enjoy. They therefore did all in their power to convince poor Psyche that her lover must be some monster, so hideous that he dare not brave the broad light of day, lest he should make her loathe him, and further added, that, if she were not very careful, he would probably end by devouring her.

They thereupon advised poor troubled Psyche to conceal a lamp and dagger in her lover's apartment, and to gaze upon him in secret, when his eyes were closed in sleep. If the light of the lamp revealed, as they felt sure it would, the hideous countenance and distorted form of a monster, they bade her use the dagger to kill him. Then, satisfied with their work, the sisters departed, leaving Psyche alone to carry out their evil suggestions.

When safe at home once more, the sisters constantly brooded over the tale Psyche had poured into their ears, and, hoping to secure as luxurious a home and as fascinating a lover, they each hurried off in secret to the mountain gorge, cast themselves over the precipice, and—perished.

Night having come, bringing the usually so welcome Cupid, Psyche, tortured with doubt, could with difficulty conceal her agitation. After repeated efforts to charm her from her silent mood, Cupid fell asleep; and, as soon as his regular breathing proclaimed him lost in slumber, Psyche noiselessly lighted her lamp, seized her dagger, and, approaching the couch with great caution, bent over her sleeping lover. The lamp, which she held high above her head, cast its light full upon the face and form of a handsome youth.

> Now trembling, now distracted; bold,
> And now irresolute she seems;
> The blue lamp glimmers in her hold,
> And in her hand the dagger gleams.
> Prepared to strike, she verges near,
> Then, the blue light glimmering from above,
> The hideous sight expects with fear—
> And gazes on the god of Love.
>
> APOLLONIUS

Psyche's heart beat loudly with joy and pride as she beheld, instead of the monster, this graceful youth; and as she hung over him, enraptured, she forgot all caution. An inadvertent motion tipped her lamp, and one drop of burning oil, running over the narrow brim, fell upon Cupid's naked shoulder.

The sudden pain made him open his eyes with a start. The lighted lamp, the glittering dagger, the trembling Psyche, told the whole story. Cupid sprang from the couch, seized his bow and arrows, and, with a last sorrowful, reproachful glance at Psyche, flew away through the open window, exclaiming—

OPPOSITE PAGE: PSYCHE AND THE EARTHLY PARADISE. Edward Burne-Jones.

> "Farewell! There is no Love except with Faith,
> And thine is dead! Farewell! I come no more!"
>
> LEWIS MORRIS

PSYCHE FORSAKEN

When he had vanished into the dusky air without, the balmy night winds ceased to blow; and suddenly a tempest began to rage with such fury, that poor frightened Psyche dared not remain alone in the palace, but hastened out into the gardens, where she soon lost consciousness of her misery in a deep swoon. When she opened her eyes once more, the storm had ceased, the sun was high in the heavens, and palace and gardens had vanished.

Poor Psyche lingered there the following and many succeeding nights, vainly hoping for Cupid's return, and shedding many bitter tears of repentance. Finally she resolved to commit suicide, and, with that purpose in view, plunged into a neighboring river; but the god of the stream caught and carried her ashore, where his daughters, the water nymphs, restored her to life. Thus forced to live, Psyche wandered about disconsolate, seeking Cupid, and questioning all she met, the nymphs, Pan, and Ceres, who compassionately listened to her confession of love for her husband.

> Not as the earthly loves which throb and flush
> Round earthly shrines was mine, but a pure spirit,
> Lovelier than all embodied love, more pure
> And wonderful; but never on his eyes
> I looked, which still were hidden, and I knew not
> The fashion of his nature; for by night,
> When visual eyes are blind, but the soul sees,
> Came he, and bade me seek not to inquire
> Or whence he came or wherefore. Nor knew I
> His name. And always ere the coming day,
> As if he were the Sun god, lingering
> With some too well loved maiden, he would rise
> And vanish until eve.
>
> LEWIS MORRIS

Ceres had often seen Cupid, and had heard that very morning that he was having a wound in his shoulder dressed by Venus: so she advised Psyche to go to the Goddess of Beauty, to enter her service, and to perform every task with cheerful alacrity, knowing that such a course would ultimately bring about a meeting and reconciliation between the lovers.

Psyche gratefully accepted and followed Ceres's advice, and labored early and late to satisfy her exacting mistress, who appointed such difficult tasks, that the poor girl would never have been able to accomplish them had she not been aided by all the beasts and insects, who loved her dearly.

PSYCHE'S JOURNEY TO HADES

Venus repeatedly tested her fidelity and endurance, and finally resolved, as a crucial experiment, to send her to Hades to fetch a box of beauty ointment, for which Proserpina alone had the recipe. Directed by Zephyrus, her old friend, Psyche encountered the terrors of Hades in safety, delivered her message, and in return received a small box. The gates of Hades were closed behind her, and she had nearly finished her last task, when she suddenly fancied that it would be wise to appropriate a little of the magic preparation to efface the traces of sleepless nights and many tears.

The box, however, contained naught but the spirit of Sleep, who, pouncing upon Psyche, laid her low by the roadside. Cupid, passing by, saw her there, marked the ravages of grief, remembered his love and her suffering, and, wrestling with the spirit, forced him to reënter the narrow bounds of his prison, and woke Psyche with a loving kiss.

> "Dear, unclose thine eyes.
> Thou mayst look on me now. I go no more,
> But am thine own forever."
>
> LEWIS MORRIS

Then, hand in hand, they winged their flight to Olympus, entered the council hall; and there Cupid presented Psyche, his chosen bride, to the assembled deities, who all promised to be present at the nuptial ceremony. Venus even, forgetting all her former envy, welcomed the blushing bride, who was happy ever after.

FOLLOWING PAGES: CHARON AND PSYCHE. John Rodham Spencer Stanhope.

The ancients, for whom Cupid was an emblem of the heart, considered Psyche the personification of the soul, and represented her with butterfly wings; that little insect being another symbol of the soul, which cannot die.

BERENICE'S HAIR

One of the latest myths concerning Venus is that of Berenice, who, fearing for her beloved husband's life, implored the goddess to protect him in battle, vowing to sacrifice her luxuriant hair if he returned home in safety. The prayer was granted, and Berenice's beautiful locks laid upon Venus's shrine, whence they, however, very mysteriously disappeared. An astrologer, consulted concerning the supposed theft, solemnly pointed to a comet rapidly coming into view, and declared that the gods had placed Berenice's hair among the stars, there to shine forever in memory of her wifely sacrifice.

WORSHIP OF VENUS

Venus, goddess of beauty, is represented either entirely naked, or with some scanty drapery called a "cestus." Seated in her chariot, formed of a single pearl shell, and drawn by snow-white doves, her favorite birds, she journeyed from shrine to shrine, complacently admiring the lavish decorations of jewels and flowers her worshipers provided. The offerings of young lovers were ever those which found most favor in her sight.

> Venus loves the whispers
>   Of plighted youth and maid,
> In April's ivory moonlight
>   Beneath the chestnut shade.
> MACAULAY

Numerous ancient and some modern statues of this goddess grace the various art galleries, but among them all the most perfect is the world-renowned Venus de Milo.

Venus's festivals were always scenes of graceful amusements; and her votaries wore wreaths of fresh, fragrant flowers, the emblem of all natural beauty.

MERCURY

BIRTH OF MERCURY

As already repeatedly stated in the course of this work, Jupiter was never a strictly faithful spouse, and, in spite of his wife's remonstrances, could not refrain from indulging his caprice for every pretty face he met along his way. It is thus, therefore, that he yielded to the charms of Maia, goddess of the plains, and spent some blissful hours in her society. This divine couple's happiness culminated when they first beheld their little son, Mercury (Hermes, Psychopompus, Oneicopompus), who was born in a grotto on Mount Cyllene, in Arcadia—

> Mercury, whom Maia bore,
> Sweet Maia, on Cyllene's hoary top.
> VIRGIL (Cowper's tr.)

This infant god was quite unlike mortal children, as will readily be perceived by the numerous pranks he played immediately after his birth. First he sprang from his mother's knee, grasped a tortoise shell lying on the ground, bored holes in its sides, stretched strings across its concavity, and, sweeping his hands over them, produced strains of sweetest music, thus inventing the first lyre.

> So there it lay, through wet and dry,
> As empty as the last new sonnet,
> Till by and by came Mercury,
> And, having mused upon it,
> "Why here," cried he, "the thing of things
> In shape, material, and dimension!
> Give it but strings, and, lo, it sings,
> A wonderful invention."
> LOWELL

Mercury's Theft

Being very hungry toward evening, young Mercury escaped from his sleeping mother, and sallied out in search of food. He had not gone very far, before he came to a wide meadow, where Apollo's herds were at pasture. The oxen were fat and sleek; and the mischievous little god, after satisfying himself that they were young, and therefore promised to be tender and juicy, drove fifty of them off to a secluded spot, taking good care to envelop their feet in leafy branches, so they would leave no traces. Then, his hiding place being reached in safety, Mercury coolly killed two of the oxen, which he proceeded to eat.

Apollo soon missed his cattle, and began to search for some clew to their hiding place or to the thief. He could, however, discover nothing but some broken twigs and scattered leaves. Suddenly he remembered that the babe whose birth had been announced early that morning in high Olympus had been appointed god of thieves. He therefore lost no more time in useless search and conjecture, but strode off to Mount Cyllene, where he found Mercury peacefully sleeping in his cradle. With a rude shake, the sun god roused him from his slumbers, and bade him restore the stolen cattle. Mercury pretended innocence, until Apollo, exasperated, dragged him off to Olympus, where he was convicted of the theft, and condemned to restore the stolen property. Mercury yielded to the decree, produced the remaining oxen, and, in exchange for the two missing, gave Apollo the lyre he had just fashioned.

This, like most other myths, admits of a natural explanation. Apollo (the Sun) was supposed by the ancients to possess great herds of cattle and sheep, the clouds; and Mercury, the personification of the wind, born in the night, after a few hours' existence waxes sufficiently strong to drive away the clouds and conceal them, leaving no trace of his passage except a few broken branches and scattered leaves.

Mercury's Wand, Cap, and Shoes

The gift of the lyre pleased Apollo so well, that he in return wished to make a present to Mercury, and gave him a magic wand, called Caduceus, which had the power of reconciling all conflicting elements. Mercury, anxious to test it, thrust it between two quarreling snakes, who immediately wound themselves in amity around it. This so pleased him, that he bade them remain there forever, and used the wand on all occasions.

Opposite Page: MERCURY (DETAIL FROM CEILING FRESCO).
Giovani Battista Tiepolo.

> A snake-encircl'd wand;
> By classic authors term'd Caduceus
> And highly fam'd for several uses.
>
> GOLDSMITH

Mercury was in due time appointed messenger of the gods, who, to make him fleet of foot, presented him with winged sandals, the Talaria, which endowed him with marvelous rapidity of motion. As these sandals did not seem quite sufficient, however, the gods added the winged cap, Petasus, to the winged shoes.

> Foot-feather'd Mercury appear'd sublime
> Beyond the tall tree tops; and in less time
> Than shoots the slanted hail-storm, down he dropt
> Towards the ground; but rested not, nor stopt
> One moment from his home; only the sward
> He with his wand light touch'd, and heavenward
> Swifter than sight was gone.
>
> KEATS

Mercury was not only the messenger of the gods, but was also appointed god of eloquence, commerce, rain, wind, and the special patron of travelers, shepherds, cheats, and thieves.

STORY OF IO

Jupiter often intrusted to Mercury messages of a delicate nature, and always found him an invaluable ally; but the faithful messenger was never so much needed or so deeply appreciated as during Jupiter's courtship of Io, the peerless daughter of the river god Inachus.

To avoid Juno's recriminations, Jupiter had carried on this affair with even more than his usual secrecy, visiting his beloved only when quite certain that his wife was asleep, and taking the further precaution of spreading a cloud over the spot where he generally met her, to shield her from all chance of being seen from Olympus.

One fine afternoon, all conditions being favorable, Jupiter hastened down to earth to see Io, and began to stroll with her up and down the river edge. They heeded not the noonday heat, for the cloud over their heads screened them from the sun's too ardent rays.

From some cause Juno's slumbers were less protracted than usual, and she soon arose from her couch to look about her realm, the atmosphere, and convince herself that all was well. Her attention was soon attracted by an opaque, immovable cloud near the earth,—a cloud which had no business there, for had she not bidden them all lie still on the blue until she awoke? Her suspicions being aroused by the presence of this cloud, she sought her husband in Olympus, and, not finding him, flew down to earth, brushing the cloud aside in her haste.

Jupiter, thus warned of her coming, had but time to change the maiden beside him into a heifer, ere his wife alighted and inquired what he was doing there. Carelessly the god pointed to the heifer, and declared he had been whiling away the time by creating it; but the explanation failed to satisfy Juno, who, seeing no other living creature near, suspected that her spouse had been engaged in a clandestine flirtation, and had screened its fair object from her wrath only by a sudden transformation.

Dissimulating these suspicions with care, Juno begged her husband to give her his new creation, which request he could not refuse, but granted most reluctantly, thus adding further confirmation to her jealous fears. The Queen of Heaven then departed, taking Io with her, and placed her under the surveillance of Argus, one of her servants, who possessed myriad eyes, but one half of which he closed at a time.

> The eyes of Argus, sentinel of Heaven:
> Those thousand eyes that watch alternate kept,
> Nor all o'er all his body waked or slept.
> STATIUS (Elton's tr.)

ARGUS'S WATCH

She bade him watch the heifer closely, and report anything unusual in its actions. One day, therefore, as he was watching his charge pasture by the river, Argus heard her relate to her father, Inachus, the story of her transformation, and immediately imparted his discovery to Juno, who, advising still closer watchfulness, sent him back to his post.

Jupiter, in the mean while, was in despair; for days had passed without his being able to exchange a word with Io, or deliver her from her imprisonment. Finally he called Mercury to his aid, and bade him devise some plan to rescue her. Armed with a handful of poppies, Mercury approached Argus, and offered to while away the time by telling him tales.

As Mercury was the prince of story-tellers, this offer was not to be despised, and Argus joyfully accepted; but instead of exerting himself to be entertaining, Mercury droned out such lengthy, uninteresting stories, that Argus soon closed half his eyes in profound sleep. Still talking in the same monotonous way, Mercury softly shook the poppies over the giant's head, until one by one the remaining eyelids closed, and Argus was wrapped in complete slumber.

Then Mercury seized the giant's sword, and with one well-directed blow severed his head from the huge trunk. Only one half of the task was successfully accomplished; and while Mercury was driving the heifer away, Juno discovered his attempt, and promptly sent an enormous gadfly to torment the poor beast, who, goaded to madness by its cruel stings, fled wildly from one country to another, forded streams, and finally plunged into the sea, since called Ionian. After swimming across it, she took refuge in Egypt, where Jupiter restored her to all her girlish loveliness, and where her son Epaphus was born, to be the first king and the founder of Memphis.

> In coming time that hollow of the sea
> Shall bear the name Ionian, and present
> A monument of Io's passage through,
> Unto all mortals.
>
> E. B. BROWNING

Juno mourned the loss of her faithful Argus most bitterly, and, gathering up his myriad eyes, scattered them over the tail of her favorite bird, the peacock, to have some memento of her faithful servant ever near her.

> From Argus slain a painted peacock grew,
> Fluttering his feathers stain'd with various hue.
>
> MOSCHUS

OPPOSITE PAGE: MERCURY ABOUT TO BEHEAD ARGUS.
Ubaldo Gandolfi.

This story also is an allegory. Io personifies the moon, restlessly wandering from place to place; Argus, the heavens, whose starry eyes keep ceaseless watch over the moon's every movement; Mercury is the rain, whose advent blots out the stars one by one, thus killing Argus, who else was never known to close all his eyes at once.

MERCURY'S OFFICES AND WORSHIP

To Mercury was intrusted the charge of conducting the souls of the departed to Hades, and when occupied in this way he bore the name of Psychopompus, while, when addressed as conductor of Dreams, he was Oneicopompus.

> Gently as a kiss came Death to sever
> From spirit flesh, and to the realm of gloom
> The pallid shades with fearless brow descended
> To Hades, by the winged god attended.
>
> BOYESEN

He was one of the twelve principal gods of Olympus, and was widely worshiped. Temples, altars, and shrines were dedicated to his service throughout the ancient countries. His statues were considered sacred boundary marks, and their removal punished by death. Solemn annual festivals were held in Rome in Mercury's honor in the month of May, and from him received their name of Mercuralia.

MARS

Mars's Character

Mars (Ares), son of Jupiter and Juno, was the god of war, the personification of the angry clouded sky, and, although but little worshiped in Greece, was one of the principal Roman divinities. He is said to have first seen the light in Thrace, a country noted for its fierce storms and war-loving people.

> Infant Mars, where Thracia's mountains rose,
> Press'd with his hardy limbs th' incrusted snows.
> Statius (Elton's tr.)

Never sated with strife and bloodshed, this god preferred the din of battle to all other music, and found no occupation so congenial as the toils and dangers of war. No gentle deeds of kindness were ever expected from him; no loving prayers were ever addressed to him; and the ancients felt no love for him, but, on the contrary, shuddered with terror when his name was mentioned.

Mars was generally represented in a brilliant suit of armor, a plumed helmet on his proud young head, a poised spear in one muscular hand, and a finely wrought shield in the other, showing him ever ready to cope with a foe.

Mars's Attendants

His attendants, or some say his children, sympathized heartily with his quarrelsome tastes, and delighted in following his lead. They were Eris (Discord), Phobos (Alarm), Metus (Fear), Demios (Dread), and Pallor (Terror).

Bellona, or Enyo, goddess of war, also accompanied him, drove his chariot, parried dangerous thrusts, and watched over his general safety. Mars and Bellona were therefore worshiped together in the selfsame temple, and their altars were the only ones ever polluted by human sacrifices.

And to the fire-ey'd maid of smoky war,
All hot and bleeding, will we offer them:
The mailed Mars shall on his altar sit,
Up to the ears in blood.

SHAKESPEARE

STORY OF OTUS AND EPHIALTES

As strife was his favorite element, Mars was very active indeed during the war between the gods and giants, but in his martial ardor he frequently forgot all caution. On one occasion he was obliged to surrender to Otus and Ephialtes,—two giants, who, though but nine years of age, were already of immense stature, since they increased in height at the rate of nine inches each month.

Proud of their victory over the God of War, these giants bore him off in triumph, and bound him fast with iron chains slipped through iron rings. Day and night they kept watch over him; and even when they slept, the rattle of the chains, whenever any one of the gods attempted to set him free, woke them up, and frustrated all efforts to deliver him. During fifteen weary months poor Mars lingered there in durance vile, until Mercury, the prince of thieves, noiselessly and deftly slipped the chains out of the rings, and restored him to freedom.

In revenge for the cruel treatment inflicted by Otus and Ephialtes, Mars prevailed upon Apollo and Diana to use their poisoned arrows, and thus rid the world of these two ugly and useless giants.

THE AREOPAGUS

Of a fiery disposition, Mars was never inclined to forgive an injury; and when Halirrhothius, Neptune's son, dared to carry off his daughter Alcippe, Mars hotly pursued the abductor, and promptly slew him. Neptune, angry at this act of summary justice, cited the God of War to appear before a tribunal held in the open air, on a hill near the newly founded city of Athens.

It was then customary for such cases to be tried at night, in utter darkness, so that the judges might not be influenced by the personal appearance of either plaintiff or defendant; and no rhetoric of any kind was allowed, that their minds might remain quite unbiased. Mars appeared before the judges, simply stated his case, and was acquitted. Since then the hill upon which his trial took place has been called the

Areopagus (Ares's Hill) or Mars' Hill, and the judges of the principal court of justice at Athens received the name of Areopagitæ.

Mars's Children

Although such a partisan of strife, Mars was not impervious to softer emotions, and passionately returned the devotion of Venus, who bore him three beautiful children,—Harmonia, Cupid, and Anteros. Mars also fell in love with a beautiful young Vestal named Ilia, a descendant of Æneas, who, in spite of the solemn pledge not to listen to a lover's pleadings until her time of service at the goddess Vesta's altar was accomplished, yielded to Mars's impetuous wooing, and consented to a clandestine union.

Romulus and Remus

Although secretly married, Ilia continued to dwell in the temple until the birth of her twin sons Romulus and Remus. Her parents, hearing she had broken her vows, commanded that she should suffer the prescribed punishment of being buried alive, and that the children should be exposed to the teeth and claws of the wild beasts of the forest. The double sentence was ruthlessly carried out, and the young mother perished; but, contrary to all previsions, the babes survived, and, after having been suckled for a time by a she-wolf, were found and adopted by a shepherd.

Romulus and Remus throve under this man's kind care, and grew up strong and fearless. When they reached manhood, they longed for a wider sphere for their youthful activity, and, leaving the mountain where they had grown up, journeyed out into the world to seek their fortunes. After some time they came to a beautiful hilly country, where they decided to found a great city, the capital of their future realm. Accordingly the brothers began to trace the outline of their city limits, and, in doing so, quarreled over the name of the prospective town.

Blinded by anger, Romulus suddenly raised the tool he held, and struck Remus such a savage blow that he fell to the ground, slain by his brother in a fit of passion. Alone now, Romulus at first vainly tried to pursue his undertaking, but, being soon joined by a number of adventurers as wicked and unscrupulous as he, they combined their forces, and built the celebrated city of Rome.

MARS AND VENUS. Peter Paul Rubens.

Then, with his nurse's wolf-skin girt,
Shall Romulus the line assert,
Invite them to his new raised home,
And call the martial city Rome.
VIRGIL (Conington's tr.)

As founder of this city, Romulus was its first king, and ruled the people with such an iron hand that his tyranny eventually became unbearable. The senators, weary of his exactions and arbitrary measures, finally resolved to free themselves of his presence. Taking advantage of an eclipse, which plunged the city in sudden darkness at noonday, and which occurred while all were assembled on the Forum, the magistrates slew Romulus, cut his body into pieces, and hid them under their wide togas.

QUIRINUS

When the light returned, and the terrified and awestruck people, somewhat reassured, looked about them for their king, they were told he had gone, never to return, carried off by the immortal gods, who wished him to share their abode and dignity. The senators further informed the credulous population that Romulus was to be henceforth worshiped as a god under the name of Quirinus, and gave orders for the erection of a temple on one of the seven hills, which since then has been known as Mount Quirinal. Yearly festivals in Romulus's honor were ever after held in Rome, under the name of Quirinalia.

Well pleased with the new city of Rome and its turbulent, lawless citizens, Mars took it under his special protection; and once, when a plague was raging which threatened to destroy all the people, the Romans rushed in a body to his temple, and clamored for a sign of his favor and protection.

THE ANCILE

Even while they prayed, it is said, a shield, Ancile, fell from heaven, and a voice was distinctly heard to declare that Rome would endure as long as this token of the god's good will was preserved. The very same day the plague ceased its frightful ravages, and the Romans, delighted with the result of their petitions, placed the heavenly shield in one of their principal temples.

Then, in constant dread lest some of their enemies should succeed in stealing it, they caused eleven other shields to be made, so exactly like the heaven-sent Ancile, that none but the guardian priests, the Salii, who kept continual watch over them, could detect the original from the facsimiles. During the month of March, which, owing to its blustery weather, was dedicated to Mars and bore his name, the ancilæ were carried in a procession all through the city, the Salii chanting their rude war songs, and executing intricate war dances.

A Roman general, ere setting out on any warlike expedition, always entered the sanctuary of Mars, touched the sacred shield with the point of his lance, shook the spear in the hand of the god's effigy, and called aloud, "Mars, watch over us!"

Worship of Mars

A common superstition among the Roman soldiery was, that Mars, under the name of Gradivus, marched in person at the head of their army, and led them on to victory. Mars's principal votaries were therefore the Roman soldiers and youths, whose exercising ground was called, in his honor, the Campus Martius, or Field of Mars. All the laurel crowns bestowed upon victorious generals were deposited at the foot of his statues, and a bull was the customary thank offering after a successful campaign.

> The soldier, from successful camps returning
> With laurel wreath'd, and rich with hostile spoil,
> Severs the bull to Mars.
>
> Prior

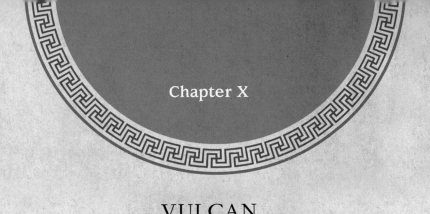

VULCAN

VULCAN'S FALL

Vulcan, or Hephæstus, son of Jupiter and Juno, god of fire and the forge, seldom joined the general council of the gods. His aversion to Olympus was of old standing. He had once been tenderly attached to his mother, had lavished upon her every proof of his affection, and had even tried to console her when she mourned Jupiter's neglect. On one occasion, intending to punish Juno for one of her usual fits of jealousy, Jupiter hung her out of heaven, fast bound by a golden chain; and Vulcan, perceiving her in this plight, tugged at the chain with all his might, drew her up, and was about to set her free, when Jupiter returned, and, in anger at his son's interference in his matrimonial concerns, kicked him out of heaven.

The intervening space between heaven and earth was so great, that Vulcan's fall lasted during one whole day and night, ere he finally touched the summit of Mount Mosychlus, in the Island of Lemnos.

> From morn
> To noon he fell, from noon to dewy eve,
> A summer's day; and with the setting sun
> Dropt from the zenith like a falling star,
> On Lemnos th' Ægean isle.
>
> MILTON

Of course, to any one but a god such a terrible fall would have proved fatal; and even Vulcan did not escape entirely unharmed, for he injured one of his legs, which accident left him lame and somewhat deformed for the remainder of his life.

VULCAN'S FORGE

Now, although Vulcan had risked so much and suffered so greatly in taking his mother's part, she never even made the slightest attempt to ascertain whether he had reached the earth in safety. Hurt by her indifference and ingratitude, Vulcan vowed never again to return to Olympus, and withdrew to the solitudes of Mount Ætna, where he established a great forge in the heart of the mountain, in partnership with the Cyclopes, who helped him manufacture many cunning and useful objects from the metals found in great profusion in the bosom of the earth.

Among these ingenious contrivances were two golden handmaidens gifted with motion, who attended the god wherever he went, and supported his halting footsteps.

> Two golden statues, like in form and look
> To living maidens, aided with firm gait
> The monarch's steps.
>
> HOMER (Bryant's tr.)

THE GOLDEN THRONE

Vulcan also devised a golden throne with countless hidden springs, which, when unoccupied, did not present an extraordinary appearance; but as soon as any one ventured to make use of it, the springs moved, and, the chair closing around the person seated upon it, frustrated all attempts to rise and escape from its treacherous embrace.

Vulcan dispatched this throne, when completed, to his mother, who, delighted with its beauty and delicate workmanship, proudly seated herself upon it, and found herself a prisoner. In vain she strove to escape, in vain the gods all gallantly rushed to her assistance. Their united strength and skill proved useless against the cunning springs.

Finally Mercury was sent to Vulcan, primed with a most diplomatic request to honor high Olympus with his presence; but all Mercury's eloquence and persuasions failed to induce the god of the forge to leave his sooty abode, and the messenger god was forced to return alone and report the failure of his attempt. Then the gods deliberated anew, and decided to send Bacchus, god of wine, hoping his powers of persuasion would prove more effective.

Armed with a flask of his choicest vintage, Bacchus presented himself before Vulcan, and offered him a refreshing draught. Vulcan, predisposed to thirst, and incited to drink by the very nature of his labor, accepted the offered cup, and allowed himself to be beguiled into renewing his potations, until he was quite intoxicated.

APOLLO IN THE FORGE OF VULCAN.
Diego Velázquez.

In this condition, Bacchus led him passive to Olympus, made him release the Queen of Heaven, and urged him to embrace his father and crave forgiveness.

Although restored to favor, Vulcan would not remain permanently in Olympus, but preferred to return to his forge and continue his labors. He undertook, however, the construction of magnificent golden palaces for each of the gods upon the Olympian heights, fashioned their sumptuous furniture from precious metals, and further embellished his work by a rich ornamentation of precious stones.

> Then to their starry domes the gods depart,
> The shining monuments of Vulcan's art:
> Jove on his couch reclin'd his awful head,
> And Juno slumber'd on the golden bed.
>
> HOMER (Pope's tr.)

Aided by the Cyclopes, Vulcan manufactured Jupiter's weapons, the dread thunderbolts, whose frightful power none could withstand, and Cupid's love-inspiring darts.

VULCAN'S LOVES

Vulcan, in spite of his deformity, extreme ugliness, and well-known aversion to any home but his sooty forge, was none the less prone to fall in love with the various goddesses. He first wooed Minerva, who, having sworn never to marry, contemptuously dismissed his suit. To console Vulcan for this rebuff, and at the same time punish the Goddess of Beauty, who, according to some mythologists, had refused even his addresses, Jupiter bestowed upon him the fair hand of Venus, and sent her and her mischievous train of Loves and Graces to reside in the dark caves of Mount Ætna.

Amused by all the strange sights and sounds, the goddess at first seemed quite contented; but after a time Vulcan's gloomy abode lost all its attractions: so she forsook her ill-favored husband, and went in search of another, more congenial mate.

Some time after, Vulcan married one of the Graces, who, however, seems to have also soon wearied of his society, for she deserted him.

Vulcan's children were mostly monsters, such as Cacus, Periphetes, Cercyon, etc., all of whom play an important part in heroic mythology. He is also the reputed father of Servius Tullius, sixth king of Rome, by a slave Ocrisia, whom he was wont to visit in the guise of a bright flame, which played harmlessly about her.

Vulcan was worshiped by all blacksmiths and artisans, who recognized him as their special patron, and venerated him accordingly.

> Those who labor
> The sweaty forge, who edge the crooked scythe,
> Bend stubborn steel, and harden gleaming armor,
> Acknowledge Vulcan's aid.
>
> PRIOR

Great festivals, the Vulcanalia and the Hephæstia, were celebrated in honor of this god, who is generally represented as a short, muscular man, with one leg shorter than the other, a workman's cap on his curly locks, a short upper garment, and a smith's tools in his hand.

NEPTUNE

When Jupiter assigned to each of his brothers a separate portion of the universe, he decreed that Neptune, or Poseidon, should govern all the waters upon the face of the earth, and be sole monarch of the ocean.

> Neptune, the mighty marine god, I sing;
> Earth's mover, and the fruitless ocean's king.
> That Helicon and th' Ægean deeps dost hold.
> O thou earth-shaker; thy command, twofold
> The gods have sorted; making thee of horses
> The awful tamer, and of naval forces
> The sure preserver. Hail, O Saturn's birth!
> Whose graceful green hair circles all the earth.
> Bear a benign mind; and thy helpful hand
> Lend all, submitted to thy dread command.
>
> HOMER (Chapman's tr.)

Before this new ruler made his appearance, the Titan Oceanus had wielded the scepter of the sea; and regretfully he now resigned it to his youthful supplanter, whom he nevertheless admired sincerely, and described in glowing colors to his brothers.

Have ye beheld the young God of the Seas,
My dispossessor? Have ye seen his face?
Have ye beheld his chariot, foam'd along
By noble winged creatures he hath made?
I saw him on the calmed waters scud,
With such a glow of beauty in his eyes,
That it enforc'd me to bid sad farewell
To all my empire.

KEATS

NEPTUNE'S EXILE

Neptune, the personification as well as the god of the sea, was of an exceedingly encroaching disposition. Dissatisfied with the portion allotted him, he once conspired to dethrone Jupiter; but, unfortunately for the success of his undertaking, his plot was discovered before he could put it into execution, and Jupiter, in punishment for his temerity, exiled him to earth. There he was condemned to build the walls of Troy for Laomedon, king of that city, who, in return, promised a handsome compensation.

Apollo, also banished from heaven at that time, volunteered to aid Neptune by playing on his lyre, and moving the stones by the power of sweet sounds. The task satisfactorily ended, Laomedon, an avaricious and dishonest king, refused the promised guerdon, whereupon Neptune created a terrible monster, which came upon the shore, devoured the inhabitants, devastated everything within his reach, and inspired all with great terror.

A great serpent from the deep,
Lifting his horrible head above their homes,
Devoured the children.

LEWIS MORRIS

To save themselves from the awful death which threatened them all, the Trojans consulted an oracle, who advised the sacrifice of a beautiful virgin, and promised the monster would disappear as soon as he had devoured the appointed victim.

THE VOYAGE OF THE CARDINAL INFANTE FERDINAND OF SPAIN
FROM BARCELONA TO GENOA IN APRIL 1663, WITH NEPTUNE
CALMING THE TEMPEST.
Peter Paul Rubens.

STORY OF HESIONE

A young girl was therefore chosen by lot, led down to the seashore, and chained by
the priest's own hands to a slimy rock. As soon as her mourning friends had forsaken
her, the hideous serpent came out of his lair in the waves, and devoured her; then he
vanished, and nothing more was heard of him for a whole year, at the end of which
time he reappeared, and resumed his former depredations, which were only checked
by the sacrifice of a second virgin.

Year after year, however, he returned, and year after year a fair girl was doomed to perish, until finally the lot fell upon Hesione, the king's only daughter. He could not bear the thought of the terrible fate awaiting her, and tried every means in his power to save her. As a last resort he sent heralds to publish far and wide that the king would give a great reward to any man who would dare attack and succeed in slaying the monster.

Hercules, on his return from the scene of one of his stupendous labors, heard the proclamation, and, with no other weapon than the oaken club he generally carried, slew the monster just as he was about to drag poor Hesione down into his slimy cave. Laomedon was, of course, overjoyed at the monster's death, but, true to his nature, again refused the promised reward, and by his dishonesty incurred the hatred and contempt of this hero also. Some time after, having finished his time of servitude with Eurystheus, Hercules, aided by a chosen band of adventurers, came to Troy to punish him for his perfidy. The city was stormed and taken, the king slain, and his wife and children carried to Greece as captives. There Hesione became the bride of Telamon; while her brother Podarces, later known as Priam, was redeemed by his people and made King of Troy.

Laomedon's failure to pay his just debts was the primary cause of the enmity which Apollo and Neptune displayed towards the Trojans during their famous war with the Greeks.

NEPTUNE'S CONTESTS

Their term of exile ended, the gods were reinstated in their exalted positions, and hastened to resume their former occupations; but, in spite of the severe lesson just received, Neptune was not yet cured of his grasping tendencies. Not long after his return from Troy, he quarreled with Minerva for the possession of the then recently founded city of Athens, then nameless, and entered into the memorable contest in which he was signally defeated. He also disputed the sovereignty of Trœœzene with Minerva, and that of Corinth with Apollo. In the latter instance, the disputants having chosen Briareus as umpire, the prize was awarded to him as the most powerful of all the gods except Jupiter.

NEPTUNE'S POWER

As god of the sea, Neptune did not generally remain in Olympus, but dwelt way down in the coral caves of his kingdom, over which he ruled with resistless sway. By one word he could stir up or calm the wildest storm, and cause the billows to roar with fury or subside into peaceful ripples.

> He spake, and round about him called the clouds
> And roused the ocean,—wielding in his hand
> The trident,—summoned all the hurricanes
> Of all the winds, and covered earth and sky
> At once with mists, while from above the night
> Fell suddenly.
>
>   HOMER (Bryant's tr.)

The rivers, fountains, lakes, and seas were not only subject to his rule, but he could also cause terrible earthquakes at will, and, when he pleased, raise islands from the deep, as he did when Latona entreated him to shelter her from Juno's persecutions.

Neptune is said to have loved the goddess Ceres, and to have followed her during her prolonged search for her daughter, Proserpina. Annoyed by his persistent wooing, the goddess, to escape him, assumed the form of a mare; but the God of the Sea, not at all deceived by this stratagem, straightway assumed the form of a horse, in which guise he contentedly trotted after her and renewed his attentions.

NEPTUNE'S WIVES

The offspring of this equine pair was Arion, a wonderful winged steed, gifted with the power of speech, whose early education was intrusted to the Nereides. They trained him to draw his father's chariot over the waves with incredible rapidity, and parted with him regretfully when he was given to Copreus, Pelops's son. This marvelous horse passed successively into Hercules's and Adrastus's hands; and the latter won all the chariot races, thanks to his fleetness.

On another occasion, Neptune, having fallen deeply in love with a maiden named Theophane, and fearful lest some one of her numerous suitors should find favor in her eyes before he had time to urge his wooing, suddenly changed her into a sheep, and conveyed her to the Island of Crumissa, where he assumed the guise of a ram, and, in this metamorphosed condition, carried on his courtship, which eventually proved successful. The offspring of this union was the golden-fleeced ram which bore Phryxus in safety to the Colchian shores, and whose pelt was the goal of the Argonautic expedition.

Neptune also loved and married Medusa in the days of her youth and beauty, and when some drops of blood fell from her severed head into the salt sea foam, he produced from them the graceful winged steed Pegasus.

Neptune is also said to be the father of the giants Otus and Ephialtes, of Neleus, Pelias, and Polyphemus.

AMPHITRITE

The Queen of the Ocean, Neptune's own true and lawful wife, was a Nereid, one of the fifty daughters of Doris and Nereus—the personification of the calm and sunlit aspect of the sea. Her name was Amphitrite, or Salacia. At first she was in great awe of her distinguished suitor, and in her fear fled at his approach, leaving him no chance to admire any of her charms, except the grace and celerity with which she managed to flit, or rather glide, out of his sight.

> Along the deep
> With beauteous ankles, Amphitrite glides.
> HESIOD (Elton's tr.)

This conduct grieved Neptune so sorely, that he sent a dolphin to plead his cause, and persuade the fair nymph to share his throne. The messenger, carefully instructed beforehand, carried out the directions with such skill, that Amphitrite formally consented to become Neptune's wife.

The King of the Deep was so overjoyed at these good tidings, that he transferred the dolphin to the sky, where he forms a well-known constellation. Neptune and Amphitrite in due time became the happy parents of several children, among whom the most celebrated is Triton, whose body was half man and half fish, and who gave his name to all his male descendants.

STORY OF IDAS AND MARPESSA

Like all other gods, Neptune took a lively interest in men's affairs, and sometimes interfered in their behalf. On one occasion, for instance, he even lent his beautiful chariot to a youth by the name of Idas, who, loving a maiden dearly, and unable to win her father's consent to their union, had resolved to kidnap her. Marpessa, for such was the lady's name, allowed herself to be carried off without protest; and the lovers were blissfully speeding along in Neptune's chariot, when her father, Evenus, perceiving their escape, started in pursuit of them. In spite of the most strenuous efforts, he could not overtake the fleeing pair, and in his anger plunged into a river, where he was drowned, and which from him received the name of Evenus.

Idas and Marpessa were just congratulating themselves upon their narrow escape, when suddenly Apollo appeared before them, and, checking their steeds, declared he loved the maiden too, and would not tamely yield her up to a rival.

This was quite equivalent to a challenge; and Idas, stepping down from the chariot, was about to engage in the fight, when suddenly out of a clear sky a thunderbolt came crashing down to earth, and an imperious voice was heard to declare that the quarrel could be settled by Marpessa only, and that she should freely choose the suitor she preferred as husband.

The maiden glanced at both her lovers, and quickly reviewed their respective attractions. Remembering that Apollo, being immortal, would retain all his youthful bloom when her more ephemeral beauty had vanished, and that he would then probably cease to love her, she held out her hand to Idas, declaring she preferred to link her fate to that of a mortal, who would grow old when she did, and love her as long as they both lived. This choice was approved by Jupiter; and the lovers, after reaching a place of safety, returned the wondrous chariot to Neptune, with many grateful thanks for his timely aid.

Neptune's Attendants

All the Nereides, Tritons, and lesser sea divinities formed a part of Neptune and Amphitrite's train, and followed closely when they rode forth to survey their kingdom.

Neptune had, besides this, many subordinates, whose duty it was to look after various seas, lakes, rivers, fountains, etc., confided to their special care. In harmony with their occupations, these divinities were either hoary river gods (such as Father Nile), slender youths, beautiful maidens, or little babbling children. They seldom left the cool waves of their appointed dwellings, and strove to win Neptune's approbation mostly by the zeal they showed in the discharge of their various duties.

Proteus, too, another inferior deity, had the care of the flocks of the deep, and he always attended Neptune when it was safe to leave his great herds of sea calves to bask on the sunny shores.

> In ages past old Proteus, with his droves
> Of sea calves, sought the mountains and the groves.
>
> COWPER

PROTEUS

In common with all the other gods, Proteus enjoyed the gift of prophecy, and had the power to assume any shape he pleased. The former gift he was wont to exercise very reluctantly; and when mortals wished to consult him, he would change his form with bewildering rapidity, and, unless they clung to him through all his changes, they could obtain no answer to their questions.

> Shouting [we] seize the god: our force t' evade,
> His various arts he soon r esumes in aid:
> A lion now, he curls a surgy mane;
> Sudden, our hands a spotted pard restrain;
> Then, arm'd with tusks, and lightning in his eyes,
> A boar's obscener shape the god belies:
> On spiry volumes, there, a dragon rides;
> Here, from our strict embrace a stream he glides;
> And last, sublime, his stately growth he rears,
> A tree, and well-dissembled foliage wears.
>
> HOMER (Pope's tr.)

But if these manifestations proved unavailing to drive his would-be hearers away, the god answered every question circumstantially.

Amphitrite, Neptune's wife,—generally represented as a beautiful nude nymph, crowned with seaweed, and reclining in a pearl-shell chariot drawn by dolphins, or sea-horses,—was worshiped with her husband.

WORSHIP OF NEPTUNE

Neptune, majestic and middle-aged, with long, flowing hair and beard, wearing a seaweed crown, and brandishing a trident, or three-pronged fork, was widely worshiped throughout Greece and Italy, and had countless shrines. His principal votaries were the seamen and horse trainers, who often bespoke his aid.

OPPOSITE PAGE: THE TRIUMPH OF AMPHITRITE. Hugues Taraval.

Hail, Neptune, greatest of the gods!
Thou ruler of the salt sea floods;
Thou with the deep and dark-green hair,
That dost the golden trident bear;
Thou that, with either arm outspread,
Embosomest the earth we tread:
Thine are the beasts with fin and scales,
That round thy chariot, as it sails,
Plunging and tumbling, fast and free,
All reckless follow o'er the sea.

ARION

Many large temples were dedicated exclusively to the worship of Neptune, and games were frequently celebrated in his honor. The most noted of all were undoubtedly the Isthmian Games,—a national festival, held every four years at Corinth, on the isthmus of the same name. Hither people came from all points of the compass, and all parts of the then known world, either to witness or to take part in the noted wrestling, boxing, and racing matches, or in the musical and poetical contests.

PLUTO

Pluto (Dis, Hades, Orcus, Aïdoneus), son of Cronus and Rhea, received as his share of the world the supervision of the Infernal Regions, situated beneath the earth, and was also appointed god of the dead and of riches, for all precious metals are buried deep in the bosom of the earth.

> Blinded Plutus, didst thou dwell
> Nor in land nor fathomed sea,
> But only in the depths of hell,—
> God of riches! Safe from thee
> Man himself might happy be.
>
> TIMOCREON OF RHODES

This god inspired all men with a great fear. They never spoke of him without trembling, and fervently prayed that they might never see his face; for, when he appeared on the surface of the earth, it was only in search of some victim to drag down into his dismal abode, or to make sure there was no crevice through which a sunbeam might glide to brighten its gloom and dispel its shadows. Whenever the stern god set out on one of these expeditions, he rode in a chariot drawn by four coal-black steeds; and, if any obstacle presented itself to impede his progress, he struck it with his two-pronged fork, the emblem of his power, and the obstacle was immediately removed. It was on one of these occasions that Pluto kidnapped Proserpina, the fair goddess of vegetation, daughter of Ceres, whom he set on his throne in Hades, and crowned his queen.

Worship of Pluto

Pluto is always represented as a stern, dark, bearded man, with tightly closed lips, a crown on his head, a scepter and a key in hand, to show how carefully he guards those who enter his domains, and how vain are their hopes to effect their escape. No temples were dedicated to him, and statues of this god are very rare. Human sacrifices were sometimes offered on his altars; and at his festivals, held every hundred years, and thence called Secular Games, none but black animals were slain.

Hades

His kingdom, generally called Hades, was very difficult of access. According to Roman traditions, it could only be entered at Avernus, but the Greeks asserted that there was another entrance near the Promontory of Tænarum. Both nations agreed, however, in saying that it was an almost impossible feat to get out again if one were rash enough to venture in.

> To the shades you go a down-hill, easy way;
> But to return and re-enjoy the day,
> This is a work, a labor!
>
> Virgil

To prevent all mortals from entering, and all spirits from escaping, Pluto placed a huge three-headed dog, called Cerberus, to guard the gate.

> There in state old Cerberus sate,
> A three-headed dog, as cruel as Fate,
> Guarding the entrance early and late.
>
> Saxe

From thence a long subterranean passage, through which shadowy spirits glided incessantly, led to the throne room, where Pluto and Proserpina sat in state, clad in their sable robes. From the foot of this throne flowed the rivers which channeled the Lower World. One, the Cocytus, rolled salt waves, composed of naught but the tears flowing continually from the eyes of the criminals condemned to hard labor in Tartarus, the portion of Hades reserved for the exclusive use of the wicked.

Cocytus, named of lamentation loud
Heard on the rueful stream.

HOMER

RIVERS OF HADES

To separate this section from the remainder of his realm, Pluto surrounded it with the Phlegethon, a river of fire; while the Acheron, a black and deep stream, was to be passed by all souls ere they reached Pluto's throne and heard his decree. The current of this river was so swift, that even the boldest swimmer could not pass over; and, as there was no bridge, all the spirits were obliged to rely upon the aid of Charon, an aged boatman, who plied the only available skiff—a leaky, worm-eaten punt—from shore to shore. Neither would he allow any soul to enter his bark, unless he was first given a small coin, called the obolus, the ferryman's fare, which the ancients carefully laid under the tongue of the dead, that they might pass on to Pluto without delay. Charon's leaky boat no sooner touched the shore than a host of eager spirits pressed forward to claim a place. The cruel boatman repulsed them roughly, and brandished his oars, while he leisurely selected those he would next ferry across the stream.

The shiv'ring army stands,
And press for passage with extended hands.
Now these, now those, the surly boatman bore;
The rest he drove to distance from the shore.

VIRGIL (Dryden's tr.)

All those who could not produce the required obolus were obliged to wait one hundred years, at the end of which time Charon reluctantly ferried them over free of charge.

There was also in Hades the sacred river Styx, by whose waters the gods swore their most irrevocable oaths; and the blessed Lethe, whose waters had the power to make one forget all unpleasant things, thus preparing the good for a state of endless bliss in the Elysian Fields.

Lethe, the river of oblivion, rolls
Her wat'ry labrinth, whereof who drinks,
Forthwith his former state and being forgets,
Forgets both joy and grief, pleasure and pain.

MILTON

THE JUDGES

Near Pluto's throne were seated the three judges of Hades, Minos, Rhadamanthus, and Æacus, whose duty it was to question all newly arrived souls, to sort out the confused mass of good and bad thoughts and actions, and place them in the scales of Themis, the blindfolded, impartial goddess of justice, who bore a trenchant sword to indicate that her decrees would be mercilessly enforced. If the good outweighed the evil, the spirit was led to the Elysian Fields; but if, on the contrary, the evil prevailed, the spirit was condemned to suffer in the fires of Tartarus.

Where his decrees
The guilty soul within the burning gates
Of Tartarus compel, or send the good
To inhabit, with eternal health and peace,
The valley of Elysium.

AKENSIDE

THE FURIES

The guilty souls were always intrusted to the three snake-locked Furies (Erinnyes, or Eumenides), who drove them with their stinging lashes to the gates of Tartarus. These deities, who were sisters, and children of Acheron and Nyx, were distinguished by the individual names of Alecto, Tisiphone, and Megæra, and with Nemesis, goddess of revenge, were noted for their hard hearts and the merciless manner in which they hurried the ghosts intrusted to their care over the fiery flood of the Phlegethon, and through the brazen gates of their future place of incessant torment.

There rolls swift Phlegethon, with thund'ring sound,

His broken rocks, and whirls his surges round.

On mighty columns rais'd sublime are hung

The massy gates, impenetrably strong.

In vain would men, in vain would gods essay,

To hew the beams of adamant away.

Here rose an iron tow'r: before the gate,

By night and day, a wakeful Fury sate,

The pale Tisiphone; a robe she wore,

With all the pomp of horror, dy'd in gore.

VIRGIL (C. Pitt's tr.)

CHARON CARRYING SOULS ACROSS THE RIVER STYX.
Alexander Litovchenko.

THE THREE FATES. Paul Thumann.

THE FATES

The three Fates (Mœræ, Parcæ), sisters, also sat near Pluto's throne. Clotho, the youngest, spun the thread of life, in which the bright and dark lines were intermingled. Lachesis, the second, twisted it; and under her fingers it was now strong, now weak.

> Twist ye, twine ye! even so,
> Mingle shades of joy and woe,
> Hope, and fear, and peace, and strife,
> In the thread of human life.
>
> SCOTT

Atropos, the third sister, armed with a huge pair of shears, remorselessly cut short the thread of life,—an intimation that another soul would ere long find its way down into the dark kingdom of Hades.

TARTARUS

When the gates of Tartarus turned on their hinges to receive the newcomer, a chorus of cries, groans, and imprecations from within fell upon his ear, mingled with the whistling of the whips incessantly plied by retributive deities.

> What sounds were heard,
> What scenes appeared,
> O'er all the dreary coasts!
>   Dreadful gleams,
>   Dismal screams,
>   Fires that glow,
>   Shrieks of woe,
>   Sullen moans,
>   Hollow groans,
> And cries of tortured ghosts.
>
> ADDISON

THE DANAIDES

Many victims renowned while on earth for their cruelty found here the just punishment of their sins. Attention was first attracted by a group of beautiful maidens, who carried water to fill a bottomless cask. Down to the stream they hastened, a long procession, filled their urns with water, painfully clambered up the steep and slippery bank, and poured their water into the cask; but when, exhausted and ready to faint from fatigue, they paused to rest for a moment, the cutting lash fell upon their bare shoulders, and spurred them on to renewed efforts to complete a task so hopeless that it has become proverbial.

These fair maidens were the Danaides, daughters of Danaus, who had pledged his fifty daughters to the fifty sons of his brother Ægyptus. The marriage preparations were all completed, when Danaus suddenly remembered an ancient prophecy which had quite escaped his memory, and which foretold that he would perish by the hand of his son-in-law.

It was now too late to prevent the marriages, so, calling his daughters aside, he told them what the oracle had said, and, giving them each a sharp dagger, bade them slay their husbands on their wedding night. The marriages were celebrated, as was customary, with mirth, dance, and song; and the revelry continued until late at night, when, the guests having departed, the newly married couples retired. But as soon as Danaus's daughters were quite certain their husbands were fast asleep, they produced their daggers and slew their mates.

> Danaus arm'd each daughter's hand
> To stain with blood the bridal bed.
>
> EURIPIDES (Potter's tr.)

One of the brides only, Hypermnestra, loved her husband too dearly to obey her father's command, and, when morning broke, only forty-nine of Ægyptus's sons were found lifeless. The sole survivor, Lynceus, to avenge his brothers' death, slew Danaus, thus fulfilling the ominous prophecy; while the gods, incensed by the Danaides's heartlessness, sent them to Hades, where they were compelled to fill the bottomless cask.

Tantalus

Tartarus also detained within its brazen portals a cruel king named Tantalus (the father of Niobe), who, while on earth, had starved and ill-treated his subjects, insulted the immortal gods, and on one occasion had even dared to cook and serve up to them his own son Pelops. Most of the gods were immediately aware of the deception practiced upon them, and refused the new dish; but Ceres, who was very melancholy on account of the recent loss of her daughter, paid no heed to what was offered her, and in a fit of absent-mindedness ate part of the lad's shoulder.

The gods in pity restored the youth to life, and Ceres replaced the missing shoulder with one of ivory or of gold. Driven away from his kingdom, which was seized by the King of Troy, Pelops took refuge in Greece, where he ruled the extensive peninsula, the Peloponnesus, which still bears his name.

To punish the inhuman Tantalus, the gods then sent him to Tartarus, where he stood up to his chin in a stream of pure water, tormented with thirst; for, whenever he stooped to drink, the waters fled from his parched lips. Over his head hung a branch of luscious fruit. His hunger was as intolerable as his thirst; but, whenever he clutched at the fruit, the branch swung upward, and eluded his eager grasp.

> Above, beneath, around his hapless head,
> Trees of all kinds delicious fruitage spread.
> The fruit he strives to seize; but blasts arise,
> Toss it on high, and whirl it to the skies.
> HOMER (Pope's tr.)

This singular punishment inflicted upon Tantalus gave rise to the expression "to tantalize."

Sisyphus

Another criminal was Sisyphus, who, while king of Corinth, had misused his power, had robbed and killed travelers, and even deceived the gods. His reprehensible conduct was punished in Tartarus, where he was condemned to roll a huge stone to the top of a very steep hill; and just as he reached the summit, and fancied his task done, the rock would slip from his grasp and roll to the foot of the hill, thus obliging him to renew all his exertions.

With many a weary step, and many a groan,
Up the high hill he heaves a huge round stone;
The huge round stone, resulting with a bound,
Thunders impetuous down, and smokes along the ground.
Again the restless orb his toil renews,
Dust mounts in clouds, and sweat descends in dews.

HOMER (Pope's tr.)

SALMONEUS

Salmoneus, another king, had vainly tried to make his subjects believe he was Jupiter. To that effect, he had once driven over a brazen bridge to imitate the roll of thunder, and, to simulate the thunderbolts, had thrown lighted torches down upon the multitude, purposely assembled below.

Th' audacious wretch four fiery coursers drew:
He wav'd a torch aloft, and, madly vain,
Sought godlike worship from a servile train.
Ambitious fool, with horny hoofs to pass
O'er hollow arches of resounding brass,
To rival thunder in its rapid course,
And imitate inimitable force!

VIRGIL (Dryden's tr.)

This insolent parody so incensed Jupiter, that he grasped one of his deadliest thunderbolts, brandished it aloft for a moment, and then hurled it with vindictive force at the arrogant king. In Tartarus, Salmoneus was placed beneath an overhanging rock, which momentarily threatened to fall, and crush him under its mass.

He was doomed to sit under a huge stone,
Which the father of the gods
Kept over his head suspended.
Thus he sat in continual dread of its downfall,
And lost to every comfort.

PINDAR

TITYUS

Still farther on was the recumbent form of Tityus, a giant whose body covered nine acres of ground. He had dared offer an insult to Juno, and in punishment was chained like Prometheus, while a vulture feasted on his liver.

> There Tityus was to see, who took his birth
> From heav'n, his nursing from the foodful earth:
> Here his gigantic limbs, with large embrace,
> Infold nine acres of infernal space.
> A rav'nous vulture in his open side
> Her crooked beak and cruel talons try'd:
> Still for the growing liver digg'd his breast,
> The growing liver still supply'd the feast.
> VIRGIL (Dryden's tr.)

IXION

Here in Tartarus, too, was Ixion, king of the Lapithæ, who had been given the hand of Dia in marriage on condition that he would give her father a stipulated sum of money in exchange, but who, as soon as the maiden was his, refused to keep his promise. The father-in-law was an avaricious man, and clamored so loudly for his money, that Ixion, to be rid of his importunities, slew him. Such an act of violence could not be overlooked by the gods: so Jupiter summoned Ixion to appear before him and state his case.

Ixion pleaded so skillfully, that Jupiter was about to declare him acquitted, when he suddenly caught him making love to Juno, which offense seemed so unpardonable, that he sent him to Tartarus, where he was bound to a constantly revolving wheel of fire.

> Proud Ixion (doom'd to feel
> The tortures of the eternal wheel,
> Bound by the hand of angry Jove)
> Received the due rewards of impious love.
> SOPHOCLES (Francklin's tr.)

Elysian Fields

Far out of sight and hearing of the pitiful sounds which so constantly rose out of Tartarus, were the Elysian Fields, lighted by a sun and moon of their own, decked with the most fragrant and beautiful of flowers, and provided with every charm that nature or art could supply. No storms or wintry winds ever came to rob these fields of their springlike beauty; and here the blessed spent eternity, in pleasant communion with the friends they had loved on earth.

> Patriots who perished for their country's rights,
> Or nobly triumphed in the fields of fight:
> There holy priests and sacred poets stood,
> Who sang with all the raptures of a god:
> Worthies whose lives by useful arts refined;
> With those who leave a deathless name behind,
> Friends of the world, and fathers of mankind.

BACCHUS

Among all the mortal maidens honored by the love of Jupiter, king of the gods, none was more attractive than Semele, daughter of Cadmus and Harmonia.

> For Semele was molded in the form
> Of elegance; the beauty of her race
> Shone in her forehead.
>
> NONNUS (Elton's tr.)

STORY OF SEMELE

Although conscious of these superior attractions, Semele was excessively coy, and it was only with the greatest difficulty that Jupiter, disguised as a mortal, could urge his love suit. When he had at last obtained a hearing, he told her who he was, calculating upon the effect which such a revelation must necessarily produce.

He was not mistaken in his previsions, for Semele, proud of having attracted the greatest among the gods, no longer offered any resistance, and consented to their union. Their love grew and prospered, and Jupiter came down from Olympus as often as possible to enjoy the society of his beloved. His frequent absences finally aroused Juno's suspicions, and, as usual, she spared no pains to discover what powerful charm could draw him from her side. After a few days she knew all, and straightway determined to have her revenge, and punish her fickle spouse. To accomplish this successfully, she assumed the face and form of Beroe, Semele's old nurse, and thus entered the young princess's apartment quite unsuspected.

> Old Beroe's decrepit shape she wears,
> Her wrinkled visage, and her hoary hairs;

> Whilst in her trembling gait she totters on,
> And learns to tattle in the nurse's tone.
>
> OVID (Addison's tr.)

There she immediately entered into conversation with her supposed nursling, artfully extracted a complete confession, heard with suppressed rage how long Jupiter had wooed ere he had finally won the maiden's consent, and received a rapturous and minute catalogue of all his personal charms and a synopsis of all they had both said.

The false nurse listened with apparent sympathy; but in reality she was furious, and, to put an end to it all, asked Semele if she were quite sure he was king of the gods, as he asserted, and whether he visited her in all the pomp of his regal apparel. The maiden shamefacedly replied that he was wont to visit her in the guise of a mortal only; whereupon Beroe, with feigned indignation, told her nursling he must either be a vile impostor, or else that he did not love her as dearly as he loved Juno, in whose presence he seldom appeared except in godlike array.

With artful words she so worked upon the guileless nature of her rival, that, when Jupiter next came, the maiden used all her blandishments to extort from him a solemn oath to grant any request she chose to make. A lover is not very likely to weigh his words under such circumstances, and Jupiter took the most solemn of all the oaths to gratify her whim.

> "Bear me witness, Earth, and ye, broad Heavens
> Above us, and ye, waters of the Styx,
> That flow beneath us, mightiest oath of all,
> And most revered by the blessed gods!"
>
> HOMER (Bryant's tr.)

The promise won, the delighted Semele bade her lover speedily return to Olympus, don his own majestic form and apparel, and hasten back to her side, surrounded by all his heavenly pomp, and armed with his dreaded thunderbolts. Jupiter, horrified at this imprudent request, implored her to ask something else, and release him from a promise fraught with such danger to her; but all in vain. Semele, like many another fair lady, enjoyed having her own way, and fairly forced him to obey.

Jupiter returned to Olympus, modified his costume as much as possible, dimmed his glory wherever he could, and chose the feeblest of all his bolts, for well he knew no mere mortal could endure the shock of his full glory. Then, mounted on a pale flash of lightning, he darted back to Semele.

To keep his promise he ascends, and shrouds
His awful brow in whirlwinds and in clouds;
Whilst all around, in terrible array,
His thunders rattle, and his lightnings play.
And yet, the dazzling luster to abate,
He set not out in all his pomp and state,
Clad in the mildest lightning of the skies,
And arm'd with thunder of the smallest size:
Not those huge bolts, by which the giants slain,
Lay overthrown on the Phlegrean plain.
'Twas of a lesser mold, and lighter weight;
They call it thunder of a second-rate.
For the rough Cyclops, who by Jove's command
Temper'd the bolt and turn'd it to his hand,
Work'd up less flame and fury in its make,
And quench'd it sooner in the standing lake.
Thus dreadfully adorn'd, with horror bright,
Th' illustrious god, descending from his height,
Came rushing on her in a storm of light.

OVID (Addison's tr.)

But, although so much milder than usual, this apparition was more than poor Semele's human nerves could bear, and she dropped to the floor in a swoon at the first glimpse of her lover. Oblivious of all but her alarming condition, Jupiter sprang to her side; but the lightning which played about his head set fire to the whole palace, which was reduced to ashes.

BIRTH OF BACCHUS

Semele herself perished, burned to death; and the only person in all the building who escaped uninjured was Bacchus (Liber, Dionysus), the infant son of Jupiter and Semele, who was saved by his father's powerful hand. Jupiter was at first inconsolable at the death of Semele; and, to testify to all mortals how fondly he had loved her, he brought her spirit up to heaven, where he raised her to the rank of a deity.

> Semele of the flowing hair,
> Who died in Thunder's crashing flame,
> To deified existence came.

HOMER

The infant Bacchus was first intrusted to the care of his aunt Ino, the second wife of Athamas, King of Thebes, who nursed him as tenderly as if he had been her own child. But all her love could not avail to screen him from the effects of Juno's persistent hatred: so Jupiter, fearing lest some harm might befall his precious son, bade Mercury convey him to the distant home of the Nysiades,—nymphs who guarded him most faithfully.

Juno, not daring to continue her persecutions, wreaked all her anger upon poor Ino and her unhappy household by sending the Fury Tisiphone to goad Athamas to madness. In a fit of deluded frenzy, he pursued his wife and children as if they were wild beasts. One of his sons, Learchus, fell beneath his arrows; and, to escape his murderous fury, Ino plunged headlong into the sea with her second child in her arms. The gods, in pity for her sufferings, changed her into the goddess Leucothea, and her son into a sea deity by the name of Palæmon.

BACCHUS'S ATTENDANTS

When still but a youth, Bacchus was appointed god of wine and revelry, and intrusted to the guidance of Silenus, a satyr, half man and half goat, who educated him, and accompanied him on all his travels; for he delighted in roaming all over the world, borne by his followers, or riding in his chariot drawn by wild beasts, while his tutor followed him, mounted on an ass, supported on either side by an attendant.

> And near him rode Silenus on his ass,
> Pelted with flowers as he on did pass.

KEATS

Bacchus's train was very large indeed, and composed of men and women, nymphs, fauns, and satyrs, all crowned with ivy leaves, who drank wine,—a drink compounded for their express use out of water and sunshine,—ate grapes, danced and sang, and loudly proclaimed him their chosen leader.

> "We follow Bacchus! Bacchus on the wing,
> A conquering!
> Bacchus, young Bacchus! good or ill betide,
> We dance before him thorough kingdoms wide."
>
> KEATS

The most unruly among his female followers were the Bacchantes, who delighted in revelry, and were in a perpetual state of intoxication as they went with him from land to land, where he taught the people the cultivation of the vine and the art of making wine. He traveled thus, it is said, throughout Greece and Asia Minor, and even ventured as far as India and Ethiopia.

BACCHUS AND THE PIRATES

During these long journeys, Bacchus, as was inevitable, met with many adventures, which have been fertile themes for poetry and art. On one occasion, having strayed away from his followers and lost his way, Bacchus laid himself down upon the sand on the seashore to rest. Some pirates, sailing by, saw the handsome young sleeper, and noiselessly bore him off to their vessel, intending to sell him as a slave in Egypt.

They were already quite far out at sea when the god awoke, and gazed around him in mute wonder at his surroundings. When fully roused, he bade the seamen take him back to land, but they merely replied by laughter and mockery. Their amusement was cut short, however, for the ship came to a sudden standstill; and, when they leaned over the sides to ascertain why their oars could no longer propel it onward, they saw a vine grow out of the sea, and twine its branches and tendrils with lightning-like velocity around oars, mast, and rigging, thus transforming the vessel into a floating arbor. Then a sound of music and revelry greeted their astonished ears, and Bacchus's followers came thronging over the ship's sides, riding on wild beasts, and chanting the praises of their god and of his favorite beverage.

> In chorus we sing of wine, sweet wine,
> Its power benign, and its flavor divine.
>
> MARTINEZ DE LA ROSA

These extraordinary sights and sounds so bewildered the poor sailors, that they lost all presence of mind, and jumped overboard into the sea, where they were drowned and changed into dolphins.

THE TRIUMPH OF BACCHUS. Cornelis de Vos.

On another occasion, Silenus, after a great carousal, lost his way in the forest, and helplessly wandered from place to place in search of his companions, until he finally came to the court of Midas, King of Lydia, of ass's ears fame.

THE CURSE OF GOLD

Midas no sooner beheld the red nose and bloated appearance of the wanderer, than he recognized him as Bacchus's tutor, and volunteered to lead him back to his divine pupil. Delighted to see Silenus again, Bacchus promised Midas any reward he wished; whereupon Midas, who was an avaricious old king, fell upon his knees, and humbly besought the god to grant that all he touched might be changed into gold.

> "Give me," says he (nor thought he ask'd too much),
> "That with my body whatsoe'er I touch,
> 　Changed from the nature which it held of old,
> 　May be converted into yellow gold."
> 　　　　　　　　　　　　　　OVID (Croxall's tr.)

Bacchus immediately signified that his prayer was granted; and Midas, overjoyed at the success of his bold venture, wandered back to his palace, testing his new-won power, which changed all to gold at a mere touch of one of his fingers.

> 　　Down from a lowly branch a twig he drew,
> 　　The twig straight glitter'd with a golden hue.
> 　　He takes a stone, the stone was turn'd to gold:
> 　　A clod he touches, and the crumbling mold
> 　　Acknowledged soon the great transforming power,
> 　　In weight and substance like a mass of ore.
> 　　He pluck'd the corn, and straight his grasp appears
> 　　Fill'd with a bending tuft of golden ears.
> 　　An apple next he takes, and seems to hold
> 　　The bright Hesperian vegetable gold:
> 　　His hand he careless on a pillar lays,
> 　　With shining gold the fluted pillars blaze.
> 　　　　　　　　　　　　　　OVID (Croxall's tr.)

The sight of these and many other wonders, wrought by a mere touch, filled his heart with joy; and in his elation he bade his servants prepare a sumptuous feast, and invite all his courtiers to share his merriment. His commands were obeyed with the utmost celerity, and Midas beamed with satisfaction as he took his place at the head of the board, and viewed the choice dishes and wines prepared for his delectation.

Here, too, however, a new revelation awaited him; for cloth, plate, and cup turned to gold, as did the food and drink as soon as they met his eager lips.

> Whose powerful hands the bread no sooner hold,
> But all its substance is transform'd to gold:
> Up to his mouth he lifts the savory meat,
> Which turns to gold as he attempts to eat:
> His patron's noble juice of purple hue,
> Touch'd by his lips, a gilded cordial grew,
> Unfit for drink; and, wondrous to behold,
> It trickles from his jaws a fluid gold.
> The rich poor fool, confounded with surprise,
> Starving in all his various plenty lies.
>
> OVID (Croxall's tr.)

In the midst of plenty, the gnawing pangs of hunger now made themselves felt; and the precious gift, which prevented his allaying them, soon lost all its attractions. With weary feet, Midas now retraced the road he had traveled in his pride a few hours before, again cast himself at Bacchus's feet, and this time implored him to take back the inconvenient gift, which prevented him from satisfying his natural appetites.

His distress seemed so real, that Bacchus bade him go and wash in the Pactolus River, if he would be rid of the power which had so soon turned into a curse. Midas hastened off to the river and plunged in its tide, noting that even its sands all turned to gold beneath his tread; since when,

> Pactolus singeth over golden sands.
>
> GRAY

NAXOS

Bacchus's favorite place of resort was the Island of Naxos, which he visited after every journey. During one of his sojourns there, he discovered a fair maiden lying alone on the sandy shore. Ariadne, for such was the girl's name, had been forsaken there by her lover, Theseus, who had sailed away while she slept. As soon as she awoke, she called her faithless lover; but no answering sound fell upon her ear except the mocking tones of Echo. Her tears flowed freely as she beat her breast in despair; but suddenly her lamentations ceased, as she caught the faint sound of music floating toward her on the summer breeze. Eagerly turning toward the pleasant music, she caught sight of a merry procession, headed by the God of Wine.

> "And as I sat, over the light blue hills
> There came a noise of revelers: the rills
> Into the wide stream came of purple hue—
>   'Twas Bacchus and his crew!
> The earnest trumpet spake, and silver thrills
> From kissing cymbals made a merry din—
>   'Twas Bacchus and his kin!
> Like to a moving vintage down they came,
> Crown'd with green leaves, and faces all on flame;
> All madly dancing through the pleasant valley."
>
>   KEATS

BACCHUS AND ARIADNE

Bacchus, the first to perceive the fair mourner, hastened to her side, and brought all his powers of persuasion into play to console her. His devotion at last induced her to forget her recreant lover, and, after a short courtship, Bacchus won her as a bride.

Their wedding was the gayest ever seen, and the feasting lasted for several days. The bridegroom presented the bride with a crown adorned with seven glittering stars,—an ornament which fitly enhanced her peerless beauty. Shortly after her marriage, however, poor Ariadne sickened and died, leaving a disconsolate widower, who took the crown she had so often worn and flung it up into the air. It rose higher and higher, until the gods fixed it in the sky, where it still forms a brilliant constellation, known as Ariadne's Crown, or Corona.

> And still her sign is seen in heaven,
> And, 'midst the glittering symbols of the sky,
> The starry crown of Ariadne glides.
>
> APOLLONIUS RHODIUS

Bacchus's lightheartedness had all vanished, and he no longer took any pleasure in music, dance, or revelry, until Jupiter, in pity for his bereavement, restored Ariadne to his longing arms, and, to prevent her being again claimed by Death, gave her immortal life.

STORY OF PENTHEUS

When but a short distance from Thebes, Bacchus once sent a herald to Pentheus, the king, to announce his approach, and bespeak a suitable reception and sumptuous entertainment. Rumors of the noise and disorder, which seemed to have been the invariable accompaniment of the god's presence, had already reached Pentheus, who therefore dismissed the herald with an insolent message, purporting that Bacchus had better remain outside of the city gates.

To avenge this insult, Bacchus inspired the Theban women with a species of dementia, which made them rush simultaneously out of the city and join his followers. Then they all clamored for permission to witness the religious rites in his honor, generally called Mysteries, which permission was graciously granted.

The king's spies reported all that had occurred, and their accounts made Pentheus long to view the ceremonies in secret. He therefore disguised himself, and hid in a bush near the consecrated place, hoping to see all without being seen; but an inadvertent movement attracted the attention of the already excited Bacchantes, who, led by Agave, the king's own mother, dragged him from his hiding place and tore him limb from limb.

WORSHIP OF BACCHUS

Bacchus, god of wine, was worshiped throughout the ancient world, and festivals without number were held in his honor. The most noted were the Greater and Lesser

FOLLOWING PAGES: MARRIAGE OF BACCHUS AND ARIADNE.
Hendrik van Balen.

Dionysia, the Liberalia, and the Bacchanalia, where the wildest merrymaking and license were freely indulged in by all participants.

> Bacchus, on thee they call, in hymns divine,
> And hang thy statues on the lofty pine:
> Hence plenty every laughing vineyard fills,
> Thro' the deep valleys and the sloping hills;
> Where'er the god inclines his lovely face,
> More luscious fruits the rich plantations grace.
> Then let us Bacchus' praises duly sing,
> And consecrated cakes, and chargers bring,
> Dragg'd by their horns let victim goats expire,
> And roast on hazel spits before the sacred fire.
>
> Come, sacred sire, with luscious clusters crown'd,
> Here all the riches of thy reign abound;
> Each field replete with blushing autumn glows,
> And in deep tides for thee the foaming vintage flows.
>
> VIRGIL (Warton's tr.)

Bacchus is generally represented as a handsome youth, crowned with ivy or grape leaves and clusters, bearing the thyrsus, an ivy-circled wand, as scepter, and riding in a chariot drawn by panthers or leopards.

CERES AND PROSERPINA

Ceres (Demeter), daughter of Cronus and Rhea, and one of Jupiter's numerous consorts, was goddess of agriculture and civilization. Her manifold cares were shared by her daughter, Proserpina (Cora, Pherephatta, Persephone), the goddess of vegetation. Whenever her duties permitted, this fair young goddess hastened off to the Island of Sicily, her favorite place of resort, where she wandered about all day long, attended by a merry girlish train, gathering flowers, on the green slopes of Mount Ætna, and danced with the nymphs in the beautiful plain of Enna.

One day, weary of labor, Proserpina called these fair playmates to join her and spend a merry day gathering flowers.

> And one fair morn—
> Not all the ages blot it—on the side
> Of Ætna we were straying. There was then
> Summer nor winter, springtide nor the time
> Of harvest, but the soft unfailing sun
> Shone always, and the sowing time was one
> With reaping.
>
> LEWIS MORRIS

PLUTO KIDNAPS PROSERPINA

The maidens sang merry lays as they wound their long garlands; and their joyous voices and ripples of silvery laughter attracted the attention of Pluto, just then driving past in his dark chariot drawn by four fiery coal-black steeds. To ascertain whence these sounds proceeded, the god stepped out of his car, and cautiously peeped through the thick foliage.

He saw Proserpina sitting on a mossy bank, almost buried in many-hued blossoms, her laughing companions picturesquely grouped around her. One glance sufficed to convince Pluto of her loveliness and grace, and to make him feel that his happiness depended on the possession of this bright young creature.

Long ere this, he had tried to persuade one after another of the goddesses to share his gloomy throne; but one and all had refused the honor, and declined to accompany him to a land where the sun never shone, the birds never sang, and the flowers never bloomed. Hurt and disappointed by these rebuffs, Pluto had finally registered a solemn vow never to go wooing again; and so, instead of gently inviting Proserpina to become his queen, he resolved to kidnap her.

Straight through the bushes he strode, direct to the spot where she was seated. The noise of crackling branches and hasty footsteps made the assembled maidens swiftly turn. One glance sufficed to identify the intruder, for none but he could boast of such a dark, lowering countenance; and all exclaimed in mingled wonder and terror at his unwonted presence in those sunlit regions.

> 'Tis he, 'tis he: he comes to us
> From the depths of Tartarus.
> For what of evil doth he roam
> From his red and gloomy home,
> In the center of the world,
> Where the sinful dead are hurled?
> Mark him as he moves along,
> Drawn by horses black and strong,
> Such as may belong to Night
> Ere she takes her morning flight.
> Now the chariot stops: the god
> On our grassy world hath trod:
> Like a Titan steppeth he,
> Yet full of his divinity.
> On his mighty shoulders lie
> Raven locks, and in his eye
> A cruel beauty, such as none
> Of us may wisely look upon.
>
> BARRY CORNWALL

Frightened by his impetuous approach, the trembling nymphs first crowded around Proserpina, who, in her astonishment and trepidation, dropped all her pretty flowers and stood motionless among them. Her uncertainty as to his purpose was only momentary, for, catching her in his brawny arms ere she could make an attempt to escape, he bore her off to his chariot, in spite of prayers and struggles, and drove away as fast as his fleet steeds could carry him.

He was soon out of hearing of the wild cries and lamentations of the nymphs, who vainly pursued him, and tried to overtake their beloved mistress. Afraid lest Ceres should come and force him to relinquish his new-won treasure, Pluto drove faster and faster, nor paused for an instant until he reached the banks of the Cyane River, whose waters, at his approach, began to seethe and roar in a menacing fashion, and spread themselves as much as possible, to check him in his flight.

Pluto quickly perceived that to attempt to cross the river in his chariot would be madness, while by retracing his footsteps he ran the risk of meeting Ceres, and being forced to relinquish his prize. He therefore decided to have recourse to other means, and, seizing his terrible two-pronged fork, struck the earth such a mighty blow, that a great crevice opened under his feet, through which horses and chariot plunged down into the darkness of the Lower World.

Proserpina turned her weeping eyes to catch a parting glimpse of the fair earth she was leaving, and then, with a fond thought of her anxious mother, who, when evening came, would vainly seek her child in all her favorite haunts, she quickly flung her girdle into the Cyane, and called to the water nymph to carry it to Ceres.

Elated by the complete success of his bold venture, and no longer fearful of immediate pursuit, the happy god strained his fair captive to his breast, pressed kisses on her fresh young cheeks, and tried to calm her terrors, as the black steeds rushed faster and faster along the dark passage, nor paused until they reached the foot of their master's throne.

> Pleased as he grasps her in his iron arms,
> Frights with soft sighs, with tender words alarms.
>
> DARWIN

FOLLOWING PAGES: THE RAPE OF PROSERPINA.
Jan Brueghel The Elder.

CERES'S SEARCH

In the mean while the sun had sunk below the Sicilian horizon; and Ceres, returning from the fields of fast-ripening grain to her own dwelling, sought for the missing Proserpina, of whom no trace could be found except the scattered flowers. Hither and thither the mother wandered, calling her daughter, and wondering where she could be, and why she did not come bounding to meet her. As time passed, and still Proserpina did not appear, Ceres's heart beat fast with apprehension, and the tears coursed down her cheeks as she rushed about from place to place, calling her daughter.

> What ails her that she comes not home?
>   Demeter seeks her far and wide,
> And gloomy-browed doth ceaseless roam
>   From many a morn till eventide.
> "My life, immortal though it be,
>   Is naught!" she cries, "for want of thee,
>   Persephone—Persephone!"
>
> INGELOW

Night came, and Ceres, kindling a torch at the volcanic fires of Mount Ætna, continued her search. Day dawned, and still the mother called, awakening the morning echoes with her longing cries for her child. Her daily duties were all neglected. The rain no longer refreshed the drooping flowers, the grain was parched by the ardent rays of the sun, and the grass all perished, while Ceres roamed over hill and dale in search of Proserpina.

Weary at last of her hopeless quest, the goddess seated herself by the wayside, near the city of Eleusis, and gave way to her overwhelming grief.

> Long was thine anxious search
> For lovely Proserpine, nor didst thou break
> Thy mournful fast, till the far-fam'd Eleusis
> Received thee wandering.
>
> ORPHIC HYMN

CERES.
Antoine Watteau.

CERES AND TRIPTOLEMUS

To avoid recognition, she had assumed the appearance of an aged crone; and as she sat there by the wayside, in tears, she attracted the compassionate inquiries of the daughters of Celeus, king of the country. Having heard her bewail the loss of her child, they entreated her to come to the palace, and, knowing nothing could so well soothe a breaking heart, offered her the charge of their infant brother Triptolemus.

Ceres, touched by their ready sympathy, accepted the offer; and when she arrived at the palace, the royal heir was intrusted to her care. Tenderly the goddess kissed the puny child's little pinched face; and at her touch the child became rosy and well, to the unbounded astonishment of the royal family and all the court.

In the night, while Ceres sat alone with her charge, it occurred to her that she might confer a still greater blessing upon him, that of immortality: so she anointed his limbs with nectar, murmured a powerful charm, and placed him upon the red-hot coals, to consume all the perishable elements left in his body.

The queen, Metaneira, who had thought it somewhat imprudent to leave the child thus alone with a stranger, now stole noiselessly into the apartment, and with a wild shriek rushed to the fire and snatched her child out of the flames, pressed him anxiously to her breast, and, after ascertaining that he was quite unharmed, turned to vent her indignation upon the careless nurse; but the aged beggar woman had vanished, and in her stead she confronted the radiant Goddess of Agriculture.

> From her fragrant robes
> A lovely scent was scattered, and afar
> Shone light emitted from her skin divine,
> And yellow locks upon her shoulders waved;
> White as from lightning, all the house was filled
> With splendor.
>
> HOMERIC HYMN

With a gentle reproof to the queen for her untimely interference, Ceres explained what she fain would have done, and vanished, to continue her wanderings in other lands. She finally returned to Italy; and, while wandering along the river banks one

OPPOSITE PAGE: A NYMPH BY THE SEA.
Wilhelm Kray.

day, the waters suddenly cast a glittering object at her feet. Stooping hastily to ascertain what it might be, she recognized the girdle her daughter had worn when she had parted from her in Sicily.

Joyfully she embraced the token, and, thinking she must now be upon Proserpina's track, hastened on until she came to a crystal fountain, by whose side she sat down to rest. Her eyes were heavy with the combined effect of tears, fatigue, and oppressive heat, and she was about to lose all consciousness of her trouble in sleep, when the murmur of the fountain increased, until she fancied it was talking; not as mortals do, but in its own silvery accents.

ARETHUSA AND ALPHEUS

The goddess was not mistaken; for a few minutes later she could distinguish words, and heard the fountain entreat her to listen, if she would hear what had befallen her child. The fountain then went on to tell how she had not always been a mere stream, but was once a nymph, called Arethusa, in Diana's train, and how, overcome by the heat, she had once sought a cool stream wherein she might bathe her heated limbs.

She soon found one, the Alpheus River, and selected a spot where the trees hung over the limpid waters, where the sand on the bottom was fine and even, and where no mortal eyes could see her as she threw aside her sandals and outer garments. She was enjoying the refreshing sensation of the water rippling around her hot limbs, and was reveling in the complete solitude, when suddenly the river, until now as smooth as a mirror, was ruffled by waves, which crept nearer and nearer to the startled nymph, until in affright she sprang out of the water.

Then a voice—the voice of the river god Alpheus—was heard, calling to her in pleading accents to stay her flight and lend an ear to his wooing; but when the impetuous god, instead of waiting for an answer to his suit, rose up out of the water and rushed to clasp her in his arms, she turned and fled in great terror. She fled, but he pursued. Over hill and dale, through forest and field, Arethusa ran, still closely followed by her too ardent lover, until, exhausted, she paused for breath, crying aloud to Diana to come to her rescue.

Her prayer was answered. A moment later she was enveloped in a thick mist and transformed into a fountain. Alpheus could no longer see her, but wandered about, bewailing her disappearance, and calling her in passionate accents.

"O Arethusa, peerless nymph! why fear
Such tenderness as mine? Great Dian, why,
Why didst thou hear her prayer? Oh that I
Were rippling round her dainty fairness now,
Circling about her waist, and striving how
To entice her to a dive! then stealing in
Between her luscious lips and eyelids thin."

KEATS

The misty cloud in which Arethusa had been enveloped by Diana's protecting care was soon blown away by a mischievous breath from Zephyrus; and Alpheus, who was still hovering near there, suddenly beholding a fountain where none had ever existed before, surmised what had happened. Changing himself into an impetuous torrent, he rushed to join his beloved, who sprang out of her mossy bed, and hurried on over sticks and stones, until Diana, seeing her new plight, opened a crevice, through which she glided away from the bright sunlight she loved so well into the depths of Pluto's realm.

While gliding there in the gloom, Arethusa had caught a glimpse of Proserpina on her sable throne, beside the stern-browed Pluto. She could not, however, pause to inquire how she came there, but hurried on breathlessly, until another crevice offered her the means of returning to the upper world, and seeing once more the blue sky and sun on the Sicilian plains.

The monotonous murmur of the fountain now subsided again into its usual undertone; and Ceres, knowing where to seek her daughter, was about to depart, when she heard the sudden rush and roar of a large body of water. She immediately turned, and beheld the torrent Alpheus, who, after a disconsolate search underground for the lost Arethusa, had found a crevice, through which he passed to join his beloved on the Sicilian plains.

Alpheus, Elis' stream, they say,
Beneath the seas here found his way,
And now his waters interfuse
With thine, O fountain Arethuse,
   Beneath Sicilian skies.

VIRGIL (Conington's tr.)

In spite of her previous efforts to escape him, Arethusa must still have been very glad to see him once more, for Ceres heard her murmur contentedly as she sank into his arms and listened to his louder tones of rapturous love.

Maidens in Greece were wont to throw fresh garlands into the Alpheus River; and it was said the selfsame flowers, carried away by his current, soon reappeared in the Sicilian fountain, carried there as love offerings by the enamored river.

> O my beloved, how divinely sweet
> Is the pure joy when kindred spirits meet!
> Like him, the river god, whose waters flow,
> With love their only light, through caves below,
> Wafting in triumph all the flowery braids
> And festal rings, with which Olympic maids
> Have decked his current, an offering meet
> To lay at Arethusa's shining feet.
> Think when at last he meets his fountain bride
> What perfect love must thrill the blended tide!
> And lost in each, till mingling into one,
> Their lot the same for shadow or for sun,
> A type of true love, to the deep they run.
>
> MOORE

CERES'S MOURNING

Now, although poor Ceres had ascertained where to find her missing daughter, her grief was not at all diminished, for she felt convinced that Pluto would never willingly relinquish her. She therefore withdrew into a dark cave to mourn unseen, and still further neglected her wonted duties.

Famine threatened to visit the people, and they prayed and clamored for her aid; but, absorbed in grief, she paid no heed to their distress, and vowed that nothing on earth should grow, with her permission, as long as her daughter was detained in Hades. In despair at this frightful state of affairs, the people then besought Jupiter to pity the sufferings they endured, and to allow Proserpina to revisit the upper world once more.

> Arise, and set the maiden free;
> Why should the world such sorrow dree
> By reason of Persephone?
>
> INGELOW

As soon as she became aware of this petition, Ceres hastened to Olympus, to join her supplications to the cries which rose from all parts of the earth; until Jupiter, wearied by these importunities, consented to Proserpina's return, upon condition, however, that she had not touched any food during the whole time of her sojourn in the Infernal Regions.

> Last, Zeus himself,
> Pitying the evil that was done, sent forth
> His messenger beyond the western rim
> To fetch me back to earth.
>
> LEWIS MORRIS

THE POMEGRANATE SEEDS

Ceres in person hastened to her daughter's new abode, and was about to lead her away in spite of Pluto, when a spirit, Ascalaphus, suddenly declared that the queen had partaken of some pomegranate seeds that very day. Proserpina could not refute the charge, and Jupiter decreed that for every seed she had eaten she should spend one month of every year in her husband's gloomy kingdom.

Thus it came about that Proserpina was condemned to spend one half the year in Hades, and could linger on the bright earth only for six months at a time.

Mercury was chosen to lead her to and from Hades; and, whenever he brought her out of her gloomy prison, the skies became blue and sunny, the grass sprang fresh and green beneath her elastic tread, the flowers bloomed along her way, the birds trilled forth their merry lays, and all was joy and brightness.

> And when, in springtime, with sweet-smelling flowers
> Of various kinds the earth doth bloom, thou'lt come
> From gloomy darkness back—a mighty joy
> To gods and mortal men.
>
> HOMERIC HYMN

Proserpina's Return

Ceres, happy once more in the possession of her beloved daughter, cheerfully and diligently attended to all her duties, and blessed the earth with plenty; but when the six months were over, and the skies wept and all nature mourned Proserpina's departure, she again returned to her cave, whence no entreaties could draw her.

As for the merry, happy-natured Proserpina, the moment Hades's portals closed behind her, she became pale and melancholy; and none would have dreamed the playful, flower-crowned Goddess of Vegetation was identical with the sad-faced, sable-vested Queen of Hades (now called Hecate), who held a pomegranate in one hand, and a torch in the other. Proserpina, like Adonis, was the personification of vegetation, visibly prosperous during the six favorable months of the year, and lurking hidden under the cold ground during the remainder of the time.

Worship of Ceres

Many beautiful temples were dedicated to Ceres and Proserpina in Greece and Italy, where yearly festivals, the Thesmophoria and the Cerealia, were celebrated with great pomp.

> To Ceres chief her annual rites be paid,
> On the green turf, beneath a fragrant shade,
> When winter ends, and spring serenely shines,
> Then fat the lambs, then mellow are the wines,
> Then sweet are slumbers on the flowery ground,
> Then with thick shades are lofty mountains crown'd.
> Let all the hinds bend low at Ceres' shrine;
> Mix honey sweet, for her, with milk and mellow wine;
> Thrice lead the victim the new fruits around,
> And Ceres call, and choral hymns resound:
> Presume not, swains, the ripen'd grain to reap,
> Till crown'd with oak in antic dance ye leap,
> Invoking Ceres, and in solemn lays,
> Exalt your rural queen's immortal praise.
>
> VIRGIL (C. Pitt's tr.)

To commemorate her long search for her daughter, Ceres returned to Eleusis, taught her former nursling, Triptolemus, the various secrets of agriculture, and gave him her chariot, bidding him travel everywhere, and teach the people how to plow, sow, and reap; and then she instituted the Eleusinia, festivals held in honor of her daughter and herself at Eleusis.

Triptolemus did not fail to carry out the goddess's instructions, and journeyed far and wide, until he finally reached the court of Lyncus, King of Scythia, where the false monarch would have treacherously slain him had not Ceres by timely interference prevented the execution of his base purpose by changing the traitor into a lynx, the emblem of perfidy.

Ceres was generally represented as a fair, matronly woman, clad in flowing draperies, sometimes crowned with wheat ears, and bearing a sheaf of grain and a sickle, or with a plow and a horn of plenty disgorging its wealth of fruit and flowers at her feet. Groves were frequently dedicated to her; and any mortal rash enough to lay the ax on one of these sacred trees was sure to incur the goddess's wrath, as is proved by the story of Erisichthon.

STORY OF ERISICHTHON

This man was evidently a freethinker, and, to show his contempt for the superstitious veneration paid to Ceres's trees, took his ax and cut down one of her sacred oaks. At his first blow, blood began to flow from the tree; but, undeterred by the phenomenon or the entreaties of the bystanders, Erisichthon continued. Finally, annoyed by the importunities of the spectators, he turned and slew one or two, and then completed his sacrilege.

Ceres, incensed by his insolence and cruelty, devised a terrible chastisement for the unfortunate man, and sent Famine to gnaw his vitals, and torment him night and day. The wretch, tortured by a hunger which no amount of food could allay, disposed of all his property to obtain the means of procuring nourishment; but his monstrous appetite continued, and, as he had but one daughter left, he sold her as a slave to obtain food.

The girl's master left her alone for a moment upon the seashore, and, in answer to her prayer, Neptune delivered her from servitude by changing her into a fisherman. When the master returned and found his slave gone, he questioned the fisherman, and, not obtaining any satisfactory information, departed. Neptune then restored the maiden to her own form, and let her return home; but, as her father sold her again, the god was obliged to interfere once more in her behalf, until at last Erisichthon, deprived of means to procure food, devoured himself.

CERES AND STELLIO

Another anecdote illustrating Ceres's power is told about a lad, Stellio, who made fun of the goddess when she was journeying, on account of the haste with which she disposed of a bowl of gruel offered by some charitable person. To punish the boy for his rudeness, Ceres flung the remainder of her gruel into his face, and changed him into a lizard.

VESTA

Worship of Vesta

Vesta, or Hestia, daughter of Cronus and Rhea, goddess of fire and of the family hearth, and guardian angel of mankind, was worshiped principally throughout Italy, although she also had shrines in Greece and Asia Minor.

The family hearth in ancient times possessed a far different signification from what it does now, and was considered the family altar, for there the father of the family was wont to offer up his daily prayers and sacrifices. "As, according to the old heathen custom, all men were regarded as enemies unless by a special compact they had been made friends, so Vesta presided especially over true and faithful dealing"; and she was therefore generally represented as pure and undefiled.

A beautiful circular temple in Rome was dedicated to Vesta's service; and here the Palladium of Troy was supposed to be preserved, together with the goddess's sacred fire, originally kindled by the rays of the sun.

This fire—an emblem of the flame of life, which the ancients fancied was kept burning within each human breast by Vesta, the life-giver—was kept constantly burning, and never allowed to go out for want of fuel or timely care. Its flames were also intended to represent the purity of the goddess, who, although wooed by many lovers,—among whom Apollo and Neptune can justly claim the precedence,—remained always a virgin.

The Romans fancied that her worship had been introduced in Italy by Æneas, their famous ancestor, who brought thither his home gods, and who, according to tradition, selected the first Vestal Virgins.

Vestal Virgins

The second king of Rome, Numa Pompilius, built a beautiful temple, and instituted various religious ceremonies, in honor of Vesta. The loveliest and noblest

among the Roman maidens were chosen to serve this goddess, and were known as Vestals, or Vestal Virgins. Admitted into the temple at the early age of six, they were compelled to serve ten years in fitting themselves to fulfill the duties they would be called upon to perform during the next decade as priestesses and guardians of the sacred fire. The last ten years were spent in instructing the novices; and, when their thirty-years' service was ended, they were at liberty either to continue in the temple, where they were treated with the greatest respect, or to leave it, and even marry, if such were their pleasure.

During their time of servitude, they were expected to keep their vows of chastity and fidelity to their patroness, and to maintain her sacred fire, under penalty of being buried alive in a vaulted chamber, fashioned for this express purpose by Numa Pompilius's order. In turn, each of the priestesses watched the fire, renewed the fuel, and fanned the flame, nor lost sight of it night or day; for the Romans considered the extinction of this sacred flame the precursor of some great public calamity.

The Vestals were, however, so pure and vigilant, that during one thousand years only eighteen failed to keep their vows satisfactorily, and suffered punishment. The Vestal Tuccia was accused of breach of faith, but, as proof of her purity, was given power to carry water in a sieve from the Tiber to the temple.

In return for the signal services the Vestals rendered to the state by maintaining this sacred fire, they enjoyed many privileges: among others, that of being preceded by a lictor with fasces when they walked abroad; of occupying the seats of honor in public ceremonies and festivities; of being buried within the city limits (a privilege granted to but very few); and of obtaining the pardon of criminals whom they met by accident on their way to the place of execution. Loved and greatly honored by all, the Vestals have become types of all things pure and lovely in woman.

> By these her trembling fires,
> Like Vesta's, ever burning; and, like hers,
> Sacred to thoughts immaculate and pure.
>
> YOUNG

The Vestal Virgins were further distinguished by a vesture of pure white linen, with a purple border and a wide purple mantle. In time of war or danger they were answerable for the preservation of the sacred fire, which they were allowed to remove

OPPOSITE PAGE: THE ANCIENT VIRGINS. Jean Raoux.

THE VESTAL TUCCIA. Domenico Corvi.

to any place of safety; and on several occasions they therefore carried it out of Rome and down the Tiber, lest it should fall into the enemy's hands.

The Vestals continued their office until the reign of Theodosius the Great, who, being converted to Christianity A.D. 380, abolished the worship of Vesta, dispersed the Vestals, and extinguished the sacred fire.

FESTIVALS

Vesta's services were held with great pomp; and her festivals, the Vestalia, were among the most beautiful and popular in Rome. Statues of this goddess—generally representing a woman of majestic beauty, clad in long robes, holding a lighted torch or lamp in one hand and a votive bowl in the other—were carried through the main streets of the city on all solemn occasions.

In public processions the Vestals had the privilege of carrying their sacred fire; while the Roman matrons, glad to swell their ranks, followed them, barefooted, chanting the praises of the good goddess Vesta.

> And from the temple brings
> Dread Vesta, with her holy things,
> Her awful fillets, and the fire
> Whose sacred embers ne'er expire.
> VIRGIL (Conington's tr.)

On these occasions great banquets were prepared before each house, all daily toil was suspended, the millstones were decked with flowers, and the very asses wont to turn them were covered with garlands and led in the processions.

Among the Romans, Vesta was not the only goddess invoked on the family hearth, for she shared that place of honor with the Lares, Manes, and Penates, who all enjoyed special veneration and sacrifices.

LARES, MANES, AND PENATES

The Lares, quite unknown to the Greeks, were two in number, the children of Mercury and Lara, a naiad famous for her beauty as well as for her extreme loquacity, which no one could check. Tradition relates that this fair maiden talked from morning till night, and told all she knew. Upon one occasion she incurred Jupiter's wrath by relating to Juno a conversation she had overheard between him and one of his numerous ladyloves.

To punish her, and at the same time prevent further tale-bearing, the king of the gods cut off Lara's tongue, and, summoning Mercury, bade him lead her down to Hades to linger there forever. But on the way to the dismal abode of the dead, the messenger god fell in love with his fair charge, who, being now effectually cured of her sole fault, was irresistibly charming; and, instead of obeying Jupiter, he made love to her, and by pantomime obtained her consent to their union. She bore him two children, who from her were called Lares, and to whom the Romans always paid divine honors, reserving special places for them on the family hearth, for they were supposed to preside over houses and families. Their statues resembled monkeys covered with the skins of dogs; while at their feet a barking dog, the symbol of their care and vigilance, was always represented.

The Manes—a name generally applied to souls when separated from the body—were also reckoned among the Roman divinities, and the illustrious ancestors of different families were often worshiped under this name.

As for the Penates, they presided over the houses and domestic affairs. Each head of a household was wont to choose his own Penates, whom he then invoked as his special patrons. The statues of the Penates were of clay, wax, ivory, silver, or gold, according to the wealth of the family whose hearth they graced, and the offerings generally made to them were a small part of each meal.

Upon removing from one house to another or from one place to another, it was customary for the head of the family to remove his household gods also, and establish them suitably before he thought of his own or his family's comfort, and in return for this kindly care the Penates blessed him with peace and prosperity.

JANUS

J anus, god of the past, present, and future, of gates, entrances, war, and peace, and patron of all beginnings, although one of the most important of all the Roman divinities, was entirely unknown to the Greeks.

According to some mythologists, he was the son of Apollo; and, although born in Thessaly, he early in life came to Italy, where he founded a city on the Tiber, to which he gave the name Janiculum. Here he was joined by the exiled Saturn, with whom he generously shared his throne. Together they civilized the wild inhabitants of Italy, and blessed them with such prosperity that their reign has often been called the Age of Gold.

> Saturn fled before victorious Jove,
> Driven down and banish'd from the realms above.
> He, by just laws, embodied all the train,
> Who roam'd the hills, and drew them to the plain;
> There fixed, and Latium called the new abode,
> Whose friendly shores concealed the latent god.
> These realms, in peace, the monarch long controlled,
> And blessed the nations with an age of gold.
>
> VIRGIL (C. Pitt's tr.)

JANUS'S TWO FACES

Janus is generally represented with two faces, turned in opposite directions, because he was acquainted with the past and future as well as with the present, and because he is considered an emblem of the sun, which opens the day at its rising, and closes the day at its setting.

In some statues he is represented with one white-haired and bearded face, and the other quite youthful in appearance, while others represent him with three and even four heads.

> Janus am I; oldest of potentates;
>   Forward I look, and backward, and below
> I count, as god of avenues and gates,
>   The years that through my portals come and go.
>
> I block the roads and drift the fields with snow;
>   I chase the wild-fowl from the frozen fen;
> My frosts congeal the rivers in their flow;
>   My fires light up the hearths and hearts of men.
>
> LONGFELLOW

The commencement of every new year, month, and day was held sacred to Janus, and at that time special sacrifices and prayers were offered up at his shrines. He also presided over all gates and avenues, and through him alone prayers were supposed to reach the immortal gods: therefore in all religious ceremonies his name was always the first invoked. From this circumstance he often appears with a key in his right hand, and a rod in his left; or, when he presides over the year, he holds the number 300 in one hand, and 65 in the other.

WORSHIP OF JANUS

He was also supposed to watch over peace and war, and had numerous temples throughout all Italy. One very celebrated temple was called Janus Quadrifons, because it was perfectly square. On each side of the building there was one door and three windows. These apertures were all symbolical,—the doors of the four seasons, and the windows of the twelve months, of the year.

In times of war the temple gates were opened wide, for the people, being in need of aid and comfort, were all anxious to enter and present their offerings; but when peace reigned, the doors were immediately closed, for the god's intercession was no longer necessary. The Romans, however, were such a belligerent people, that the temple gates were closed but thrice in more than seven centuries, and then only for a very short period.

Festivals in honor of Janus were celebrated on the first day of the new year; and one month bore the god's name, and was considered sacred to him. It was customary for friends and relatives to exchange calls, good wishes, and gifts on the first day of this month,—a Roman custom in force to this day.

ANCIENT DIVISIONS OF TIME

Janus is not the only one among the Greek and Latin divinities whose name has been given to a part of the year or week; for in Latin the names of the days are *dies Solis* (Sun day), *dies Lunæ* (Moon day), *dies Martis* (Mars's day), *dies Mercurii* (Mercury's day), *dies Jovis* (Jove's day), *dies Veneris* (Venus's day), *dies Saturni* (Saturn's day); Latin names which are still in use in legislative and judiciary acts, while in English the common nomenclature is derived from the names of the corresponding Saxon divinities.

FOLLOWING PAGE: SLEEP AND DEATH CARRYING AWAY SARPEDON OF LYCIA. Henry Fuseli.

Chapter XVII

SOMNUS AND MORS

Cave of Sleep

After leaving the joyless regions of Pluto's realm, and following the even course of the Lethe River, the ancients fancied one reached a large cave in a remote and quiet valley. This cave was the dwelling of Somnus (or Hupnos), god of sleep, and of his twin brother Mors (or Thanatos), god of death; and both were sons of the Goddess of Night, who had once ruled the whole universe. Near the entrance of the cave, shadowy forms kept constant watch, gently shaking great bunches of poppies, and, with finger to lips, enjoining silence on all who ventured near. These forms were the genii of sleep and death, represented in art as crowned with poppies or amaranths, and sometimes holding a funeral urn or a reversed torch.

Somnus and Morpheus

The cave was divided into chambers, each one darker and more silent than the one which preceded it. In one of the inner rooms, which was all draped with sable curtains, stood a downy couch, upon which reclined the monarch of sleep. His garments were also black, but all strewn with golden stars. He wore a crown of poppies on his head, and held a goblet full of poppy juice in his languid hand. His drowsy head was supported by Morpheus, his prime minister, who watched incessantly over his prolonged slumbers, and hindered any one from troubling his repose.

FOLLOWING PAGES: MORPHEUS. Jean-Bernard Restout.

Deep in a cavern dwells the drowsy god:
Whose gloomy mansion nor the rising sun,
Nor setting, visits, nor the lightsome noon:
But lazy vapors round the region fly,
Perpetual twilight, and a doubtful sky;
No crowing cock does there his wings display,
Nor with his horny bill provoke the day:
Nor watchful dogs, nor the more wakeful geese,
Disturb with nightly noise the sacred peace:
Nor beast of nature, nor the tame, are nigh,
Nor trees with tempest rock'd, nor human cry;
But safe repose, without an air of breath,
Dwells here, and a dumb quiet next to death.

   An arm of Lethe, with a gentle flow,
Arising upwards from the rock below,
The palace moats, and o'er the pebbles creeps,
And with soft murmurs calls the coming sleeps;
Around its entry nodding poppies grow,
And all cool simples that sweet rest bestow;
Night from the plants their sleepy virtue drains,
And passing, sheds it on the silent plains:
No door there was the unguarded house to keep,
On creaking hinges turn'd to break his sleep.

   But in the gloomy court was rais'd a bed,
Stuff'd with black plumes, and on an ebon sted:
Black was the covering too, where lay the god,
And slept supine, his limbs display'd abroad.
About his head fantastic visions fly,
Which various images of things supply,
And mock their forms; the leaves on trees not more,
Nor bearded ears in fields, nor sands upon the shore.

OVID (Dryden's tr.)

Dreams and Nightmares

All around the bed and over it hovered throngs of exquisite spirits, the Dreams, who stooped to whisper their pleasant messages in his ear; while in the distant corners of the apartment lurked the hideous Nightmares. The Dreams were often dispatched to earth under Mercury's charge, to visit mortals.

Two gates led out of the valley of sleep,—one of ivory, and the other of horn. The Dreams which passed through the glittering gates of ivory were delusive, while those which passed through the homely gate of horn were destined to come true in the course of time.

> Of dreams, O stranger, some are meaningless
> And idle, and can never be fulfilled.
> Two portals are there for their shadowy shapes,
> Of ivory one, and one of horn. The dreams
> That come through the carved ivory deceive
> With promises that never are made good;
> But those which pass the doors of polished horn,
> And are beheld of men, are ever true.
>
> HOMER (Bryant's tr.)

Dreams were also frequently sent through the gates of horn to prepare mortals for misfortunes, as in the case of Halcyone.

Story of Ceyx and Halcyone

Ceyx, King of Thessaly, was once forced to part from his beloved wife, Halcyone, to travel off to Delphi to consult the oracle. With many tears this loving couple parted, and Halcyone watched the lessening sail until it had quite vanished from sight; then she returned to her palace to pray for her husband's safe return. But, alas! the gods had decreed they should never meet again on earth; and, even while Halcyone prayed, a tempest arose which wrecked Ceyx's vessel, and caused him and all his crew to perish in the seething waves.

Day after day the queen hastened down to the seashore, followed by her attendants, to watch for the returning sails of her husband's vessel; and night after night she lay on her couch, anxiously expecting the morrow, which she ever fancied would prove auspicious. The gods, seeing her anxiety, and wishing to prepare her to receive the news of his death, and especially to view with some composure his corpse, which they had decided should be washed ashore, sent a Dream to visit her.

After assuming the face and form of Ceyx, the Dream glided away through the gate of horn, hastened to Halcyone's bedside, and whispered that her husband was dead, and that his body was even now being cast up on the smooth, sandy beach by the salt sea waves. With a wild cry of terror and grief, Halcyone awoke, and hastened to the seashore to convince herself that the dream had been false; but she had no sooner reached the beach, than the waves washed her husband's corpse to her feet.

To endure life without him seemed too great a task for poor Halcyone, who immediately cast herself into the sea, to perish beside him. Touched by grief so real and intense, the gods changed both bodies into birds, since known as Halcyon birds, and decreed they should ever live on the waters. These birds were said to build their nests and hatch their young on the heaving billows, and to utter shrill cries of warning to the seamen whenever a storm threatened, bidding them prepare for the blast, and hasten to shelter in port, if they would not encounter the mournful fate of poor Ceyx.

MORS

Mors, god of death, occupied one of the corners of Somnus's cave. He was a hideous, cadaverous-looking deity, clad in a winding sheet, and held an hourglass and a scythe in his hand. His hollow eyes were fixed upon the sands of time; and when they had run out, he knew some life was about to end, and sallied forth, scythe in hand, to mow down his prey with relentless joy.

Needless to say, this cruel deity was viewed by the ancients with fear and dislike, and no homage was offered him.

These two divinities were, however, but of slight importance in the general scheme of ancient mythology, in which Proserpina was generally regarded as the emblem of death, and they were therefore more like local divinities. The Lacedæmonians paid the most heed to them, and invariably placed their statues side by side.

MORPHEUS

As for Morpheus, the son as well as the prime minister of Somnus, he was also called the god of sleep, and mortals were wont to intercede for his good offices. He is generally represented as a sleeping child of great corpulence, and with wings. Morpheus held a vase in one hand, and poppies in the other, which he gently shook to induce a state of drowsiness,—according to him, the acme of bliss.

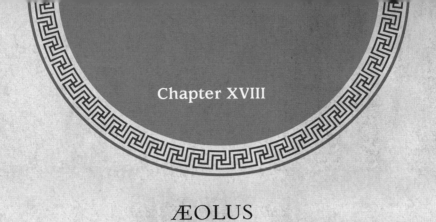

ÆOLUS

Not very far away from the quiet realm of Somnus and Mors, but on the surface of the earth, were the Æolian Islands, now known as the Lipari Islands, where Æolus, god of the storm and winds, governed a very unruly and turbulent population.

ÆOLUS'S CHILDREN

He is said to have received his royal dignity from the fair hands of Juno, and he was therefore specially eager to obey all her behests. He is commonly reputed to have married Aurora, or Eos, who gave him six sons: i.e., Boreas, the north wind; Corus, the northwest wind; Aquilo, the west wind; Notus, the southwest wind; Eurus, the east wind; and lastly, Zephyrus, the gentle and lovable south wind, whose mission it was to announce to mortals the return of ever-welcome spring.

Æolus's five elder sons were of a noisy, roving, mischievous, turbulent disposition, and peace and quiet were utterly impossible to them. To prevent their causing serious disasters, he therefore ruled them with a very strict hand, kept them very closely confined in a great cave, and let them loose only one at a time, to stretch their limbs and take a little exercise.

> Æolus in a cavern vast
> With bolt and barrier fetters fast
> Rebellious storm and howling blast.
> They with the rock's reverberant roar
> Chafe blustering round their prison door:
> He, throned on high, the scepter sways,
> Controls their moods, their wrath allays.
>
> VIRGIL (Conington's tr.)

Although very unruly indeed, the winds always obeyed their father's voice, and at his command, however reluctant, returned to their gloomy prison, where they expended their impotent rage in trying to shake its strong walls.

According to his own mood, or in conformity with the gods' request, Æolus either sent the gentler winds to play among the flowers, or, recalling them, let the fiercest of all his children free, with orders to pile up the waves mountain-high, lash them to foam, tear the sails of all the vessels at sea, break their masts, uproot the trees, tear the roofs off the houses, etc.,—in short, to do all the harm they possibly could.

> Now rising all at once, and unconfin'd,
> From every quarter roars the rushing wind:
> First, from the wide Atlantic Ocean's bed,
> Tempestuous Corus rears his dreadful head,
> Th' obedient deep his potent breath controls,
> And, mountain-high, the foamy flood he rolls;
> Him the Northeast encountering fierce, defied,
> And back rebuffeted the yielding tide.
> The curling surges loud conflicting meet,
> Dash their proud heads, and bellow as they beat;
> While piercing Boreas, from the Scythian strand,
> Plows up the waves and scoops the lowest sand.
> Nor Eurus then, I ween, was left to dwell,
> Nor showery Notus in th' Æolian cell,
> But each from every side, his power to boast,
> Ranged his proud forces to defend the coast.
>
> LUCAN

Æolus, king of the winds, shared with Dædalus the honor of inventing the sails which propel the ships so swiftly over the tide. It was he, too, who, according to Homer, bound all his children but one in a leather bag, which he gave to Ulysses when the latter visited Æolia. Thanks to this gift, Ulysses reached the shores of Ithaca, and would have landed in safety, had not his men, in view of port, untied the sack to investigate its contents, and thus set free the angry winds, who stirred up the most frightful tempest in mythic annals.

OPPOSITE PAGE: JUNO ASKING ÆOLUS TO RELEASE THE WINDS.
Francois Boucher.

TEMPLE OF ÆOLUS

The ancients, and especially the Athenians, paid particular attention to the winds, to whom they dedicated a temple, which is still extant, and generally known as the Tower of the Winds, or the Temple of Æolus. This temple is hexagonal, and on each side a flying figure of one of the winds is represented.

Eurus, the east wind, was generally depicted "as a young man flying with great impetuosity, and often appearing in a playful and wanton humor." Notus, or Auster, the southwest wind, "appeared generally as an old man, with gray hair, a gloomy countenance, a head covered with clouds, a sable vesture, and dusky wings," for he was considered the dispenser of rain and of all sudden and heavy showers. Zephyrus, mild and gentle, had a lapful of flowers, and, according to the Athenian belief, was wedded to Flora, with whom he was perfectly happy, and visited every land in turn. Corus, the northwest wind, drove clouds of snow before him; while Aquilo, dreadful in appearance, caused cold shivers to run down one's back at his mere sight. Boreas, rough and shivering too, was the father of rain, snow, hail, and tempests, and was therefore generally represented as veiled in impenetrable clouds. His favorite place of abode was in the Hyperborean Mountains, from whence he sallied forth on wild raids. During one of these excursions he carried off Orithyia, who always fled at his approach. But all her fleetness could not save her: she was overtaken, and borne away to the inaccessible regions of snow and ice, where he detained her, and made her his wife. She became the mother of Zetes and Calais,—who took part in the Argonautic expedition, and drove away the Harpies,—and of two daughters, Cleopatra and Chione.

On another occasion, Boreas, having changed himself into a horse and united himself to the mares of Dardanus, King of Troy, became the father of twelve steeds so swift that none could overtake them.

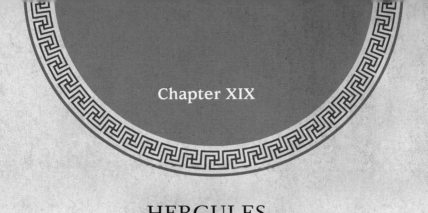

HERCULES

Unto this thy son it shall be given,
With his broad heart to win his way to heaven;
Twelve labors shall he work; and all accurst
And brutal things o'erthrow, brute men the worst;
And in Trachinia shall the funeral pyre
Purge his mortalities away with fire;
And he shall mount amid the stars, and be
Acknowledg'd kin to those who envied thee,
And sent these den-born shapes to crush his destiny.

THEOCRITUS (Hunt's tr.)

The ancients were not content to worship the gods only, but also offered up sacrifices to a few mortals, who, by their heroic deeds and virtuous lives, had won both admiration and respect. Foremost among these heroes—generally designated by the title of demigods—is Hercules (Heracles, Alcides), son of Jupiter and Alcmene, a mortal princess.

JUNO PERSECUTES HERCULES

As soon as the tidings of Hercules's birth reached Olympus, Juno began to plot how to destroy her rival's child. Two colossal serpents with poisonous fangs were therefore dispatched by her orders to attack the babe in its cradle. The monsters crept along noiselessly, entered the palace unseen, twined themselves around the cradle, and were about to crush the child to death in their folds, when, to the utter astonishment of the helpless attendants, little Hercules caught them fast by the neck in each tiny hand and strangled them, thus giving the first proof of the marvelous strength which was to make him famous.

INFANT HERCULES STRANGLING SERPENTS IN HIS CRADLE.
Sir Joshua Reynolds.

First two dread Snakes at Juno's vengeful nod
Climb'd round the cradle of the sleeping God;
Waked by the shrilling hiss, and rustling sound,
And shrieks of fair attendants trembling round,
Their gasping throats with clenching hands he holds;
And Death untwists their convoluted folds.

DARWIN

When Juno perceived how easily Hercules had escaped from the danger which threatened him, she deemed it useless to make another attempt to take his life, but decided to vex his proud spirit by inflicting many petty annoyances, and to prevent his enjoying any lasting peace or happiness.

To achieve this purpose, she first extorted from Jupiter a decree that condemned Hercules to serve his cousin Eurystheus—a mean and cowardly prince who ruled over the kingdom of Argos—for a certain number of years.

Hercules's education was carefully attended to by Chiron, a learned Centaur, who taught him how to use all the different weapons, and trained him in all kinds of athletic sports. The years passed by happily and swiftly, until at last the time came when Hercules's education was completed, and the whole world lay before him, full of pleasant possibilities, and rich with many attractions.

HERCULES'S CHOICE

The youthful hero, dismissed by his instructor, now set out to seek his fortunes. He had not gone very far, however, before he met two beautiful women, who immediately entered into conversation with him, and drew from him a confession that he was in search of adventures. The women, Arete (Virtue) and Kakia (Vice), each offered to be his guide, but bade him choose which he preferred to follow.

Kakia, to induce him to follow her guidance, promised riches, ease, consideration, and love; while Arete, a modest maiden, warned him that in her wake he would be obliged to wage incessant war against evil, to endure hardships without number, and spend his days in toil and poverty.

Silently Hercules pondered for a while over these two so dissimilar offers, and then, mindful of his tutor's oft-repeated instructions, rose from his seat by the wayside, and, turning to Arete, declared himself ready to obey any command she might choose to give him.

Young Hercules with firm disdain
Braved the soft smiles of Pleasure's harlot train;
To valiant toils his forceful limbs assign'd,
And gave to Virtue all his mighty mind.

Darwin

Courageously he then trod along the rough and thorny path she pointed out, and patiently performed the various tasks she assigned him, delivering the oppressed, defending the weak, and redressing all wrongs.

Hercules's Madness

In reward for these good actions he received the hand of Megara, daughter of Creon, King of Thebes, in marriage, and by her had three children, whom he tenderly loved. But Juno was not at all satisfied to see him leading such a peaceful and prosperous life, and to interrupt its even course drove the hero mad.

In a fit of delirium he threw his offspring into the fire, and, we are told, slew his dearly beloved wife. Then only he recovered his senses, and suffered agonies of sorrow and remorse for the terrible crimes he had unwittingly committed. In his grief he withdrew to the mountain solitudes, where he would probably have lingered all the remainder of his life, had not Mercury come to get him, and announced that he was to serve Eurystheus, King of Argos, for a twelvemonth.

Hercules in Servitude

The messenger god then offered to lead him to his appointed taskmaster. But when Hercules learned he was doomed to be a slave, he fell into such a passion, that he nearly lost his reason again; and instead of killing noxious beasts, and winning the people's blessings by his deeds of kindness, he wandered about stupidly and aimlessly, until he finally perceived how vain was his attempt to struggle against fate, and urged by his chosen adviser, Arete, voluntarily offered his services to Eurystheus, who informed him that he must accomplish twelve great labors ere he could again be free.

Nemean Lion

Eager to begin the appointed tasks, Hercules set out first to find and destroy a monstrous lion, whose den was in the Nemean Forest. Far and wide, throughout the whole neighborhood, this monster committed his depredations, carrying off cattle and sheep, men, women, and children, to devour at his ease. All warned Hercules of the danger and difficulty of the undertaking, described the failure of countless previous attempts to slay the monster, and prophesied that he would never return alive. The hero would not be dissuaded, but entered the forest, tracked the lion to his den, grasped him by the throat, and strangled him as he had strangled the snakes in his infancy. He then skinned the monster, whose shaggy pelt became his favorite covering.

> So from Nemea's den Alcides strode,
> The lion's yellow spoil around his shoulders flow'd.
>
> Flaccus (Elton's tr.)

Hydra of Lerna

On his return to Argos to report the successful termination of his first task, Hercules was told to repair to the marshes of Lerna, where lurked a seven-headed serpent, the Hydra, and put an end to its career of rapacity, for this snake devoured man and beast. Armed with a great sword, Hercules succeeded in cutting off one of the seven heads; but he had no sooner done so, than, to his dismay, he saw seven other heads suddenly spring from the bleeding stump. To prevent a repetition of this unpleasant miracle, Hercules bade his friend Iolaus, who had accompanied him thither to view his prowess, take a lighted brand and sear the wounds as soon as inflicted. Thanks to this wise plan, the monster was finally slain, although a friendly crab sent by Juno to defend Hydra continually pinched Hercules's feet. The hero, angry at this intervention, crushed the crab, which, however, received its reward, for the Queen of Heaven placed it in the sky as the constellation of Cancer (the Crab). The country was thus freed from its long state of thraldom; but, before leaving the scene of his second labor, Hercules dipped his arrows in the Hydra's venomous blood, knowing well that any wound they inflicted, however slight, would be sure to prove fatal.

STAG OF CERYNEA

The third task appointed by Eurystheus was the capture of the golden-horned, brazen-footed stag of Cerynea, whose fleetness was such that he seemed scarcely to touch the ground. Hercules was obliged to pursue this animal for many a weary mile before he could overtake him; and he only managed the capture by driving him into a deep snowdrift, in a distant northern land, from which he extricated him, and carried him home in triumph.

ERYMANTHIAN BOAR

The same success crowned his fourth labor, the capture of the wild boar of Erymanthus in Arcadia. Attacked by the Centaurs during the performance of this labor, Hercules turned his deadly arrows upon them, and accidentally wounded his beloved tutor Chiron, who was coming to settle the dispute. Vainly the hero applied every healing herb. The wound was mortal, and Chiron died; but in reward for his good offices the gods transferred him to the sky, where he is known as the constellation Sagittarius.

AUGEAN STABLES

Hercules was next sent to Augeas, King of Elis, who had immense droves of cattle. The stables usually occupied by these animals were in an incredibly filthy state, as they had not been cleaned in years; and now Hercules was given the task to remove the accumulated filth, and make a complete purification of the premises.

Close by these stables rushed a torrent, or rather a river, the Alpheus. Hercules, with one glance, saw the use he could make of this rushing stream, which he dammed and turned aside from its course, so that the waters passed directly through the stables, carrying away all impurities, and finally washing them perfectly clean.

Nothing else
Could clean the Augean stables.
WORDSWORTH

OPPOSITE PAGE: HERCULES AND THE HYDRA.
Antonio del Pollaiolo.

When Hercules saw that the work of purification was thoroughly accomplished, he guided the stream back to its original bed, and returned home to announce that the fifth labor was accomplished. The fabulous filth of the Augean stables, and the radical methods employed for their cleansing, have given rise to proverbial expressions still in current use.

CRETAN BULL

Hercules next journeyed off to Crete to accomplish his sixth task, the capture of a mad bull given by Neptune to Minos, king of the island. The god had sent the animal with directions that he should be offered up in sacrifice; but Minos, charmed with his unusual size and beauty, resolved to keep him, and substituted a bull from his own herds for the religious ceremony.

Angry at seeing his express command so wantonly disobeyed, Neptune maddened the bull, which rushed wildly all over the island, causing great damage. This was the animal that Hercules, with his usual strength and skill, caught and bound fast, thus finishing the sixth task.

DIOMEDES'S STEEDS

He then hastened on to Thrace, where Diomedes, the king, kept some fine coursers, which were fed on human flesh. In order to obtain a sufficient supply of fresh meat for his horses, Diomedes had decreed that all strangers who ventured into his kingdom should be seized, and, when sufficiently fat, executed, and served up in his horses' mangers. To punish Diomedes for this long-continued barbarity, Hercules fed him to his own horses, which were then led off to Eurystheus, as a token that the seventh labor was done.

HIPPOLYTA'S GIRDLE

Now, at the court of Eurystheus was his beautiful daughter, Admete, a vain princess, who delighted in dress and jewels, and who was never happier than when she obtained some new ornament or article of apparel. One day Admete heard a traveler describe a girdle worn by Hippolyta, queen of the Amazons, and was immediately seized by the desire to possess the ornament.

She imparted this wish to Eurystheus, who, delighted to gratify her as long as he could do so without taking any personal risk or trouble, sent Hercules in quest of the coveted jewel. The journey to the land of the Amazons—a fierce, warlike nation of women—was long and dangerous; but Hercules traveled on undaunted, nor paused, except when his services were needed in furthering some good work for mortals, until he reached their land, presented himself before their queen, and boldly explained the cause of his presence. Hippolyte listened to his explanation and request with queenly condescension, promised to consider the matter, and in the mean while bade him feast and rest in her palace.

Hercules would have succeeded in this undertaking without any trouble, had not Juno suddenly remembered his existence, and resolved to continue her never entirely forgotten persecutions. In the guise of an Amazon, she mingled among the women, and artfully spread the report that Hercules had really come to kidnap their queen, and that the pretended quest of the girdle was a mere excuse, and only intended to distract their attention from his real purpose. The Amazons yielded implicit belief to these rumors, flew to arms, and surrounded their queen.

> The Amazons array their ranks,
> In painted arms of radiant sheen
> Around Hippolyte the queen.
> VIRGIL (Conington's tr.)

The assembled force then attacked Hercules, who met their onslaught single-handed, defeated them, and finally bore away the prize he had risked so much to obtain. It was on his homeward journey from this expedition that he saved Hesione, Laomedon's daughter, from the jaws of the sea monster who was about to devour her, as he had devoured many a fair Trojan maid before her.

STYMPHALIAN BIRDS

Eurystheus, well pleased with the manner in which Hercules had accomplished eight out of the twelve tasks, bade him now go forth and slay the dangerous, brazen-clawed birds which hovered over the stagnant waters of Lake Stymphalus. The poisoned arrows now served him in good stead, and enabled him to put a speedy end to the whole flock.

HERCULES OBTAINING THE GIRDLE OF HYPPOLITA.
Nicolaus Knüpfer.

> His arrows slew
> The monsters hov'ring fell Stymphalus round.
>
> CATULLUS

CATTLE OF GERYONES

Hercules was next told to capture the divine cattle of Geryones, a giant of Erythea. On his way home with this marvelous herd, Hercules paused on Mount Aventine, where, during the night, the loathsome giant Cacus stole some of his cows. To punish him for this theft, Hercules forced his way into his cave, attacked him, and, after a memorable encounter, slew him. The animals were soon after delivered into the hands of Eurystheus, who then sent Hercules in search of the Golden Apples of the Hesperides.

HESPERIAN APPLES

This commission sadly perplexed Hercules, for he did not know in what portion of the world he would find these apples, which had been given to Juno as a wedding present, and which she had intrusted to the care of the Hesperides, daughters of Hesperus, god of the West. After numerous journeys and many inquiries, Hercules discovered that these maidens had carried these apples off to Africa, hung them on a tree in their garden, and placed the dragon Ladon at its foot to guard their treasures night and day. Unfortunately, no one could tell Hercules in what part of Africa the garden of the Hesperides might be situated: so he set out at a venture, determined to travel about until he gained some information. On his way he met with many adventures, and saw many strange sights. For instance, he first met the nymphs of the Eridanus River, and, questioning them about the golden apples, was told to consult old Nereus, god of the sea, who would probably be able to give him some information on the subject.

Hercules, having surprised this aged divinity while asleep on the seashore, held him fast, in spite of the multitudinous transformations he underwent in the vain hope of frightening his would-be interlocutor away. In answer to Hercules's question, he finally very reluctantly bade him seek Prometheus, who alone would be able to direct him aright.

In obedience to this advice, Hercules went to the Caucasian Mountains, where, on the brink of a mighty precipice, he found Prometheus, still bound with adamantine chains, and still a prey to the ravenous vulture. To spring up the mountain side, kill the cruel bird, snap the adamantine chains, and set free the benefactor of all mankind, was the work of but a few minutes for such a hero as Hercules; and, in gratitude for the deliverance he had so long sought in vain, Prometheus directed Hercules to his brother Atlas, telling him he would be sure to know where the apples could be found.

PYGMIES

Hercules wended his way to Africa, where Atlas dwelt, and on his way passed through the land of a diminutive race of men, called Pygmies, who were so small that they lived in constant dread of their neighbors, so much larger and stronger than they, and of the cranes, which passed over their country in great flocks, and sometimes alighted to devour their harvests.

To guard against these constant inroads, the Pygmies finally accepted the services of Antæus, a giant son of Gæa, who generously offered to defend them against all their enemies. When these little people, therefore, saw Hercules's mighty form looming up in the dim distance, they called aloud for fear, and bade Antæus go forth and kill the new invader, who, they wrongly fancied, had evil designs against them.

Proud of his strength, Antæus went to meet Hercules, and defied him. A fierce struggle was the immediate result of this challenge, and, as the combatants were of equal size and strength, the victory seemed very uncertain. At last Hercules felt his great strength begin to fail, and noticed that every time his adversary touched the ground he seemed to renew his vigor. He therefore resolved to try and win by strategy, and, watching his opportunity, seized Antæus round the waist, raised him from the ground, and held him aloft in his powerful embrace.

The giant struggled with all his might to get free; but Hercules held him fast, and felt him grow weaker and weaker, now that he was no longer sustained by his mother Earth, from whom he derived all his strength, until at last his struggles ceased, and he hung limp and lifeless in Hercules's crushing embrace.

> Lifts proud Antæus from his mother-plains,
> And with strong grasp the struggling giant strains;
> Back falls his fainting head and clammy hair,
> Writhe his weak limbs, and flits his life in air.
>
> DARWIN

ATLAS

Now that the gigantic defender of the Pygmies no longer blocked his way, Hercules traveled onward in search of Atlas, whom he finally found supporting the heavens on his broad shoulders. Atlas listened attentively to all Hercules had to say, declared he knew where the apples could be found, and promised to get them if the hero would only relieve him of his burden for a little while. Glad to accomplish his purpose so easily, Hercules allowed the burden of the heavens to be transferred to his shoulders, and Atlas hastened off to fulfill his part of the agreement.

From afar the giant saw the golden fruit glittering in the sunshine. Stealthily he drew near, entered the gardens, slew the dragon in his sleep, plucked the apples, and returned unmolested to the place where he had left Hercules. But his steps became slower and slower; and as he neared the hero, he could not help thinking with horror of the burden he must so soon resume, and bear for centuries, perhaps, without relief.

This thought oppressed him. Freedom was so sweet, that he resolved to keep it, and, coolly stepping up to Hercules, announced that he would carry the golden apples to Eurystheus, and leave him to support the heavens in his stead. Feigning a satisfaction which he was very far from feeling, Hercules acquiesced, but detained Atlas for a moment, asking him to hold the heavens until he could place a cushion on his shoulders. Good-natured, as giants proverbially are, Atlas threw the apples on the grass beside him, and assumed the incumbent weight; but Hercules, instead of preparing to resume it, picked up the apples, leaving Atlas alone, in the same plight as he had found him, there to remain until some more compassionate hero should come and set him free.

> There Atlas, son of great Iapetus,
> With head inclined and ever-during arms,
> Sustains the spacious heavens.
>
> HESIOD

It was during the course of one of his mighty labors, that Hercules, with one wrench of his powerful arm, tore a cleft in the mountains, and allowed the waters of the Sea to flow into Oceanus; and ever since, the rocks on either side of the Strait of Gibraltar have borne the name of Hercules's Pillars.

The twelfth and last task appointed by Eurystheus was the most difficult of all to perform. Hercules was commanded to descend into Hades and bring up the dog Cerberus, securely bound.

But for the last, to Pluto's drear abode
Through the dark jaws of Tænarus he went,
To drag the triple-headed dog to light.

EURIPIDES (Potter's tr.)

This command, like all the others, was speedily obeyed; but Eurystheus was so terrified at the aspect of the triple-headed dog, from the foam of whose dripping jaws the nightshade sprang, that he took refuge in a huge jar, and refused to come out until Hercules had carried the monster back to his cave.

OLYMPIAN GAMES

The twelve appointed labors were finished; the time of bondage was ended; and Hercules, a free man, could wander at his own sweet will, and enjoy the happiness of freedom. A roaming existence had, from force of habit, become a necessity: so the hero first journeyed to Olympia, where he instituted games to be celebrated every fifth year in honor of Jupiter, his father. Thence he wandered from place to place, doing good, and came to the house of Admetus, where he was surprised to find all the court in mourning.

His sympathetic inquiries soon brought forth a full account of Alcestis's sacrifice of her own life to insure the immortality of her husband. The hero's heart was touched by the king's loneliness; and he again braved the terrors of Hades, and brought Alcestis back from the grave, and restored her to her husband's arms.

Hercules took a prominent part in many heroic enterprises. Among others, he joined in the Argonautic expedition, in the battle between the Centaurs and Lapithæ, in the war of the gods and giants, and in the first siege of Troy, which proved successful.

HERCULES AND OMPHALE

But the hero, although so lately escaped from servitude, was soon obliged to return into bondage; for in a fit of anger he slew a man, and was condemned by the assembled gods to serve Omphale, Queen of Lydia, for a certain lapse of time.

No great deeds were now required of Hercules, whose strength was derided by his new mistress, and who, governing him easily by his admiration for her, made him submit to occupations unworthy of a man, and, while he was busy spinning, decked herself in his lion's skin, and brandished his renowned club.

His lion spoils the laughing Fair demands,
And gives the distaff to his awkward hands.

DARWIN

However unworthy these effeminate tasks may seem for such a hero, they proved very agreeable indeed to Hercules, who, having fallen in love with his new mistress, seemed to wish nothing better than to remain her slave forever, and end his days in idleness and pleasure. Great labors were awaiting his mighty arm, however; and the gods, at the appointed time, freed him from his bondage to the Lydian queen, and bade him go forth and do all the good in his power.

HERCULES AND DEIANEIRA

In the course of his wanderings, Hercules next met Deianeira, daughter of Œneus, and, having fallen in love with her, expressed a desire to marry her. But unfortunately another suitor, the river god Achelous, had already won the father's consent.

Achelous came,
The river god, to ask a father's voice,
And snatched me to his arms.

SOPHOCLES (Francklin's tr.)

So sure was this suitor of his attractions, that he did not even deem it necessary to secure the maiden's good graces; and when Hercules made known his love, she immediately promised to marry him, if he would only free her from the lover her father would fain force upon her. Delighted to be able to win his bride and punish his rival at the same time, Hercules challenged Achelous; and now began a wrestling match, the fame of which has come down to us through all the intervening centuries.

Achelous was an opponent worthy of Hercules, and, besides, took advantage of his power to change his form at will, further to perplex and harass the sturdy hero. At last he assumed the shape of a bull, and with lowered horns rushed toward Hercules, intending to toss him aside. The hero, skillfully avoiding his first onset, seized him by one of his great thickset horns, and held it so firmly that all the bull's efforts to free himself from his powerful grasp were vain, until the horn broke.

The Goddess of Plenty, the Attican Fortuna, a witness of this strange combat, appropriated the broken horn, stuffed her treasures in its hollow, and was so well

pleased with the effect, that she decreed it should henceforth be one of her attributes. The fight, only temporarily suspended, was now resumed with redoubled ardor, for each of the lovers was intent upon winning the hand of the fair Deianeira.

> Warm, and more warm the conflict grows:
> Dire was the noise of rattling bows,
> Of front to front opposed, and hand to hand:
> Deep was the animated strife
> For love, for conquest, and for life.
>
> SOPHOCLES (Francklin's tr.)

The victory, though long uncertain, finally rested with Hercules, who triumphantly departed with his hard-won bride, for his destiny would not permit him to tarry long in any place. Instead of wandering alone now, with none to cheer or sympathize, Hercules had Deianeira ever at his side; and after many days they came to the river Evenus, whose usually shallow and peaceful waters were swollen and turbid, for violent rainstorms had recently swept over that portion of the country.

STORY OF NESSUS

Hercules paused for a moment to contemplate the stream, and glanced about for some safe mode to transport Deianeira across. While he was thus considering, a Centaur by the name of Nessus came to his assistance, and proposed to carry the fair young bride to the other shore in complete safety, if she would but consent to mount upon his broad back.

> The hoary centaur, who was wont for hire
> To bear the traveler o'er the rapid flood
> Of deep Evenus: not with oars or sail
> He stemm'd the torrent, but with nervous arm
> Opposed and pass'd it; me, when first a bride,
> I left my father's hospitable roof
> With my Alcides, in his arms he bore
> Athwart the current.
>
> SOPHOCLES (Francklin's tr.)

OPPOSITE PAGE: HERCULES AND OMPHALE. Peter Paul Rubens.

Hercules, only too glad to avail himself of the Centaur's kind offer of assistance, quickly helped Deianeira to mount, saw them descend into the water, and prepared to follow, holding his bow and arrows aloft in one hand, and breasting the waves with the other.

Now, the Centaur Nessus did not often have the good fortune to carry such a pretty passenger as Deianeira over the river, and as he swam he made up his mind to gallop off with her as soon as he reached the opposite shore. All his strength and energy, therefore, were called into requisition; and when he reached the shore, instead of pausing to allow his fair burden to dismount, he set off as fast as he could run.

Nessus's Robe

A loud shriek from Deianeira attracted Hercules' attention, and a second later one of his poisoned arrows had brought the would-be ravisher to the ground, pierced through the heart. With dying accents the Centaur Nessus professed repentance, and bade Deianeira take his robe,—but slightly stained with the blood which gushed from the wound inflicted by the poisoned arrow,—and keep it carefully, for it had magic power; and if she ever found her husband's love waning, he assured her, that, could she but induce him to put it on, all his early affection would revive, as pure and fervent as during their honeymoon.

> "Take
> This white robe. It is costly. See, my blood
> Has stained it but a little. I did wrong:
> I know it, and repent me. If there come
> A time when he grows cold—for all the race
> Of heroes wander, nor can any love
> Fix theirs for long—take it and wrap him in it,
> And he shall love again."
>
> LEWIS MORRIS

Deianeira gratefully accepted the proffered gift, and promised to treasure it up carefully, although she sincerely hoped she would never be called upon to make use of it. Years passed by. Hercules often left Deianeira to deliver the oppressed and relieve

OPPOSITE PAGE: ALLEGORY OF FORTUNE. Salvatore Rosa.

the suffering, for people came from great distances to ask for his aid; and although his absences were sometimes prolonged, he always returned to her side, as loving as ever, and she had no cause for complaint. Finally duty took him back to the court of Eurytus, where he beheld Iole, whom he had seen and loved in the beginning of his career, but whom he had been obliged to leave to fulfill his arduous tasks. She was still young and charming, and his first glance into her sweet face rekindled all his former passion. Day after day he lingered by her side, forgetful of duty, Deianeira, and all but his first dream of love and happiness. When absent, Deianeira was wont to hear rumors of his heroic achievements; but on this occasion the only report which reached her ear was that he had returned to his allegiance to his first love, and this roused her jealousy, so long dormant.

Deianeira's Jealousy

Finally she heard that Hercules was wending his way homeward again, and her heart bounded with joy, but only to sink more heavily when told that he was accompanied by Iole and a numerous train. Then she remembered the long-forgotten gift of the Centaur. With trembling hands she sought the glittering robe, gave it to a messenger, and bade him hasten to meet Hercules, and prevail upon him to wear it for his triumphant return. The messenger, Lichas, hastened to do her bidding, and Deianeira waited with fast-beating heart for the success of her venture.

> I only wish the charm may be of power
> To win Alcides from this virgin's love,
> And bring him back to Deianeira's arms.
> SOPHOCLES (Francklin's tr.)

Lichas acquitted himself faithfully of his errand; and Hercules, viewing the costly garment, and anxious to appear to his best advantage before the bright eyes of Iole, immediately donned the richly embroidered robe.

Hercules's Death

He had no sooner put it on, than the Centaur's poisoned blood began its deadly work. First he experienced a burning, stinging sensation, which ran like fire through every vein. Vainly he tried to tear off the fatal garment. It clung to his limbs, and the poison ate its way into his flesh, until the pain was greater than he could bear.

In his rage at the trick which had been played upon him, he seized Lichas—the unfortunate bearer of the poisoned robe—by the foot, and flung him from the heights of Mount Œta down into the sea, where he perished.

> And Lichas from the top of Œta threw
> Into th' Euboic Sea.
>
> MILTON

Then, resolved to end these unendurable torments by a death worthy of his whole life, Hercules called his servants, and bade them build his funeral pyre on the mountain peak; but they, in tears, refused to obey, for they could not bear the thought of parting with their beloved master. Commands and entreaties alike failed to move them: so Hercules climbed up the mountain side alone, tore up the huge oaks by their roots, flung them one upon the other until he had raised a mighty pile, upon which he stretched his colossal, pain-racked limbs, and bade his friend Philoctetes set fire to the stupendous mass.

At first Philoctetes also refused to do his bidding; but, bribed by the promise of the world-renowned poisoned arrows, he finally consented to do as Hercules wished, and the red flames rose higher and higher, the wood crackled and burned, and the hero was soon enveloped in sheets of flame, which purged him from all mortality.

Then Jupiter came down from his glorious abode, caught the noble soul in his mighty arms, and bore it off to Olympus, there to dwell in happiness forever with Hebe, the fair goddess of youth, whose hand was given him in marriage.

> Till the god, the earthly part forsaken,
> From the man in flames asunder taken,
> Drank the heavenly ethers' purer breath.
> Joyous in the new, unwonted lightness,
> Earth's dark, heavy burden lost in death.
> High Olympus gives harmonious greeting

FOLLOWING PAGES: THE ABDUCTION OF DEIANEIRA BY THE CENTAUR NESSUS.
Louis-Jean-François Lagrenée.

To the hall where reigns his sire adored;
Youth's bright goddess, with a blush at meeting,
Gives the nectar to her lord.

SCHILLER (S. G. B.'s tr.)

WORSHIP OF HERCULES

Hercules, the special divinity of athletic sports and of strength, was principally worshiped by young men. He is generally represented in art as a tall, powerfully built
man, with a small, bearded head, a lion's skin carelessly thrown over his shoulder,
and leaning upon a massive club.

Great Alcides, stooping with his toil,
Rests on his club.

POPE

It is said that some of the games celebrated at Olympia were held in his honor,
although originally instituted by him in honor of Jupiter, his father. The Nemean
Games, celebrated in the forest of Nemea, the scene of his first great labor, were the
principal games held in Greece in commemoration of his noble deeds and early death.

PERSEUS

ACRISIUS AND DANAE

The life of Acrisius, King of Argos, had been a burden to him ever since the unfortunate day when an oracle had predicted that he would be killed by his grandson. Until then the king had been very fond of his only child, Danae, and until then, too, had thought with pride of the time when he would bestow her hand in marriage upon the noblest of all who came to woo.

Now his plans were all changed, and his only wish was to keep her unmated,—a somewhat difficult task, for the maiden was very fair, and Acrisius knew that the wily God of Love would endeavor to find some way to outwit him and bring his plans to naught. After much thought, Acrisius decided to lock Danae up in a brazen tower, around which he stationed guards to prevent any one from even approaching the captive princess.

But, although safely concealed from the eyes of men, Danae was plainly seen by the everlasting gods; and Jupiter, looking down from Olympus, beheld her in all her loveliness and in all her loneliness. She was seated on top of her brazen tower, her eyes wistfully turned toward the city, where girls of her age enjoyed freedom, and were allowed to marry when they pleased.

THE SHOWER OF GOLD

Jupiter, pitying her isolation and admiring her beauty, resolved to go down and converse with her for a little while. To avoid being seen, he changed himself into a golden shower, and gently dropped down on the turret beside her, where his presence and spirited conversation soon won the maiden's heart.

> Danae, in a brazen tower
> Where no love was, loved a shower.
> SHELLEY

This first successful visit was frequently repeated, and Danae no longer felt lonely and deserted, for Jupiter spent most of his time with her, pursuing his courtship most diligently, and finally winning her to a secret marriage, to which no one offered the slightest objection, as no one suspected his visits, which he continued quite unmolested.

BIRTH OF PERSEUS

But one morning the guards rushed in terror to Acrisius's palace to announce that Danae, his daughter, had given birth to a son, who, on account of his beauty, was called Perseus. The king no sooner learned this astonishing news, than he flew into a great rage, vowed that mother and child should perish, and dispatched the guards to fetch the unfortunate victims.

Acrisius, however, was not cruel enough to stain his own hands with his child's blood, or to witness her execution: so he ordered that she should be placed in an empty cask with her helpless infant, and exposed to the fury of the waves. These orders were speedily executed; and Danae's heart sank with terror when she felt the cask buffeted about by the great waves far out of sight of land, and out of all reach of help. Clasping her babe close to her bosom, she fervently prayed the gods to watch over them both, and bring them in safety to some hospitable shore.

> When round the well-fram'd ark the blowing blast
> Roar'd, and the heaving whirlpools of the deep
> With rough'ning surge seem'd threatening to o'erturn
> The wide-tost vessel, not with tearless cheeks
> The mother round her infant gently twined
> Her tender arm, and cried, "Ah me! my child!
> What sufferings I endure! thou sleep'st the while,
> Inhaling in thy milky-breathing breast
> The balm of slumber."
>
> SIMONIDES (Elton's tr.)

Danae at Seriphus

Her piteous prayer was evidently heard, for, after much tossing, the cask was finally washed ashore on the Island of Seriphus, where Polydectes, the king, kindly received mother and child. Here Perseus, the golden-haired, grew to manhood, and here made his first appearance in games and combats.

In the mean while, Polydectes had fallen in love with Danae, and expressed his desire to marry her; but Danae did not return his affections, and would not consent. Angry at her persistent refusal of his proposals, Polydectes wished to compel her to obey, and thereby incurred the wrath of young Perseus, who loudly declared that none should dare force his mother as long as he were there to defend her. This boast did not at all allay the monarch's wrath; and, hoping to get rid of the young boaster, he bade him go forth and slay Medusa, if he wished to convince people that his bravery was real.

The Gorgons

This Medusa was one of the three Gorgons. Her sisters, Euryale and Stheno, although immortal, had never had any claims to beauty; but Medusa, when only a girl, had been considered very handsome indeed. Her home, in a land where the sun never shone, was very distasteful to her, so she entreated Minerva to let her go and visit the beautiful sunny south.

But when Minerva refused to grant her wish, she reviled the goddess, and declared that nothing but a conviction that mortals would no longer consider her beautiful if they but once beheld Medusa, could have prompted this denial. This presumptuous remark so incensed Minerva, that, to punish her for her vanity, she changed her beautiful curling locks into hissing, writhing serpents, and decreed that one glance into her still beautiful face would suffice to change the beholder into stone.

Fatal Beauty! thou didst seem
The phantom of some fearful dream.
Extremes of horror and of love
Alternate o'er our senses move,
As, rapt and spellbound, we survey
The horrid coils which round thee play,
And mark thy wild, enduring smile,
Lit by no mortal fire the while,
Formed to attract all eyes to thee,
And yet their withering blight to be;
Thy power mysterious to congeal
And from life's blood its warmth to steal,
To petrify the mortal clay
In its first gleam of wild dismay,
Is a dread gift to one like thee,
Cursed with a hateful destiny.

MRS. ST. JOHN

PERSEUS'S QUEST

The gods, who had carefully watched over Perseus through his childhood and youth, now decided to lend him their aid, so that he might successfully accomplish the great task of slaying Medusa. Pluto lent him a magic helmet, which made the wearer invisible at will; Mercury attached his own winged sandals to the youth's heels, to endow him with great rapidity of flight; while Minerva armed him with her own mirror-like shield, the dreadful Ægis.

Minerva thus to Perseus lent her shield;
Secure of conquest, sent him to the field:
The hero acted what the queen ordain'd,
So was his fame complete.

PRIOR

THE GRÆÆ

Thus equipped, Perseus flew northward until he came to the land of perpetual darkness, the home of the Grææ, three horrible sisters, who possessed but one eye and one tooth, which they handed about and used in turn, and who were the only living beings cognizant of the place where Medusa dwelt.

Invisible by virtue of his magic helmet, Perseus drew near the cave without fear of detection, and intercepted the eye while on its way from one sister to another. As soon as it was safe in his possession, he spoke to them, promising to restore it if they would only give him accurate directions for finding Medusa. The sisters, eager to recover the treasured eye, immediately gave the desired information; and Perseus, having honorably fulfilled his share of the contract, departed in search of Medusa.

DEATH OF MEDUSA

Perseus at last perceived the Gorgons' home in the dim distance; and, as he was fully aware of Medusa's petrifying proclivities, he advanced very cautiously, holding his shield before him at such an angle that all surrounding objects were clearly reflected on its smooth, mirrorlike surface.

He thus discovered Medusa asleep, raised his sword, and, without looking at anything but her mirrored form, severed her head from her body, seized it in one hand, and, holding it persistently behind his back, flew away in great haste, lest the two remaining Gorgons should fall upon him and attempt to avenge their sister's death.

BIRTH OF SNAKES

Perseus then swiftly winged his way over land and sea, carefully holding his ghastly trophy behind him; and as he flew, Medusa's blood trickled down on the hot African sand, where it gave birth to a race of poisonous reptiles destined to infest the region in future ages, and cause the death of many an adventurous explorer. The drops which fell into the sea were utilized by Neptune, who created from them the famous winged steed called Pegasus.

FOLLOWING PAGES: PERSEUS, UNDER THE PROTECTION OF MINERVA, TURNS PHINEUS TO STONE BY BRANDISHING THE HEAD OF MEDUSA.
Jean-Marc Nattier.

And the life drops from thy head
On Libyan sands, by Perseus shed,
Sprang a scourging race from thee—
Fell types of artful mystery.

MRS. ST. JOHN

The return journey was long and wearisome, and on his way the hero had many adventures. Once, when flying high above a mountainous country, he caught a glimpse of Atlas, his pale face turned up to the heavens, whose weight he had patiently borne for many a long year,—a burden which seemed all the more grievous after the short taste of freedom he had enjoyed while Hercules stood in his place,—

Supporting on his shoulders the vast pillar
Of Heaven and Earth, a weight of cumbrous grasp.

ÆSCHYLUS (Potter's tr.)

ATLAS PETRIFIED

When Atlas saw Perseus flying toward him, hope revived, for he remembered that Fate had decreed that it was this hero who was to slay the Gorgon; and he thought, that, if he could but once gaze upon her stony face, he would be free from pain and weariness forever. As soon as the hero was within hearing, Atlas therefore addressed him as follows:—

"Hasten now, Perseus, and let me look upon the Gorgon's face, for the agony of my labor is well-nigh greater than I can bear." So Perseus hearkened unto the word of Atlas, and he unveiled before him the dead face of Medusa. Eagerly he gazed for a moment on the changeless countenance, as though beneath the blackness of great horror he yet saw the wreck of her ancient beauty and pitied her for her hopeless woe. But in an instant the straining eyes were stiff and cold; and it seemed to Perseus, as he rose again into the pale yellow air, that the gray hairs which streamed from the giant's head were like the snow which rests on the peak of a great mountain, and that in place of the trembling limbs he saw only the rents and clefts on a rough hillside.

Thus the mere sight of Medusa changed Atlas into the rugged mountains which have since borne his name; and, as their summits are lost in the clouds, the ancients supposed they sustained the full weight of the heavenly vault.

Story of Andromeda

Thence Perseus flew on until he reached the seashore, where a strange sight greeted him. Away down on the "rock-bound coast," so near the foaming billows that their spray continually dashed over her fair limbs, a lovely maiden was chained fast to an overhanging rock. This maiden was the Princess Andromeda. To atone for the vanity of her mother, Cassiopeia, who claimed she was fairer than any of the sea nymphs, she had been exposed there as prey for a terrible sea monster sent to devastate the homes along the coast.

An oracle, when consulted, declared that the monster would not depart until Andromeda was sacrificed to his fury; and Perseus could even now perceive the receding procession which had solemnly accompanied her to the appointed place of sacrifice, and chained her fast.

At the same time, too, he saw the waters below the maiden lashed to foam by the monster's tail, and the scales of his hideous body slowly rising up out of the water. Fascinated by this horrible sight, the maiden's eyes were fixed on the monster. She did not see the rapid approach of her deliverer, who, dauntless, drew his sword from its scabbard, and, swooping down, attacked the monster, cheered by the shouts of the people, who had seen him, and now rushed back to witness the slaying of their foe.

> On the hills a shout
> Of joy, and on the rocks the ring of mail;
> And while the hungry serpent's gloating eyes
> Were fixed on me, a knight in casque of gold
> And blazing shield, who with his flashing blade
> Fell on the monster. Long the conflict raged,
> Till all the rocks were red with blood and slime,
> And yet my champion from those horrible jaws
> And dreadful coils was scathless.
>
> Lewis Morris

Of course, this fierce struggle could have but one conclusion; and when Perseus had slain the monster, freed Andromeda from her chains, and restored her to the arms of her overjoyed parents, they immediately offered any reward he might be pleased to claim. When he, therefore, expressed a desire to marry the maiden he had so bravely rescued, they gladly gave him her hand, although in early youth the princess had been promised to her uncle Phineus.

PHINEUS PETRIFIED

Preparations for the marriage were immediately begun; and the former suitor, who had been too cowardly to venture a single blow to deliver her from the monster, prepared to fight the rival who was about to carry off his promised bride. Unbidden he came to the marriage feast with a number of armed followers, and was about to carry off Andromeda, when Perseus suddenly bade his adherents stand behind him, unveiled the Medusa head, and, turning its baleful face toward Phineus and his followers, changed them all into stone.

The interrupted marriage feast was now resumed; and when it was over, Perseus took his bride to Seriphus. There, hearing that Polydectes had dared to ill treat his mother because she still refused to accede to his wishes and become his wife, he changed the importunate king into a rock by showing him his Medusa trophy, gave the kingdom to the king's brother, and, accompanied by wife and mother, returned to his native land. The borrowed helmet, sandals, and shield were all duly restored to their respective owners, and the Medusa head was given to Minerva in token of gratitude for her help. Greatly pleased with this gift, the goddess set it in the center of her terrible Ægis, where it retained all its petrifying power, and served her in many a fight.

RETURN TO ARGOS

Arrived at Argos, Perseus discovered that a usurper had claimed his grandfather's throne. To hurl the unlawful claimant from his exalted seat, and compel him to make full restitution and atonement, was but a trifle for the hero who had conquered Medusa; and Acrisius, now old and weak, was taken from the prison where he languished, and restored to his wonted honors, by the very youth he had been taught to fear.

But the gods' decree was always sure to be fulfilled sooner or later; and one day, when Perseus was playing quoits, he accidentally killed his grandfather. To remain at Argos, haunted by the memory of this involuntary crime, was too painful for him: so he exchanged his kingdom for another, that of Mycenæ, which he ruled wisely and well. When Perseus died, after a long and glorious reign, the gods, who had always loved him, placed him among the stars, where he can still be seen, with his wife Andromeda, and mother-in-law Cassiopeia.

PRECEDING PAGES: PERSEUS AND ANDROMEDA.
Charles-André van Loo.

THESEUS

W hen yet but a very young man, Ægeus, King of Athens, journeyed off to Trœzene, where he fell in love with and married a pretty young princess by the name of Æthra. For some reason, which mythologists do not make known, the king was forced to return alone to Athens; but ere he departed he concealed his sword and sandals beneath a stone, bidding his wife remember, that, as soon as the strength of their son Theseus permitted, he must raise the rock, appropriate sword and sandals, and come and join him in Athens, where he should be introduced to the people as his son and heir. These instructions given, Ægeus bade a fond farewell to his wife and infant son, and returned home.

As the years passed by, they brought strength, beauty, and wisdom to Theseus, whose fame began to be published abroad. At last Æthra deemed him strong enough to raise the rock beneath which his father's trusty weapon lay; and, conducting him to the spot where it was, she told him the whole story, and bade him try his strength.

Theseus immediately obeyed. With a mighty effort he raised the rock, and, to his great satisfaction, found the sword and sandals in a perfect state of preservation. Sword in hand, he then set out for Athens,—a long and dangerous journey. He proceeded slowly and cautiously, for he knew that many dangers lurked along his pathway, and that ere he reached his father's city he would have to encounter both giants and monsters, who would strive to bar his way.

Periphetes

He was not at all mistaken in his previsions; for Trœzene was scarcely lost to sight ere he came across the giant Periphetes, son of Vulcan, who stood in the road and attacked with a huge club, whose blows were generally fatal, all who strove to pass. Adroitly evading the giant's first onslaught, Theseus plunged his sword deep into his huge side ere he could renew the attack, and brought him lifeless to the ground.

SINIS

Theseus then disarmed his fallen foe, and, retaining the club for future use, continued his journey in peace, until he came to the Isthmus of Corinth, where two adventures awaited him. The first was with a cruel giant named Sinis, nicknamed The Pine-bender, whose usual practice was to bend some huge pine until its top touched the ground, and call to any unsuspecting passer-by to seize it and lend him a helping hand for a moment. Then, as soon as the innocent stranger had complied with his request, he would suddenly let go the pine, which, freed from his gigantic grasp, sprang back to its upright position, and hurled the unfortunate traveler way up in the air, to be dashed to pieces against the rocky mountain side.

Theseus, who had already heard of the giant's stratagem, skillfully eluded the danger, and finally caused Sinis to perish by the same cruel death which he had dealt out to so many others.

SCIRON

In one place the Isthmus of Corinth was exceedingly narrow, and the only practicable pathway led along a rocky ledge, guarded by a robber named Sciron, who forced all who tried to pass him to wash his feet. While the traveler was thus engaged, and knelt in the narrow pathway to do his bidding, he would suddenly raise his foot, kick him over the side, and hurl him down into the sea below, where a huge tortoise was ever waiting with gaping jaws to devour the victims.

Instead of yielding to Sciron's exactions, Theseus drew his sword, and by his determined bearing so terrified the robber, that he offered him a free passage. This offer, however, did not satisfy Theseus, who said he would sheathe his sword only on condition that Sciron performed for him the menial office he had imposed upon so many others. Sciron dared not refuse, and obeyed in fear and trembling; but he was doomed never to molest any one again, for Theseus kicked him over the precipice, into the breakers, where the tortoise feasted upon his remains with as keen a relish as upon former victims.

CERCYON AND PROCRUSTES

After disposing of another world-renowned robber, Cercyon (The Wrestler), Theseus encountered Procrustes (The Stretcher), a cruel giant, who, under pretext of entertainment, deluded travelers into entering his home, where he had two beds of very different dimensions,—one unusually short, the other unusually long. If the unfortunate traveler were a short man, he was put to bed in the long bedstead, and his limbs were pulled out of joint to make him fit it; but if, on the contrary, he were tall, he was assigned the short bed, and the superfluous length of limb was lopped off under the selfsame pretext. Taking Procrustes quite unawares, Theseus gave him a faint idea of the sufferings he had inflicted upon others by making him try each bed in turn, and then, to avoid his continuing these evil practices, put an end to his wretched existence.

Theseus successfully accomplished a few more exploits of a similar character, and finally reached Athens, where he found that his fame had preceded him.

> In days of old, there liv'd of mighty fame,
> A valiant prince, and Theseus was his name:
> A chief, who more in feats of arms excell'd,
> The rising nor the setting sun beheld.
>
> MORRIS

MEDEA'S DRAUGHT

The first tidings that there reached his ear were that Ægeus had just married Medea, the enchantress; but, although these tidings were very unwelcome, he hastened on to his father's court, to make himself known, and receive the welcome promised so many years before. Medea, seated by Ægeus's side, no sooner saw the young stranger draw near, than she knew him, and foresaw that he had come to demand his rights. To prevent his making known claims which might interfere with the prospects of her future offspring, she hastily mixed a deadly poison in a cup, which she filled with fragrant wine, and bade Ægeus offer it to the stranger.

The monarch was about to execute her apparently hospitable purpose, when his eye suddenly rested upon the sword at Theseus's side, which he immediately recognized. One swift glance into the youth's open face convinced him that Æthra's son stood before him, and he eagerly stretched out his arms to clasp him to his heart. This sudden movement upset the goblet, and the poisonous contents, falling upon a dog lying at the king's feet, caused his almost instantaneous death. Seeing her crime discovered and Theseus recognized, Medea quickly mounted her magic dragon car, and fled to Media, whence she never returned.

Tribute to the Minotaur

One day, some time after his arrival at Athens, Theseus heard a sound of weeping and great lamentation throughout all the city, and in reply to his wondering inquiries was told, that ever since an unfortunate war between the Cretans and Athenians, the latter, who had been vanquished, were obliged to pay a yearly tribute of seven youths and as many maidens, destined to serve as food for the Minotaur. Further questions evolved the fact that the Minotaur was a hideous monster, the property of Minos, King of Crete, who kept it in an intricate labyrinth, constructed for that express purpose by Dædalus, the far-famed architect.

> There lived and flourished long ago, in famous Athens town,
> One Dædalus, a carpenter of genius and renown;
> ('Twas he who with an augur taught mechanics how to bore,—
> An art which the philosophers monopolized before.)
>
> > SAXE

Dædalus and Icarus

This labyrinth was so very intricate, that those who entered could not find their way out; and even Dædalus and his son Icarus, after many days' attempt, found they could not leave it. Rather than remain imprisoned forever, Dædalus then manufactured wings for himself and for his son, and determined to make use of them to effect his escape.

> Now Dædalus, the carpenter, had made a pair of wings,
> Contrived of wood and feathers and a cunning set of springs,
> By means of which the wearer could ascend to any height,
> And sail about among the clouds as easy as a kite.
>
> > SAXE

After repeated cautions to his son not to venture too high, lest the sun's heat should melt the wax fixing the feathers to the frame, Dædalus bade Icarus don his plumage and fly to a country where they would be free, promising to follow him thither very shortly.

ICARUS AND DÆDALUS. Charles Paul Landon.

"My Icarus!" he says; "I warn thee fly
  Along the middle track: nor low, nor high;
  If low, thy plumes may flag with ocean's spray;
  If high, the sun may dart his fiery ray."

OVID (Elton's tr.)

ARIADNE. John William Waterhouse.

Delighted with this new mode of travel, Icarus flew swiftly along. Little by little he forgot the danger and his father's caution, and rose up higher and higher, until he could bask in the direct rays of the ardent sun. The heat, which seemed so grateful after his chilly flight, soon softened and melted the wax on his wings; and Icarus, no longer supported by the light feathers, sank down faster and faster, until he fell into the sea, where he was drowned, and which, in memory of him, bears the name of Icarian to this day.

These varied details kindled Theseus's love of adventure, and still further strengthened him in his sudden resolve to join the mournful convoy, try his strength against the awful Minotaur, and, if possible, save his country from further similar exactions.

> While Attica thus groan'd, with ills opprest;
> His country's wrongs inflam'd brave Theseus' breast;
> Instant his gen'rous soul resolv'd to save
> Cecrops's great offspring from a timeless grave.
>
> CATULLUS

Even his father's tears and entreaties were powerless to move him from his purpose, and, the hour having come, he embarked upon the black-sailed vessel which was to bear the yearly tribute to Crete, promising to change the black sails for snowy white ones if he were fortunate enough to return victorious.

TALUS

Favorable winds soon wafted the galley to distant Crete, and as they sailed along the coast, searching for the harbor, they were challenged by the brazen giant Talus, who walked daily thrice around the whole island, killing, by contact with his red-hot body, all who had no business to land on that coast. Knowing, however, that the black-sailed galley brought a fresh supply of youths and maidens for the terrible Minotaur, Talus let it pass unharmed; and the victims were brought into the presence of Minos, who personally inspected each new freight-load, to make sure he was not being cheated by the Athenians.

ARIADNE'S CLEW

At the monarch's side stood his fair daughter Ariadne, whose tender heart was filled with compassion when she beheld the frail maidens and gallant youths about to perish by such a loathsome death. Theseus, by right of his birth, claimed the precedence, and proffered a request to be the first victim,—a request which the king granted with a sardonic smile, ere he returned unmoved to his interrupted feast.

Unnoticed by all, Ariadne slipped out of the palace, and, under cover of the darkness, entered the prison where Theseus was confined. There she tremblingly offered him a ball of twine and a sharp sword, bidding him tie one end of the twine to the entrance of the labyrinth, and keep the other in his hand as a clew to find the way out again should the sword enable him to kill the dreaded Minotaur. In token of gratitude for this timely assistance, Theseus solemnly promised Ariadne to take her with him to Athens as his bride, were he only successful in his undertaking.

At dawn the next day Theseus was conducted to the entrance of the labyrinth, and there left to await the tender mercies of the Minotaur. Like all heroes, he preferred to meet any danger rather than remain inactive: so, mindful of Ariadne's instructions, he fastened his twine to the entrance, and then boldly penetrated into the intricate ways of the labyrinth, where many whitening bones plainly revealed the fate of all who had preceded him.

THESEUS AND THE MINOTAUR

He had not gone very far before he encountered the Minotaur,—a creature more hideous than fancy can paint,—and he was obliged to use all his skill and ingenuity to avoid falling a prey to the monster's appetite, and all his strength to lay him low at last.

The Minotaur slain, Theseus hastily retraced his footsteps.

> And the slender clew,
> Prepar'd in secret by th' enamor'd maid,
> Thro' the curv'd labyrinth his steps convey'd.
>
> CATULLUS

THESEUS'S ESCAPE

Arrived at the place where his ship rode at anchor, he found his companions and Ariadne awaiting him, and, springing on board, bade the sailors weigh anchor as quickly as possible. They were almost out of reach of the Cretan shores, when Talus came into view, and, perceiving that his master's prisoners were about to escape, leaned forward to catch the vessel by its rigging. Theseus, seeing this, sprang forward, and dealt the giant such a blow, that he lost his balance and fell into the deep sea, where he was drowned, and where thermal springs still bear witness to the heat of his brazen body.

Ariadne Forsaken

The returning vessel, favored by wind and tide, made but one port, Naxos; and here youths and maidens landed to view the beautiful island. Ariadne strayed apart, and threw herself down upon the ground to rest, where, before she was aware of it, sleep overtook her. Now, although very brave, Theseus was not very constant. He had already grown weary of Ariadne's love; and, when he saw her thus asleep, he basely summoned his companions, embarked with them, and set sail, leaving her alone upon the island, where Bacchus soon came to console her for the loss of her faithless lover.

Theseus's Punishment

Theseus, having committed a deed heinous in the eyes of gods and men, was doomed to suffer just punishment. In his preoccupation he entirely forgot his promise to change the black sails for white; and Ægeus, from Attica's rocky shore, seeing the sable sails when the vessel was yet far from land, immediately concluded that his son was dead, and in his grief cast himself into the sea since known as the Ægean, where he perished.

> As from a mountain's snowy top are driv'n
> The rolling clouds, by the rude blasts of heav'n;
> So from the mem'ry of lost Theseus fled
> Those dictates, which before his reason sway'd:
> But now his father from the ramparts' height,
> All bath'd in tears, directs his eager sight;
> O'er the wide sea, distended by the gale,
> He spies, with dread amaze, the lurid sail.
>
> Catullus

Theseus's Reign and Marriage

Theseus, on entering the city, heard of his father's death; and when he realized that it had been caused by his carelessness, he was overwhelmed with grief and remorse. All the cares of royalty and the wise measures he introduced for the happiness of his people could not divert his mind from this terrible catastrophe: so he finally resolved to resign his authority and set out again in search of adventures, which might help him forget his woes. He therefore made an excursion into the land of the Amazons, where Hercules had preceded him, and whence he brought back Hippolyte, whom he married. Theseus was now very happy indeed, and soon all his hopes were crowned by the birth of a son, whom he called Hippolytus. Shortly after this joyful event, the Amazons invaded his country under pretext of rescuing their kidnapped queen, and in the battle which ensued Hippolyte was accidentally wounded by an arrow, and breathed her last in Theseus's arms.

Theseus next set out with an Athenian army to fight Pirithous, king of the Lapithæ, who had dared to declare war; but when the armies were face to face, the two chiefs, seized with a sudden liking for each other, simultaneously cast down their weapons, and, falling on each other's necks, embraced, and swore an eternal friendship.

CENTAURS AND LAPITHÆ

To show his devotion to this newly won friend, Theseus consented to accompany him to the court of Adrastus, King of Argos, and witness his marriage to Hippodamia, daughter of the king. Many guests were, of course, present to witness the marriage ceremony, among others Hercules and a number of the Centaurs. The latter, struck with admiration for the bride's unusual beauty, made an attempt to kidnap her, which was frustrated by the Lapithæ, seconded by Theseus and Hercules. The terrible struggle which ensued between the conflicting parties has ever been a favorite subject in art, and is popularly known as the "Battle between the Centaurs and Lapithæ."

THESEUS IN HADES

The hotly contested bride did not, however, enjoy a very long life, and Pirithous soon found himself, like Theseus, a disconsolate widower. To avoid similar bereavement in future, they both resolved to secure goddesses, who, being immortal, would share their thrones forever. Aided by Pirithous, Theseus carried off Helen, the daughter of Jupiter, and, as she was still but a child, intrusted her to the care of his mother, Æthra, until she attained a suitable age for matrimony. Then, in return for Pirithous's kind offices, he accompanied him to Hades, where they intended to carry off Proserpina.

While they were thus engaged, Helen's twin brothers, Castor and Pollux, came to Athens, delivered her from captivity, and carried her home in triumph. As for Theseus and Pirithous, their treacherous intention was soon discovered by Pluto, who set the

FOLLOWING PAGES: THESEUS AND THE MINOTAUR.
Charles Edward Chase.

first on an enchanted rock, from which he could not descend unassisted, and bound the second to the constantly revolving wheel of his father, Ixion.

When Hercules was in Hades in search of Cerberus, he delivered Theseus from his unpleasant position, and thus enabled him to return to his own home, where he now expected to spend the remainder of his life in peace.

Phædra and Hippolytus

Although somewhat aged by this time, Theseus was still anxious to marry, and looked about him for a wife to cheer his loneliness. Suddenly he remembered that Ariadne's younger sister, Phædra, must be a charming young princess, and sent an embassy to obtain her hand in marriage. The embassy proved successful, and Phædra came to Athens; but, young and extremely beautiful, she was not at all delighted with her aged husband, and, instead of falling in love with him, bestowed all her affections upon his son, Hippolytus, a virtuous youth, who utterly refused to listen to her proposals to elope. In her anger at finding her advances scorned, Phædra went to Theseus and accused Hippolytus of attempting to kidnap her. Theseus, greatly incensed at what he deemed his son's dishonorable behavior, implored Neptune to punish the youth, who was even then riding in his chariot close by the shore. In answer to this prayer, a great wave suddenly arose, dashed over the chariot, and drowned the young charioteer, whose lifeless corpse was finally flung ashore at Phædra's feet. When the unfortunate queen saw the result of her false accusations, she confessed her crime, and, in her remorse and despair, hung herself.

Death of Theseus

As for Theseus, soured by these repeated misfortunes, he grew so stern and tyrannical, that he gradually alienated his people's affections, until at last they hated him, and banished him to the Island of Scyros, where, in obedience to a secret order, Lycomedes, the king, treacherously slew him by hurling him from the top of a steep cliff into the sea. As usual, when too late, the Athenians repented of their ingratitude, and in a fit of tardy remorse deified this hero, and built a magnificent temple on the Acropolis in his honor. This building, now used as a museum, contains many relics of Greek art. Theseus's bones were piously brought back, and inhumed in Athens, where he was long worshiped as a demigod.

JASON

At Iolcus, in Thessaly, there once reigned a virtuous king, Æson, with his good wife, Alcimede. Their happiness, however, was soon disturbed by Pelias, the king's brother, who, aided by an armed host, took forcible possession of the throne. Æson and Alcimede, in fear of their lives, were forced to resort to a hasty and secret flight, taking with them their only son, Jason.

The king and queen soon found a place of refuge, but, afraid lest their hiding place should be discovered and they should all be slain by the cruel Pelias, they intrusted their son to the Centaur Chiron, revealing to him alone the secret of the child's birth, and bidding him train him up to avenge their wrongs.

Chiron discharged his duties most faithfully, trained the young prince with great care, and soon made him the wisest and most skillful of his pupils. The years spent by Jason in the diligent acquisition of knowledge, strength, and skill, passed very quickly; and at last the time came when Chiron made known to him the secret of his birth, and the story of the wrongs inflicted by Pelias, the usurper, upon his unfortunate parents.

Jason's Vow

This tale aroused the young prince's anger, and made him solemnly vow to punish his uncle, or perish in the attempt. Chiron encouraged him to start, and in parting bade him remember that Pelias alone had injured him, but that all the rest of the human race were entitled to any aid he could bestow. Jason listened respectfully to his tutor's last instructions; then, girding his sword and putting on his sandals, he set out on his journey to Iolcus.

It was early in the spring, and the young man had not gone very far before he came to a stream, which, owing to the usual freshets of the season, was almost impassable. Jason, however, quite undaunted by the rushing, foaming waters, was about to attempt the crossing, when he saw an aged woman not far from him, gazing in helpless despair at the waters she could not cross.

Naturally kind-hearted and helpful, and, besides that, mindful of Chiron's last recommendation, Jason offered the old woman his assistance, proposing to carry her across on his back if she would but lend him her staff to lean upon. The old woman gladly accepted this offer; and a few moments later, Jason, bending beneath his strange load, was battling with the rapid current.

After many an effort, breathless and almost exhausted, Jason reached the opposite bank, and, after depositing his burden there, scrambled up beside her, casting a rueful glance at the torrent, which had wrenched off one of his golden sandals. He was about to part from the old dame with a kindly farewell, when she was suddenly transformed into a large, handsome, imperious-looking woman, whom, owing to the peacock by her side, he immediately recognized as Juno, queen of heaven. He bent low before her, and claimed her aid and protection, which she graciously promised ere she vanished from his sight.

With eager steps Jason now pressed onward, nor paused until he came in view of his native city. As he drew near, he noticed an unusual concourse of people, and upon inquiry discovered that Pelias was celebrating a festival in honor of the immortal gods. Up the steep ascent leading to the temple Jason hastened, and pressed on to the innermost circle of spectators, until he stood in full view of his enemy Pelias, who, unconscious of coming evil, continued offering the sacrifice.

THE ONE SANDAL

At last the ceremony was completed, and the king cast an arrogant glance over the assembled people. His eyes suddenly fell upon Jason's naked foot, and he grew pale with horror as there flashed into his memory the recollection of an ancient oracle, warning him to beware of the man who appeared before him wearing but one sandal. Pelias tremblingly bade the guards bring forth the uninvited stranger. His orders were obeyed; and Jason, confronting his uncle boldly, summoned him to make a full restitution of the power he had so unjustly seized.

PHRYXUS AND HELLE

To surrender power and wealth and return to obscurity was not to be thought of; but Pelias artfully concealed his displeasure, and told his nephew that they would discuss the matter and come to an amicable understanding after the banquet, which was already spread and awaiting their presence. During the festive meal, bards sang of all the heroic deeds accomplished by great men; and Pelias, by judicious flattery, stimulated Jason to attempt similar feats. At last the musicians recited the story of Phryxus and Helle, the son and daughter of Athamas and Nephele, who, to escape the cruel treatment of their stepmother, Ino, mounted a winged, golden-fleeced ram sent by Neptune to transport them to Colchis.

The ram flew over land and sea; but Helle, frightened at the sight of the waves tossing far beneath her, suddenly lost her hold on the golden fleece, and tumbled off the ram's back into a portion of the sea since known as the Hellespont,

> Where beauteous Helle found a watery grave.
>
> MELEAGER

Phryxus, more fortunate than his sister, reached Colchis in safety, and in gratitude to the gods sacrificed the ram they had sent to deliver him, and hung its golden fleece on a tree, near which he stationed a dragon to guard it night and day. The bards then went on to relate that the glittering trophy still hung there, awaiting a hand bold enough to slay the dragon and bear it off.

THE GOLDEN FLEECE

This tale and his liberal potations greatly excited the youth Jason; and Pelias, perceiving it, hypocritically regretted his inability to win the golden fleece, and softly insinuated that young men of the present generation were not brave enough to risk their lives in such a glorious cause. The usurper's crafty remarks had the desired effect; for Jason suddenly sprang from his seat, and vowed he would go in quest of the golden fleece. Pelias, quite certain that the rash youth would lose his life in the attempt, and thus cause no more trouble, with much difficulty restrained all expressions of joy, and dared him to make the attempt.

> With terror struck, lest by young Jason's hand
> His crown should be rent from him, Pelias sought
> By machinations dark to slay his foe.
> From Colchis's realm to bring the golden fleece
> He charged the youth.
>
> ORPHIC ARGONAUTICS

THE SPEAKING OAK

When Jason, sobered and refreshed by a long night's rest, perceived how foolish had been his vow, he would fain have recalled it; but, mindful of Chiron's teachings ever to be true to his word, he resolved to depart for Colchis. To secure Juno's assistance, he began by visiting her shrine at Dodona, where the oracle, a Speaking Oak, assured him of the goddess's good will and efficacious protection. Next the Speaking Oak bade him cut off one of its own mighty limbs, and carve from it a figurehead for the swift-sailing vessel which Minerva, at Juno's request, would build for his use from pine trees grown on Mount Pelion.

THE ARGO AND CREW

Jason, having finished his figurehead, found that it too had the gift of speech, and that it would occasionally vouchsafe sage counsel in the direction of his affairs. When quite completed, Jason called his vessel the Argo (swift-sailing), and speedily collected a crew of heroes as brave as himself, among whom were Hercules, Castor, Pollux, Peleus, Admetus, Theseus, and Orpheus, who were all glad to undertake the perilous journey to lands unknown. To speed them on their way, Juno then bargained with Æolus for favorable winds, and forbade any tempest which might work them harm.

> Then with a whistling breeze did Juno fill the sail,
> And Argo, self-impell'd, shot swift before the gale.
> ONOMACRITUS (Elton's tr.)

STORY OF HYLAS

On several occasions the heroes landed, either to renew their stock of provisions or to recruit their strength, but in general every delay brought them some misfortune. Once Hercules, having landed with a youth named Hylas to cut wood for new oars, bade the youth go to a neighboring spring and draw a pitcher of water to quench the thirst produced by his exertions. The youth promptly departed; but as he bent over the fountain, the nymphs, enamored with his beauty, drew him down into their moist abode to keep them company. Hercules, after vainly waiting for Hylas's return, went in search of him, but could find no trace of him, and, in his grief and disappointment at the death of his young friend, refused to continue the expedition, and, deserting the Argonauts, made his way home alone and on foot.

PHINEUS AND THE HARPIES

On another occasion, when Jason visited Phineus, the blind king of Thrace, he heard that this monarch's life was imbittered by the Harpies, vile monsters, part woman, part bird, who ate or befouled all the food placed before him, and never let him eat a mouthful in peace. Having repeated this tale to his companions, the two sons of Boreas, who were also in the Argo, begged permission to drive them away. Jason could not refuse their request; and the two youths, with drawn swords, pursued the Harpies to the Strophades Islands, where the birds promised to remain.

Jason, sailing on in the mean while, was attacked by a flock of brazen-feathered birds, which rained their sharp plumage down upon the Argonauts, wounding many of them sorely. The captain of the expedition, seeing weapons were of no avail against these foes, consulted the figurehead, and, in obedience to its directions, clashed his arms against his shield, until, terrified by the din, the brazen-feathered birds flew rapidly away, uttering discordant cries of terror.

THE SYMPLEGADES

Some time during the course of their journey the Argonauts came to the Symplegades,——floating rocks which continually crashed together, and ground to powder all objects caught between them. Jason knew he was obliged to pass between these rocks or give up the expedition: so, calculating that the speed of his vessel was equal to that of a dove on the wing, he sent one out before him. The dove flew safely between the rocks, losing only one of its tail feathers as they again clashed together. Watching his opportunity, therefore, Jason bade his men row swiftly. The Argo darted through the opening, and, when the rocks again came into contact, they merely grazed the rudder. As a vessel had passed between them unharmed, their power for evil left them, and they were chained fast to the bottom of the sea, near the mouth of the Bosporus, where they remained immovable like any other rocks.

ARRIVAL AT COLCHIS

The Argonauts, after other adventures far too numerous to recount in detail, reached the Colchian shores, and presented themselves before Æetes, the king, to whom they

FOLLOWING PAGES: THE CAPTURE OF THE GOLDEN FLEECE.
Jean-François de Troy.

made known their errand. Loath to part with his golden treasure, Æetes declared, that, before Jason could obtain the fleece, he must catch and harness two wild, fire-breathing bulls dedicated to Vulcan, and make use of them to plow a stony piece of ground sacred to Mars. This done, he must sow the field with some dragon's teeth, as Cadmus had done, conquer the giants which would spring up, and, last of all, slay the guardian dragon, or the fleece would never be his.

Medea's Aid

One of these tasks would have sufficed to dismay many a brave youth; but Jason was of the dauntless kind, and merely hastened down to his vessel to ask the figurehead how he had better proceed. On his way to the seashore he met the king's daughter, Medea, a beautiful young sorceress, who had been charmed by his modest but firm bearing, and who was quite ready to bring her magic to his aid if he would but promise to marry her. Jason, susceptible to her attractions, and free from any conflicting ties, readily agreed to her proposal, and, carrying out her directions, caught and harnessed the fiery bulls, plowed the field, and sowed it with the dragon's teeth.

> And how he yoked the bulls, whose breathings fiery glow'd,
> And with the dragons' teeth the furrow'd acres sow'd.
>
> ONOMACRITUS (Elton's tr.)

But when he saw glittering spears and helmets grow out of the ground, and beheld the close ranks of giants in full armor, he was filled with dismay, and would have fled had it been possible. However, aware that such a performance would insure his ruin, he stood his ground, and, when the phalanx was quite near him, threw a handful of dust full in the giants' faces. Blinded with the sand, the giants attacked one another, and in a short time were exterminated.

> They, like swift dogs,
> Ranging in fierceness, on each other turn'd
> Tumultuous battle. On their mother earth
> By their own spears they sank; like pines, or oaks,
> Strew'd by a whirlwind in the mountain dale.
>
> APOLLONIUS RHODIUS (Elton's tr.)

JASON AND MEDEA.
John William Waterhouse.

THE FLEECE CAPTURED

Accompanied by Medea, Jason next hastened to the tree where the dragon kept guard over his treasure. An opiate prepared by Medea's magic skill soon made the dragon forget his charge in a profound sleep, and enabled Jason to draw near enough to sever his frightful head from his hideous trunk. Jason then tore the coveted fleece from the branch where it had hung for many a year, and bore it in triumph to the Argo.

> Exulting Jason grasped the shining hide,
> His last of labors, and his envied pride.
> Slow from the groaning branch the fleece was rent.
>
> FLACCUS (Elton's tr.)

His companions, who had made ready for a hasty departure, were already seated at their oars; and, as soon as he had embarked with Medea and her attendants, the Argo shot out of the Colchian harbor.

> How softly stole from home the luckless-wedded maid,
> Through darkness of the night, in linen robe array'd;
> By Fate to Argo led, and urged by soft desire,
> Nor yet regarding aught her father's furious ire.
>
> ONOMACRITUS (Elton's tr.)

When morning dawned and Æetes awoke, he heard that the dragon was slain, the fleece stolen, his daughter gone, and the Grecian ship far out of sight. No time was lost in useless wailing, but a vessel was hurriedly launched and manned, and the king in person set out in pursuit of the fugitives, who had, moreover, taken his most precious treasure, his only son and heir, Absyrtus. Although the Colchian men were good sailors and skillful rowers, they did not catch sight of the Argo until they came near the mouth of the Danube, and Æetes wildly called to his daughter to return to her home and to her father.

> "Stay thy rash flight! and, from the distant main,—
> For oh! thou canst, my daughter,—turn again.
> Whither depart? the vessel backward steer;
> Thy friends, thy still fond father, wait thee here."
>
> FLACCUS (Elton's tr.)

DEATH OF ABSYRTUS

But Medea had no wish to be torn away from Jason's arms, and, instead of listening to her father's entreaties, urged the Argonauts to redoubled efforts. Little by little the distance between the two vessels grew less; the Colchian rowers were gaining upon the Greek; and Medea saw, that, unless she found means to delay her father, he would overtake her and compel her to return. With her own hands she therefore slew her little brother, Absyrtus, and cut his body into pieces, which she dropped over the side of the vessel one by one. Æetes, a helpless witness of this cruel, awful deed, piously collected his son's remains, and, in pausing to do so, lost sight of the Argo, and all hope of recovering his unnatural daughter: so he returned sadly to Colchis, where he buried his son's remains with due solemnity.

PELIAS DETHRONED

In the mean while, Pelias had reigned contentedly over Thessaly, confident that Jason would never return. Imagine his dismay, therefore, when he heard that the Argo had arrived, bearing Jason, now the proud possessor of the renowned golden fleece. Ere he could take measures to maintain his usurped authority, Jason appeared, and compelled him to resign the throne in favor of the rightful king, Æson.

Unfortunately, Æson was now so old and decrepit, that power had no charms for him: so Jason begged Medea to use her magic in his behalf, and restore him to the vigor and beauty of his early manhood. To gratify Jason, Medea called all her magic into play, and by some mysterious process restored Æson to all his former youth, strength, activity, and grace.

> Medea's spells dispersed the weight of years,
> And Æson stood a youth 'mid youthful peers.
>   WORDSWORTH

THE MAGIC RECIPE

As soon as Pelias's daughters heard of this miraculous transformation, they hastened to Medea and implored her to give them the recipe, that they might rejuvenate their father also. The sorceress maliciously bade them cut their father's body into small pieces, and boil them in a caldron with certain herbs, declaring that, if the directions were carefully carried out, the result would be satisfactory; but, when the too credulous maidens carried out these instructions, they only slew the father whom they had so dearly loved.

Days and years now passed happily and uneventfully for Jason and Medea; but at last their affection for each other cooled, and Jason fell in love with Glauce, or Creusa. Frantic with jealousy, Medea prepared and sent the maiden a magic robe, which she no sooner donned than she was seized with terrible convulsions, in which she died. Medea, still full of resentment against Jason, then slew her own children, and, mounting her dragon car, departed, leaving a message for Jason, purporting that the Argo would yet cause his death.

Death of Jason

Jason, a victim of remorse and despair, now led a weary and sorrowful life, and every day he wandered down to the shore, where he sat under the shade of the Argo's hulk, which was slowly rotting away. One day, while he was sitting there musing over his youthful adventures and Medea's strange prophecy, a sudden gale detached a beam, which, falling on his head, fractured his skull and caused instantaneous death.

The Argonautic expedition is emblematic of the first long maritime voyage undertaken by the Greeks for commercial purposes; while the golden fleece which Jason brought back from Colchis is but a symbol of the untold riches they found in the East, and brought back to their own native land.

THE CALYDONIAN HUNT

BIRTH OF MELEAGER

Œneus and Althæa, King and Queen of Calydon, in Ætolia, were very happy in the possession of a little son, Meleager, only a few days old, until they heard that the Fates had decreed the child should live only as long as the brand then smoking and crackling on the hearth. The parents were motionless with grief, until Althæa, with true mother's wit, snatched the brand from the fire, plunged it into an earthen jar filled with water, quenched the flames which were consuming it, and, carefully laying it aside, announced her intention to keep it forever.

Meleager, thus saved from an untimely death by his mother's presence of mind, grew up a brave and handsome youth, and joined the Argonautic expedition. While he was absent, his father omitted the yearly sacrifice to Diana, who, enraged at his neglect, sent a monstrous boar to devour his subjects and devastate his realm. Meleager, on his return, gathered together all the brave men of the country, and instituted a great hunt, whose main object was the capture or death of the obnoxious boar.

THE HUNTERS

Jason, Nestor, Peleus, Admetus, Theseus, Pirithous, and many other noted heroes, came at his call; but the attention of all the spectators was specially attracted by Castor and Pollux, and by the fair Atalanta, daughter of Iasius, King of Arcadia. This princess had led a very adventurous life; for when but a babe, her father, disappointed to see a daughter instead of the longed-for son, had exposed her on Mount Parthenium to the fury of the wild beasts. Some hunters, passing there shortly after this, found the babe fearlessly nursing from a she-bear, and in compassion carried her home, where they trained her to love the chase.

The grand Calydonian Hunt was headed by Meleager and Atalanta, who were very fond of each other, and who boldly led the rest in pursuit of the boar. From one end of the Calydonian forest to the other the boar fled, closely pursued by the hunt, and was at last brought to bay by Atalanta, who succeeded in dealing him a mortal wound. But even in his dying struggles the boar would have killed her, had not Meleager come to her rescue and given him his deathblow.

MELEAGER SLAYS HIS UNCLES

All the hunt now gathered around the boar's corpse, and watched Meleager take its spoil, which he gallantly bestowed upon Atalanta. Althæa's two brothers were present at the hunt; and, as they wished to possess the skin, they bitterly reproved their nephew on their way home for giving it to a stranger. They added taunts to this reproof, which so angered Meleager, that, in a sudden fit of passion, he slew them both. When Althæa saw her brothers' corpses, and heard that they had been slain by her son, she vowed to avenge their death, drew the carefully cherished brand from its hiding place, and threw it upon the fire burning brightly on her hearth. When the last bit of the precious wood crumbled away into ashes, Meleager died. All Althæa's affection for her son returned when his lifeless corpse was brought to her, and in her despair she committed suicide.

ATALANTA'S RACE

In the mean while, Atalanta, proud of her skill and of her spoil, had returned to her father's court, where, no other heir having appeared, she was joyfully received, and entreated to marry. Many suitors came to woo the fair princess, but most of them refrained from pressing their suit when they heard what conditions were imposed upon all who would obtain her hand; for Atalanta disapproved of marriage, and, anxious to keep her freedom, decreed that she should marry only on condition that her suitor would beat her in a foot race. If he were beaten, however, he must pay for his defeat by forfeiting his life.

THE GOLDEN APPLES

In spite of these barbarous terms, a few youths had tried to outrun her; but they failed, and their lifeless heads were exposed on the racing ground to deter all other suitors. Undaunted by these ghastly trophies, Hippomenes, or Milanion, once came to Atalanta and expressed a desire to race with her. This youth had previously obtained Venus's protection, and concealed under his garment her gift of three golden apples. Atalanta prepared for her race as usual, and, as usual, passed her rival; but just as she did so, one of the golden apples rolled at her feet. For a moment she paused, then stooped and picked it up ere she resumed the race. Her adversary had passed her and won some advance; but she soon overtook him, when a second golden apple caused a second delay. She was about to reach the goal first, as usual, when a third golden treasure tempted her to pause, and enabled Hippomenes to win the race.

> Hippomenes turns her astray
> By the golden illusions he flings on her way.
>
> MOORE

Atalanta could now no longer refuse to marry, and her nuptials were soon celebrated. In his happiness at having won such a peerless bride, Hippomenes forgot to pay the promised thanks to Venus, for which offense he and his wife were severely punished by being transformed into a pair of lions, and doomed to drag Cybele's car.

CASTOR AND POLLUX

The twin brothers Castor and Pollux, the Dioscuri, or Gemini, who had greatly distinguished themselves by their daring in the Calydonian Hunt, were made the deities of boxing, wrestling, and all equestrian exercises.

> Leda's sons I'll sound,
> Illustrious twins, that are
> For wrestling this, and for the race renown'd.
>
> HORACE

One of these twins, Castor, was a mortal, and in a combat with the sons of Aphareus was slain. Pollux, who was immortal, then implored Jupiter to allow him to die also, that he might not be parted from his brother,—a proof of brotherly affection which so touched the father of the gods, that he permitted Castor to return to life on condition that Pollux would spend half his time in Hades.

Later on, satisfied that even this sacrifice was none too great for their fraternal love, he translated them both to the skies, where they form a bright constellation, one

MELEAGER AND ATALANTA. Jacob Jordaens.

of the signs of the zodiac. Castor and Pollux are generally represented as handsome youths, mounted on snowy chargers.

> So like they were, no mortal
>   Might one from other know:
> White as snow their armor was:
>   Their steeds were white as snow.
> MACAULAY

Their appearance under certain circumstances foretold success in war, and the Romans believed that they fought at the head of their legions at the celebrated battle of Lake Regillus. Their name was also given to meteors, sometimes seen at sea, which attach themselves like balls of fire to the masts of ships,—a sure sign, according to the sailors, of fine weather and an auspicious journey.

> Safe comes the ship to haven,
>   Through billows and through gales,
> If once the Great Twin Brethren
>   Sit shining on the sails.
> MACAULAY

Festivals celebrated in honor of these twin brethren, and called the Dioscuria, were held in many places, but specially in Sparta, their birthplace, where they had world-renowned wrestling matches.

HIPPOMENES AND ATALANTA. Nicolas Columbel.

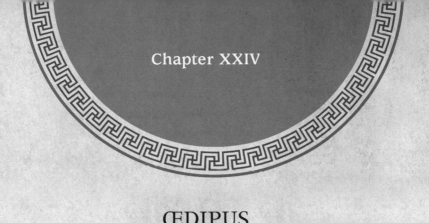

ŒDIPUS

Laius and Jocasta, King and Queen of Thebes, in Bœotia, were greatly delighted at the birth of a little son. In their joy they sent for the priests of Apollo, and bade them foretell the glorious deeds their heir would perform; but all their joy was turned to grief when told that the child was destined to kill his father, marry his mother, and bring great misfortunes upon his native city.

> Laius once,
> Not from Apollo, but his priests, receiv'd
> An oracle, which said, it was decreed
> He should be slain by his own son.
> SOPHOCLES (Francklin's tr.)

To prevent the fulfillment of this dreadful prophecy, Laius bade a servant carry the new-born child out of the city, and end its feeble little life. The king's mandate was obeyed only in part; for the servant, instead of killing the child, hung it up by its ankles to a tree in a remote place, and left it there to perish from hunger and exposure if it were spared by the wild beasts.

When he returned, none questioned how he had performed the appointed task, but all sighed with relief to think that the prophecy could never be accomplished. The child, however, was not dead, as all supposed. A shepherd in quest of a stray lamb had heard his cries, delivered him from his painful position, and carried him to Polybus, King of Corinth, who, lacking an heir of his own, gladly adopted the little stranger. The Queen of Corinth and her handmaidens hastened with tender concern to bathe the swollen ankles, and called the babe Œdipus (swollen-footed).

OPPOSITE PAGE: ŒDIPUS AND THE SPHINX. Jean Auguste Dominique.

Years passed by. The young prince grew up in total ignorance of the unfortunate circumstances under which he had made his first appearance at court, until one day at a banquet one of his companions, heated by drink, began to quarrel with him, and taunted him about his origin, declaring that those whom he had been accustomed to call parents were in no way related to him.

> A drunken rev'ler at a feast proclaim'd
> That I was only the supposed son
> Of Corinth's king.
>
> SOPHOCLES (Francklin's tr.)

ŒDIPUS CONSULTS THE ORACLE

These words, coupled with a few meaning glances hastily exchanged by the guests, excited Œdipus's suspicions, and made him question the queen, who, afraid lest he might do himself an injury in the first moment of his despair if the truth were revealed to him, had recourse to prevarication, and quieted him by the assurance that he was her beloved son.

Something in her manner, however, left a lingering doubt in Œdipus's mind, and made him resolve to consult the oracle of Delphi, whose words he knew would reveal the exact truth. He therefore went to this shrine; but, as usual, the oracle answered somewhat ambiguously, and merely warned him that fate had decreed he should kill his father, marry his mother, and cause great woes to his native city.

> I felt
> A secret anguish, and unknown to them
> Sought out the Pythian oracle; in vain;
> Touching my parents, nothing could I learn;
> But dreadful were the mis'ries it denounc'd
> Against me; 'twas my fate, Apollo said,
> To wed my mother, to produce a race
> Accursed and abhorr'd; and last, to slay
> My father.
>
> SOPHOCLES (Francklin's tr.)

ŒDIPUS LEAVES CORINTH

What! kill Polybus, who had ever been such an indulgent father, and marry the queen, whom he revered as his mother! Never! Rather than perpetrate these awful crimes, and bring destruction upon the people of Corinth, whom he loved, he would wander away over the face of the earth, and never see city or parents again.

> Lest I should e'er fulfill the dire prediction,
> Instant I fled from Corinth, by the stars
> Guiding my hapless journey.
>
>   SOPHOCLES (Francklin's tr.)

But his heart was filled with intense bitterness, and as he journeyed he did not cease to curse the fate which drove him away from home. After some time, he came to three crossroads; and while he stood there, deliberating which direction to take, a chariot, wherein an aged man was seated, came rapidly toward him.

DEATH OF LAIUS

The herald who preceded it haughtily called to the youth to stand aside and make way for his master; but Œdipus, who, as Polybus's heir, was accustomed to be treated with deference, resented the commanding tone, and refused to obey. Incensed at what seemed unparalleled impudence, the herald struck the youth, who, retaliating, stretched his assailant lifeless at his feet.

This affray attracted the attention of the master and other servants. They immediately attacked the murderer, who slew them all, thus unconsciously accomplishing the first part of the prophecy; for the aged man was Laius, his father, journeying *incognito* from Thebes to Delphi, where he wished to consult the oracle.

Œdipus then leisurely pursued his way until he came to the gates of Thebes, where he found the whole city in an uproar, "because the king had been found lifeless by the roadside, with all his attendants slain beside him, presumably the work of a band of highway robbers or assassins."

> He fell
> By strangers, murdered, for so fame reports,
> By robbers in the place where three ways meet.
>
>   SOPHOCLES (FRANCKLIN'S TR.)

Of course, Œdipus did not connect the murder of such a great personage as the King of Thebes by an unknown band of robbers, with the death he had dealt to an arrogant old man, and he therefore composedly inquired what the second calamity alluded to might be.

The Sphinx

With lowered voices, as if afraid of being overheard, the Thebans described the woman's head, bird's wings and claws, and lion's body, which were the outward presentment of a terrible monster called the Sphinx, which had taken up its station without the city gates beside the highway, and would allow none to pass in or out without propounding a difficult riddle. Then, if any hesitated to give the required answer, or failed to give it correctly, they were mercilessly devoured by the terrible Sphinx, which no one dared attack or could drive away.

While listening to these tidings, Œdipus saw a herald pass along the street, proclaiming that the throne and the queen's hand would be the reward of any man who dared encounter the Sphinx, and was fortunate enough to free the country of its terrible presence.

The Riddle

As Œdipus attached no special value to the life made desolate by the oracle's predictions, he resolved to slay the dreaded monster, and, with that purpose in view, advanced slowly, sword in hand, along the road where lurked the Sphinx. He soon found the monster, which from afar propounded the following enigma, warning him, at the same time, that he forfeited his life if he failed to give the right answer:—

> Tell me, what animal is that
> Which has four feet at morning bright,
> Has two at noon, and three at night?
> PRIOR

Œdipus was not devoid of intelligence, by any manner of means, and soon concluded that the animal could only be man, who in infancy, when too weak to stand, creeps along on hands and knees, in manhood walks erect, and in old age supports his tottering steps with a staff.

ŒDIPUS MARRIES HIS MOTHER

This reply, evidently as correct as unexpected, was received by the Sphinx with a hoarse cry of disappointment and rage as it turned to fly; but ere it could effect its purpose, it was stayed by Œdipus, who drove it at his sword's point over the edge of a neighboring precipice, where it was killed. On his return to the city, Œdipus was received with cries of joy, placed on a chariot, crowned King of Thebes, and married to his own mother, Jocasta, unwittingly fulfilling the second fearful clause of the prophecy.

THE PLAGUE

A number of happy and moderately uneventful years now passed by, and Œdipus became the father of two manly sons, Eteocles and Polynices, and two beautiful daughters, Ismene and Antigone; but prosperity was not doomed to favor him long.

Just when he fancied himself most happy, and looked forward to a peaceful old age, a terrible scourge visited Thebes, causing the death of many faithful subjects, and filling the hearts of all with great terror. The people now turned to him, beseeching him to aid them, as he had done once before when threatened by the Sphinx; and Œdipus sent messengers to consult the Delphic oracle, who declared the plague would cease only when the former king's murderers had been found and punished.

> The plague, he said, should cease,
> When those who murder'd Laius were discover'd,
> And paid the forfeit of their crime by death,
> Or banishment.
> SOPHOCLES (Francklin's tr.)

Messengers were sent in every direction to collect all possible information about the murder committed so long ago, and after a short time they brought unmistakable proofs which convicted Œdipus of the crime. At the same time the guilty servant confessed that he had not killed the child, but had exposed it on a mountain, whence it was carried to Corinth's king.

DEATH OF JOCASTA

The chain of evidence was complete, and now Œdipus discovered that he had involuntarily been guilty of the three crimes to avoid which he had fled from Corinth. The rumor of these dreadful discoveries soon reached Jocasta, who, in her despair at finding herself an accomplice, committed suicide.

Œdipus, apprised of her intention, rushed into her apartment too late to prevent its being carried out, and found her lifeless. This sight was more than the poor monarch could bear, and in his despair he blinded himself with one of her ornaments.

> He pluck'd from off the robe she wore
> A golden buckle that adorn'd her side,
> And buried in his eyes the sharpen'd point,
> Crying, he ne'er again would look on her,
> Never would see his crimes or mis'ries more,
> Or those whom guiltless he could ne'er behold,
> Or those to whom he now must sue for aid.
>
> SOPHOCLES (Francklin's tr.)

DEATH OF ŒDIPUS

Penniless, blind, and on foot, he then left the scene of his awful crimes, accompanied by his daughter Antigone, the only one who loved him still, and who was ready to guide his uncertain footsteps wherever he wished to go. After many days of weary wandering, father and daughter reached Colonus, where grew a mighty forest sacred to the avenging deities, the Furies, or Eumenides.

Here Œdipus expressed his desire to remain, and, after bidding his faithful daughter an affectionate farewell, he groped his way into the dark forest alone. The wind rose, the lightning flashed, the thunder pealed; but although, as soon as the storm was over, a search was made for Œdipus, no trace of him was ever found, and the ancients fancied that the Furies had dragged him down to Hades to receive the punishment of all his crimes.

ETEOCLES AND POLYNICES

Antigone, no longer needed by her unhappy father, slowly wended her way back to Thebes, where she found that the plague had ceased, but that her brothers had quarreled about the succession to the throne. A compromise was finally decided upon, whereby it was decreed that Eteocles, the elder son, should reign one year, and at the end of that period resign the throne to Polynices for an equal space of time, both brothers thus exercising the royal authority in turn. This arrangement seemed satisfactory to Eteocles; but when, at the end of the first year, Polynices returned from his travels in foreign lands to claim the scepter, Eteocles refused to relinquish it, and, making use of his power, drove the claimant away.

> Thou seest me banish'd from my native land,
> Unjustly banish'd, for no other crime
> But that I strove to keep the throne of Thebes,
> By birthright mine, from him who drove me thence,
> The young Eteocles: not his the claim
> By justice, nor to me his fame in arms
> Superior; but by soft, persuasive arts
> He won the rebel city to his love.
>
> SOPHOCLES (Francklin's tr.)

THE SEVEN CHIEFS BEFORE THEBES

Polynices's nature was not one to endure such a slight patiently; and he hastened off to Argos, where he persuaded Adrastus, the king, to give him his daughter in marriage, and aid him to recover his inheritance. True to his promise, Adrastus soon equipped a large army, which was led by seven determined and renowned chiefs, ready to risk all in the attempt, and either win or perish.

> Seven valiant leaders march
> To Thebes, resolved to conquer or to die.
> SOPHOCLES (Francklin's tr.)

Their bravery was of no avail, however, for Thebes was well fortified and defended; and after a seven-years' siege they found themselves no nearer their goal than at the beginning of the war. Weary of the monotony of this quarrel, the conflicting armies finally decreed that the difference should be settled by a duel between the inimical brothers, who no sooner found themselves face to face, than they rushed upon each other with such animosity that both fell.

FOLLOWING PAGES: THE BLIND ŒDIPUS COMMENDING HIS CHILDREN TO THE GODS. Bénigne Gagneraux.

By order of Jocasta's father, Creon, the corpse of Eteocles received all the honors of a Greek burial, while that of Polynices was left on the plain, a prey to the birds and wild beasts.

> Polynices's wretched carcass lies
> Unburied, unlamented, left expos'd
> A feast for hungry vultures on the plain.
> SOPHOCLES (Francklin's tr.)

ANTIGONE'S DEVOTION

Then a proclamation was issued, that, if any dared bury the body of the fallen prince, he would incur the penalty of being buried alive. Heedless of this injunction and Ismene's prayers to refrain from endangering her own life, Antigone dug a grave for her brother's remains, and, unaided, fulfilled the various customary funeral rites. Her task was almost completed, when the guards discovered her, and dragged her into the presence of Creon, who, although she was a relative and the promised wife of his son Hæmon, condemned her to death.

> Let her be carried instant to the cave,
> And leave her there alone, to live, or die;
> Her blood rests not on us: but she no longer
> Shall breathe on earth.
> SOPHOCLES (Francklin's tr.)

ANTIGONE AND HÆMON

Hæmon pleaded passionately for her life; but, when he saw his prayers were vain, he ran to the place where Antigone was confined, sprang into her narrow cell, wound his arms closely around her, and refused to leave her. There they were walled in; Antigone's sufferings were cut mercifully short by asphyxiation; and, when Hæmon saw she was no more, he, in utter despair, thrust his dagger into his side, and perished too.

> On himself bent all his wrath,
> Full in his side the weapon fix'd, but still,
> Whilst life remain'd, on the soft bosom hung

ANTIGONE AND ISMENE. Emil Teschendorf.

> Of the dear maid, and his last spirit breath'd
> O'er her pale cheek, discolor'd with his blood.
> Thus lay the wretched pair in death united,
> And celebrate their nuptials in the tomb.
>
> SOPHOCLES (Francklin's tr.)

Ismene, the last of Œdipus's unfortunate race, died of grief, and thus the prophecy was fully accomplished. The Theban war was not, however, entirely ended, for, when both brothers fell, the two armies flew to attack each other; and such was their courage, that many fell, and only one of the seven chiefs returned to Argos. There he patiently waited until the children of these brave captains were old enough to bear arms, and then proposed to them to attack Thebes and avenge their fathers' death.

The Epigoni (or those who come after), as these youths are collectively designated, received this proposal with rapture; and Thebes, again besieged, fell into their hands, and was duly sacked, burned, and destroyed, as the Delphic oracle had foretold so many years before.

BELLEROPHON

Bellerophon, a brave young prince, the grandson of Sisyphus, King of Corinth, had the great misfortune to kill his own brother while hunting in the forest. His grief was, of course, intense; and the horror he felt for the place where the catastrophe had occurred, added to his fear lest he should incur judicial punishment for his involuntary crime, made him flee to the court of Argos, where he took refuge with Prœtus, the king, who was also his kinsman.

ANTEIA'S TREACHERY

He had not sojourned there very long, before Anteia, the queen, fell in love with him; and although her husband, Prœtus, treated her with the utmost kindness, she made up her mind to desert him, and tried to induce Bellerophon to elope with her. Too honest to betray a man who had treated him as a friend, the young prince refused to listen to the queen's proposals. His refusal was to cost him dear, however; for, when Anteia saw that the youth would never yield to her wishes, she became very angry indeed, sought her husband, and accused the young stranger of crimes he had never even dreamed of committing.

Prœtus, indignant at what he deemed deep treachery on the part of an honored guest, yet reluctant to punish him with his own hand as he deserved, sent Bellerophon to Iobates, King of Lycia, with a sealed message bidding him put the bearer to death.

Quite unconscious of the purport of this letter, Bellerophon traveled gayly onward, and presented himself before Iobates, who received him very hospitably, and, without inquiring his name or errand, entertained him royally for many days. After some time, Bellerophon suddenly remembered the sealed message intrusted to his care, and hastened to deliver it to Iobates, with many apologies for his forgetfulness.

The Chimæra

With blanched cheeks and every outward sign of horror, the king read the missive, and then fell into a deep reverie. He did not like to take a stranger's life, and still could not refuse to comply with Prœtus' urgent request: so, after much thought, he decided to send Bellerophon to attack the Chimæra, a terrible monster with a lion's head, a goat's body, and a dragon's tail.

> Dire Chimæra's conquest was enjoin'd;
> A mingled monster, of no mortal kind;
> Behind, a dragon's fiery tail was spread;
> A goat's rough body bore a lion's head;
> Her pitchy nostrils flaky flames expire;
> Her gaping throat emits infernal fire.
>
> HOMER (Pope's tr.)

His principal motive in choosing this difficult task was, that, although many brave men had set forth to slay the monster, none had ever returned, for one and all had perished in the attempt.

Although very courageous, Bellerophon's heart beat fast with fear when told what great deed he must accomplish; and he left Iobates's palace very sorrowfully, for he dearly loved the king's fair daughter, Philonoe, and was afraid he would never see her again.

Minerva's Advice

While thus inwardly bewailing the ill luck which had so persistently dogged his footsteps, Bellerophon suddenly saw Minerva appear before him in all her splendor, and heard her inquire in gentle tones the cause of his too evident dejection. He had no sooner apprised her of the difficult task appointed him, than she promised him her aid, and before she vanished gave him a beautiful golden bridle, which she bade him use to control Pegasus.

Bridle in hand, Bellerophon stood pondering her words, and gradually remembered that Pegasus was a wonderful winged steed, born from the blood which fell into the foam of the sea from Medusa's severed head. This horse, as white as snow, and gifted with immortal life as well as incredible speed, was the favorite mount of Apollo and the Muses, who delighted in taking aërial flights on his broad back; and

MINERVA RESTRAINS PEGASUS WITH THE HELP OF MERCURY.
Jan Boeckhorst.

Bellerophon knew that from time to time he came down to earth to drink of the cool waters of the Hippocrene (a fountain which had bubbled forth where his hoofs first touched the earth), or to visit the equally limpid spring of Pirene, near Corinth.

Pegasus Bridled

Bellerophon now proceeded to the latter fountain, where, after lingering many days in the vain hope of catching even a glimpse of the winged steed, he finally beheld him sailing downward in wide curves, like a bird of prey. From his place of concealment in a neighboring thicket, Bellerophon watched his opportunity, and, while the winged steed was grazing, he boldly vaulted upon his back.

Pegasus, who had never before been ridden by a mortal, reared and pranced, and flew up to dizzy heights; but all his efforts failed to unseat the brave rider, who, biding his time, finally thrust Minerva's golden bit between his teeth, and immediately he became gentle and tractable. Mounted upon this incomparable steed, Bellerophon now went in search of the winged monster Chimæra, who had given birth to the Nemean lion and to the riddle-loving Sphinx.

CHIMÆRA SLAIN

From an unclouded sky Bellerophon and Pegasus swooped suddenly and unexpectedly down upon the terrible Chimæra, whose fiery breath and great strength were of no avail; for after a protracted struggle Bellerophon and Pegasus were victorious, and the monster lay lifeless upon the blood-soaked ground.

This mighty deed of valor accomplished, Bellerophon returned to Iobates, to report the success of his undertaking; and, although the king was heartily glad to know the Chimæra was no more, he was very sorry to see Bellerophon safe and sound, and tried to devise some other plan to get rid of him.

He therefore sent him to fight the Amazons; but the hero, aided by the gods, defeated these warlike women also, and returned to Lycia, where, after escaping from an ambush posted by the king for his destruction, he again appeared victorious at court.

These repeated and narrow escapes from certain death convinced Iobates that the youth was under the special protection of the gods; and this induced the king not only to forego further attempts to slay him, but also to bestow upon the young hero his daughter's hand in marriage.

BELLEROPHON'S FALL

Bellerophon, having now attained his dearest wishes, might have settled down in peace; but his head had been utterly turned by the many lofty flights he had taken upon Pegasus's back, and, encouraged by the fulsome flattery of his courtiers, he finally fancied himself the equal of the immortal gods, and wished to join them in their celestial abode.

OPPOSITE PAGE: **BELLEROPHON RIDING PEGASUS AND FIGHTING THE CHIMÆRA**. Peter Paul Rubens.

Summoning his faithful Pegasus once more, he rose higher and higher, and would probably have reached Olympus's heights, had not Jupiter sent a gadfly, which stung poor Pegasus so cruelly, that he shied viciously, and flung his too confident rider far down to the earth below.

> Bold Bellerophon (so Jove decreed
> In wrath) fell headlong from the fields of air.
>   WORDSWORTH

This fall, which would doubtless have killed any one but a mythological hero, merely deprived Bellerophon of his eyesight; and ever after he groped his way disconsolately, thinking of the happy days when he rode along the paths of air, and gazed upon the beautiful earth at his feet.

Bellerophon, mounted upon Pegasus, winging his flight through the air or fighting the Chimæra, is a favorite subject in sculpture and painting, which has frequently been treated by ancient artists, a few of whose most noted works are still extant in various museums.

This story, like many others, is merely a sun myth, in which Bellerophon, the orb of day, rides across the sky on Pegasus, the fleecy white clouds, and slays Chimæra, the dread monster of darkness, which he alone can overcome. Driven from home early in life, Bellerophon wanders throughout the world like his brilliant prototype, and, like it, ends his career in total darkness.

MINOR DIVINITIES

Naiades and Oreades

According to the ancients' belief, every mountain, valley, plain, lake, river, grove, and sea was provided with some lesser deity, whose special duty was assigned by the powerful gods of Olympus. These were, for instance, the Naiades, beautiful water nymphs, who dwelt in the limpid depths of the fountains, and were considered local patrons of poetry and song.

The Oreades, or mountain nymphs, were supposed to linger in the mountain solitudes, and guide weary travelers safely through their rocky mazes.

> Mark how the climbing Oreads
> Beckon thee to their Arcades!
>
> Emerson

Napææ and Dryades

As for the Napææ, they preferred to linger in the valleys, which were kept green and fruitful by their watchful care, in which task they were ably seconded by the Dryades, the nymphs of vegetation.

The very trees in the forest and along the roadside were supposed to be each under the protection of a special divinity called Hamadryad, said to live and die with the tree intrusted to her care.

> When the Fate of Death is drawing near,
> First wither on the earth the beauteous trees,
> The bark around them wastes, the branches fall,
> And the nymph's soul, at the same moment, leaves
> The sun's fair light.
>
> Homer

STORY OF DRYOPE

A sweet and touching story was told by the ancients of a mortal who was changed into a Hamadryad. This young girl, whose name was Dryope, was a beautiful young princess, the daughter of Baucis, so bright and clever, that all who knew her loved her dearly. Of course, as soon as she was old enough to think of marriage, a host of suitors asked her hand, each eager to win for his bride one so beautiful and gifted.

> No nymph of all Œchalia could compare,
> For beauteous form, with Dryope the fair.
>
> OVID (Pope's tr.)

Fully aware of the importance of making a wise choice, Dryope took her time, and finally decided to marry Andræmon, a worthy young prince, who possessed every charm calculated to win a fair girl's heart. The young people were duly married, and daily rejoiced in their happiness, which seemed almost too great for earth, when they became the parents of a charming little son.

Every day Dryope carried the child along the banks of a little lake close by the palace, where bloomed a profusion of gay-colored flowers.

> A lake there was, with shelving banks around,
> Whose verdant summit fragrant myrtles crown'd.
> Those shades, unknowing of the Fates, she sought,
> And to the Naiads flowery garlands brought;
> Her smiling babe (a pleasing charge) she press'd
> Between her arms.
>
> OVID (Pope's tr.)

One day, while wandering there as usual, accompanied by her sister, she saw a lotus blossom, and pointed it out to her little son. He no sooner saw the brilliant flower, than he stretched out his little hands. To please him, the fond mother plucked it and gave it to him.

She had scarcely done so, when she noticed drops of blood trickling from the broken stem; and while she stood there, speechless with wonder, a voice was heard accusing her of having slain Lotis, a nymph, who, to escape the pursuit of Priapus, god of the shade, had assumed the guise of a flower.

> Lotis the nymph (if rural tales be true),
> As from Priapus's lawless love she flew,
> Forsook her form; and fixing here became
> A flowery plant, which still preserves her name.
>
> OVID (Pope's tr.)

Recovering from her first speechless terror, Dryope turned to flee, with a pitiful cry of compassion on her pale lips, but, to her astonishment, she could not leave the spot: her feet seemed rooted to the ground. She cast a rapid glance downward to ascertain what could so impede her progress, and noticed the rough bark of a tree growing with fearful rapidity all around her.

Higher and higher it rose, from her knees to her waist, and still it crept upward, in spite of her frantic attempts to tear it away from her shapely limbs. In despair she raised her trembling hands and arms to heaven to implore aid; but, ere the words were spoken, her arms were transformed into twisted branches, and her hands were filled with leaves.

Nothing human now remained of poor Dryope except her sweet, tear-stained face; but this too would soon vanish under the all-involving bark. She therefore took hasty leave of her father, sister, husband, and son, who, attracted by her first cry, had rushed to give her all the assistance in their power. The last words were quickly spoken, but none too soon, for the bark closed over the soft lips and hid the lovely features from view.

> She ceased at once to speak, and ceased to be,
> And all the nymph was lost within the tree:
> Yet latent life through her new branches reign'd,
> And long the plant a human heat retain'd.
>
> OVID (Pope's tr.)

One of Dryope's last requests had been that her child might often play beneath her shady branches; and when the passing winds rustled through her leaves, the ancients said it was "Dryope's lone lulling of her child."

SATYRS AND PAN

The male divinities of the woods, which were also very numerous, were mostly Satyrs,—curious beings with a man's body and a goat's legs, hair, and horns. They were all passionately fond of music and revelry, and were wont to indulge in dancing at all times and in all places. The most famous among all the Satyrs was Silenus, Bacchus's tutor; and Pan, or Consentes, god of the shepherds, and the personification of nature. The latter was the reputed son of Mercury and a charming young nymph named Penelope; and we are told, that, when his mother first beheld him, she was aghast, for he was the most homely as well as the most extraordinary little creature she had ever seen. His body was all covered with goat's hair, and his feet and ears were also those of a goat.

Amused at the sight of this grotesque little divinity, Mercury carried him off to Olympus, where all the gods turned him into ridicule. Pan was widely worshiped in olden times, however; and the ancients not only decked his altars with flowers, but sang his praises, and celebrated festivals in his honor.

> He is great and he is just,
> He is ever good, and must
> Be honored. Daffodillies,
> Roses, pinks, and loved lilies,
> Let us fling, while we sing,
> Ever Holy! Ever Holy!
> Ever honored! Ever young!
> The great Pan is ever sung!
> BEAUMONT AND FLETCHER

STORY OF SYRINX

Pan was equally devoted to music, the dance, and pretty nymphs. He saw one of the nymphs, Syrinx, whom he immediately loved; but unfortunately for him, she, frightened at his appearance, fled. Exasperated by her persistent avoidance of him, Pan once pursued and was about to overtake her, when she paused, and implored Gæa to protect her. The prayer was scarcely ended, when she found herself changed into a clump of reeds, which the panting lover embraced, thinking he had caught the maiden, who had stood in that very spot a few moments before.

His deception and disappointment were so severe, that they wrung from him a prolonged sigh, which, passing through the rustling reeds, produced plaintive tones. Pan, seeing Syrinx had gone forever, took seven pieces of the reed, of unequal lengths, bound them together, and fashioned from them a musical instrument, which was called by the name of the fair nymph.

Fair, trembling Syrinx fled
Arcadian Pan, with such a fearful dread.
Poor nymph!—poor Pan!—how he did weep to find
Naught but a lovely sighing of the wind
Along the reedy stream; a half-heard strain
Full of sweet desolation—balmy pain.

KEATS

Pan was supposed to delight in slyly overtaking belated travelers and inspiring them with sudden and unfounded fears,—from him called "panic." He is generally represented with a syrinx and shepherd's crook, and a pine garland around his misshapen head.

SILVAN DEITIES

The Romans also worshiped three other divinities of nature entirely unknown to the Greeks; i.e., Silvanus, Faunus, and Fauna, the latter's wife, who had charge over the woods and plants. Priapus, god of the shade, was also a rural deity, but his worship was only known along the shores of the Hellespont.

FLORA AND ZEPHYRUS

The fairest among all the lesser gods was doubtless Flora, goddess of flowers, who married Zephyrus, the gentle god of the south wind, and wandered happily with him from place to place, scattering her favors with lavish generosity. She was principally worshiped by young girls, and the only offerings ever seen on her altars were fruits and garlands of beautiful flowers. Her festivals, generally celebrated in the month of May, were called the Floralia.

Crowds of nymphs,
Soft voiced, and young, and gay,
In woven baskets bringing ears of corn,
Roses and pinks and violets to adorn
The shrine of Flora in her early May.

KEATS

Vertumnus and Pomona

Vertumnus and Pomona were the special divinities of the garden and orchard. They are represented with pruning knives and shears, gardening implements, and fruits and flowers. Pomona was very coy indeed, and had no desire to marry. Vertumnus, enamored of her charms, did his best to make her change her mind, but she would not even listen to his pleadings.

At last the lover had recourse to stratagem, disguised himself as an aged crone, entered Pomona's garden, and inquired how it happened that such a very charming young woman should remain so long unmarried. Then, having received a mocking answer, he began to argue with her, and finally extracted an avowal, that, among all the suitors, one alone was worthy of her love, Vertumnus. Vertumnus seized the favorable opportunity, revealed himself, and clasped her to his breast. Pomona, perceiving that she had hopelessly betrayed herself, no longer refused to wed, but allowed him to share her labors, and help her turn the luscious fruit to ripen in the autumn sunshine.

Sea Deities

The lesser divinities of the sea were almost as numerous as those of the land, and included the lovely Oceanides and Nereides, together with their male companions the Tritons, who generally formed Neptune's regal train.

Story of Glaucus

One of the lesser sea gods, Glaucus, was once a poor fisherman, who earned his daily bread by selling the fish he caught in his nets. On one occasion he made an extra fine haul, and threw his net full of fish down upon a certain kind of grass, which the flapping fish immediately nibbled, and, as if endowed with extraordinary powers, bounded back into the waves and swam away.

Greatly surprised at this occurrence, Glaucus began chewing a few blades of this peculiar grass, and immediately felt an insane desire to plunge into the sea,—a desire which soon became so intense, that he could no longer resist it, but dived down into the water. The mere contact with the salt waves sufficed to change his nature; and swimming about comfortably in the element, where he now found himself perfectly at home, he began to explore the depths of the sea.

"I plung'd for life or death. To interknit
  One's senses with so dense a breathing stuff
  Might seem a work of pain; so not enough
  Can I admire how crystal-smooth it felt,
  And buoyant round my limbs. At first I dwelt
  Whole days and days in sheer astonishment;
  Forgetful utterly of self-intent;
  Moving but with the mighty ebb and flow.
  Then, like a new fledg'd bird that first doth show
  His spreaded feathers to the morrow chill,
  I try'd in fear the pinions of my will.
  'Twas freedom! and at once I visited
  The ceaseless wonders of this ocean-bed."

                                            KEATS

Glaucus was worshiped most particularly by the fishermen and boatmen, whose vessels he was supposed to guard from evil, and whose nets were often filled to overflow through his intervention.

FOLLOWING PAGES: **VERTUMNUS AND POMONA**. Peter Paul Rubens.

IMAGE CREDITS